LEWIS
HAMILTON

LEWIS HAMILTON

FIVE-TIME WORLD CHAMPION

THE BIOGRAPHY

FRANK WORRALL

JOHN BLAKE

Published by John Blake Publishing,
2.25, The Plaza,
535 Kings Road,
Chelsea Harbour,
London SW10 0SZ

www.johnblakebooks.com

www.facebook.com/johnblakebooks 🔲
twitter.com/jblakebooks 🔲

First published in hardback in 2007
This edition published in 2017

ISBN: 978 1 78946 092 6

British Library Cataloguing-in-Publication Data:

A catalogue record for this book is available from the British Library.

Design by www.envydesign.co.uk

Printed and bound in Great Britain by Clays Ltd, Elcograf S.p.A.

1 3 5 7 9 10 8 6 4 2

Papers used by John Blake Publishing are natural, recyclable products made
from wood grown in sustainable forests. The manufacturing processes conform
to the environmental regulations of the country of origin.

Every reasonable effort has been made to trace copyright-holders of material
reproduced in this book, but if any have been inadvertently overlooked the
publishers would be glad to hear from them.

John Blake Publishing is an imprint of Bonnier Books UK
www.bonnierbooks.co.uk

This book is dedicated to Shaf Karim

ACKNOWLEDGEMENTS

Special thanks to: James Hodgkinson, Sarah Fortune, Toby Buchan, and all at John Blake Publishing, and Humayra Ahmed at Bonnier Books.

Thanks to: Rupert Morrall, Kevan Manwaring, Ben Felsenburg, Colin Forshaw, Steven Gordon, Russ Forgham, Roy Stone, Tom Henderson Smith, Pravina Patel, Lee Hassall, Danny Bottono, Mick Morris and Catherine Collin.

Not forgetting: Angela, Frankie, Jude, Nat, Stephen and Bob and Barbara and Frank

CONTENTS

INTRODUCTION

It was 28 October, 2018, when Lewis Hamilton joined the immortals of motor racing: the day he won his fifth F1 crown. He lifted the drivers' world championship title in Mexico City, becoming only the third man to do so five times, drawing him level with Juan Manuel Fangio, and leaving himself just two short of Michael Schumacher's record of seven. It propelled him well beyond fellow Brit, Sir Jackie Stewart, who won it three times, making him the greatest British racing driver of all-time, and joint second greatest of all-time – with just Schuey's record of seven left to target.

After lifting the world title in Mexico, Lewis celebrated into the night. The significance of the feat had not been lost on him. He said, 'To win it with Mercedes means something, as Fangio won two championships with Mercedes. It's an incredible feeling, very surreal.'

He would later admit another, closer-to-home motivation to win – and to claim victory in his second season of an intense duel with his biggest rival, Ferrari's Sebastian Vettel. Three days before his triumph in Mexico City, Lewis's beloved granddad Davidson had passed away, aged 88. Lewis dedicated his latest success to Davidson, saying, 'My grandfather would be so proud of us, so grateful that the Hamilton name is established and that it will now go down in history. He was the godfather of the family.'

At thirty-three, Lewis had proved he was the best driver on the planet. The boy from Stevenage with humble beginnings was now a true global superstar and icon. His face adorned magazines and billboards not connected with motor racing and he was in demand for TV chat shows around the world.

Lewis Hamilton had become F1's first celebrity phenomenon. He was more, much more, than just a racing driver – but it was in motor racing where he had made his name and it would be in motor racing where his biggest dreams still lived. He was not content with five crowns: his aim was to be the greatest ever.

The road to legend had not been easy. There had also been nightmares to contend with during a six-year barren spell between his first and second crowns. Along the way, Lewis would fall out with his dad Anthony (and eventually make his peace with him in 2014), see his mentor Ron Dennis leave McLaren and then walk away himself from the legendary racing team that had been home since he was a boy. Lewis moved from McLaren to the then emergent Mercedes in 2013.

It would take him a year to settle in and for the German team to fine-tune his car but then he would show his mettle by becoming world champion for the second time.

By the time he had collected his second world title in Abu Dhabi, Lewis had become a national treasure. Similar to David Beckham at his peak, Lewis earned standing ovations wherever he went.

Yet some pundits suggested that while he was undoubtedly a winner on the track, he would never be one off it with the British public. They carped that he was too arrogant, that he was too attracted to money, bling and showbiz for the public to hold him close to their hearts. That idea was blown out of the water in December 2014 when Lewis won the BBC Sports Personality of the Year 2014 award – an accolade decided purely by the public.

Lewis had made his mark with those who previously would not have given the sport of motor racing the time of day.

This is his story, and an unlikely one at that. From his ancestral roots in Grenada, through his modest start in life in a council estate in Stevenage and years of steely determination and commitment in the lower echelons of racing, right up to his glorious debut season in F1, that initial world crown in 2008 and the joy he expressed by finally reclaiming the title in 2014 and then triumphing once again in 2015, 2017 and 2018.

Lewis Hamilton, this is your life – and long may you reign.

Frank Worrall
London, 2018

CHAPTER 1

THE REAL SPECIAL ONE

First up, a humble apology to Lewis Hamilton from myself and Damon Hill: hands up, I was one of the majority who agreed with Damon in January 2007 when he said that Lewis would probably get half a season to prove himself. I also thought maybe he'd find it all too much and be shunted quietly aside, shell-shocked, perhaps back into GP2 until he was really ready for the big-time with a more experienced driver stepping up to bolster Fernando Alonso's assault on a surely inevitable third World Drivers' title. Sorry, Lewis…

It just goes to show you how wrong you can be. Even the great Damon Hill called it incorrectly, and if anybody should know about drivers, it's him. There again, the signs that Lewis was hardly thrown in without any prior training were certainly there. There was the nine-year apprenticeship with McLaren, the usually infallible judgment of the McLaren team boss, 'Big Ron' Dennis, and Lewis' performances and results the previous season in GP2, when he roared to that Drivers' title. One thing was for certain: Lewis Hamilton was no one-season wonder. The boy is here for the long run. Finally, there was a British hero we could all praise to the ceilings.

Lewis Hamilton is the real thing: he's the Real Special One, comfortably taking the mantle that was once the preserve of Chelsea's former big-talking football manager, José Mourinho. The youngster who quickly became known as the 'Stevenage Rocket' on the Formula One circuit soon knocked down the record book skittles as he notched up one achievement after another. The first black Formula One driver, the first rookie to achieve more than two consecutive podium finishes, the first black driver to win a Formula One grand prix, only the second driver to win more than one race in his first Formula One Championship season since its inception, the first driver to achieve consecutive wins from pole position in a debut season, the youngest Briton ever to win a grand prix and the youngest driver to lead the World Championship... and, of course, the first rookie and black driver to be a serious contender for the title in his first season.

As the records show, this was a truly astonishing debut campaign, and one that was only the beginning of many achievements. By the end of the season, Lewis Hamilton was odds-on favourite to lift the coveted BBC Sports Personality of the Year award in December 2007 – in fact, five months earlier in July, bookmaker Paddy Power was refusing to take any more bets on Lewis. Thanks to him, this was also a season that changed the face of Formula One forever, bringing in a larger, more diverse audience. Motorsport was transformed from a rather dull spectator sport into one that had us all, and not just the traditional diehards, gripped with excitement as it hurtled towards a thrilling finale.

Lewis said he was taken aback by his overnight transformation from relative obscurity to worldwide fame. He said: 'It's amazing, I've received letters this week from young kids telling me that all of a sudden they want to be racing drivers. I remember when I was in the same position and now I just try to be a good role model. The fame has come all of a sudden and I'm starting to appreciate the importance of my actions – especially when young kids are looking up to me.'

Formula One expert and *Sun* contributor Chris Hockley was also stunned at the way Lewis had changed the demographic of the sport. He told me it had been an incredibly swift reversal of fortune: 'Yes, his rocket-ship rise to fame has bumped up British TV audiences for grands prix by a whopping 50 per cent. And enthusiasm for Formula One is soaring across the world – even in the stock-car domain of America, they were forced to sit up and take notice when this upstart rookie kid beat off the reigning World Champ to win the US Grand Prix.

'It's a fairytale, you see, enacted across the globe. And all of a sudden everyone, from barmaids to vicars, from paperboys to company directors, has an opinion on Lewis, and asks after his progress. No more is Formula One the preserve of anoraks, petrolheads and techno-junkies who salivate at the prospect of a 0.63 per cent increase in front aerofoil downforce eked out by Ferrari's engineers. Now wives, who decades ago gave up trying to understand their husbands' weird obsession with "watching cars go round in circles" are dallying at the telly and asking: "How's Lewis doing?" Surely it won't be long before traffic cops tell speeding motorists: "Who do you think you are, Lewis Hamilton?"'

Lewis Hamilton was certainly a breath of fresh air during 2007 – some would even argue that he was the very saviour of a Formula One that had lost its way and no longer had the ingredients to thrill. His story could be straight out of an Hollywood script, but its beauty is that it is real and the great thing about Lewis is that, in a sport littered with characters who are usually just the opposite, he is so down-to-earth. In a sport dominated by big money and star names, he was, after just one season, the biggest star of all by virtue of his extraordinary talent, skills and utter lack of pretension. He also seemed to have appeared from nowhere, although of course there's a hinterland of many years of slog and determination behind the starry tale of the boy born to be King of Formula One.

I asked one of the McLaren crew if this was why they seemed so behind their new boy. On condition of anonymity, he told me that it was one of the reasons, at the same time giving a hint of the team's thinking on the feud between Lewis and his team-mate Fernando Alonso, ever-present in his debut campaign. 'The thing is there's been all this stuff in the press with Alonso saying we favour Lewis because he is British... but that's rubbish. We're all in this together; we're all McLaren. Big Ron [Ron Dennis] wouldn't have any of that kind of thing in his team – if anything, it was Lewis as the rookie who got the slower car.

'But Lewis is a special talent – he works harder than most seasoned drivers and he's got that touch of magic that most don't have. I watch him in the practice sessions and it reminds me of why I wanted to be part of Formula One in the first place. A lot of the time it seems that Alonso's raging, that he's flat out, trying to cling on to his title, but Lewis was often beating him hands down – looking as if he hasn't broken sweat, always gracious and the crowds love him.

'The thing is, Alonso's a great driver, a great champion and a nice guy underneath it all, but Lewis is something special. Forget all the stuff about being the first black guy and all that – he could be the best driver of his generation irrelevant of all that. It gives me the shivers to be around that to see it happening and, yes, even Big Ron's got a spring in his step these days.'

Indeed, he had. There were even suggestions that, similarly to football manager Sir Alex Ferguson, the rise of a young star within his ranks had re-energised the old man of motor racing and forced him to scrap any plans for premature retirement. When Lewis won his first grand prix, the big man had tears in his eyes, although he would later claim that it was the champagne that was making them sting! It is also true that Dennis' wife Lisa has a soft spot for

Lewis. She seemed to cheer loudly when he eclipsed Alonso's lap time for pole in Montreal (1:15.707 against the Spaniard's 1:16.163).

And, in another poignant moment, I am told Big Ron rushed off to a private room after Lewis crashed during practice at the Nürburgring at the end of July 2007. A McLaren backroom boy told me that Ron could be seen holding his head in his hands. He had tears running down his face as Lewis was hurriedly taken away from the circuit to hospital with an oxygen mask over his face, a drip connected to his arm.

The son of a former British Rail worker, Lewis Hamilton is mixed-race. His father Anthony's family originates from the Caribbean island Grenada and he is the first driver of Afro-Caribbean origin to race in Formula One. Anthony scrimped and saved, at one point taking on three jobs to give his son a chance in the racing world. He has become a hugely supportive influence. Lewis later paid tribute to him, saying: 'I have been incredibly fortunate having my father's support, because I don't recall any of the other competitors [in the early karting days] coming from the same background as us – they all had wealthy parents. I know there will be setbacks during my career but I have the attitude that if it was easy to win championships everybody would be doing it.

'I guess that approach springs from the fact that, ever since I was 9 or 10, I have spent every weekend at a race-track, so I wasn't hanging out and doing stuff with my friends. I was with Dad, and was best friends with him. If you want to fit in and mix with the grown-ups you have to learn at a faster pace than other youngsters. And although I suppose I missed out on doing the silly things at school, I quickly realised I can have all the toys I want if I keep working and winning at McLaren.'

It was that brand of tunnel vision determination that put Lewis on the road to success from the age of 6, when he first excelled at karting. That talent, in turn, was to earn him a life-changing spin-off: with his now legendary meeting with Ron Dennis, as a starry-eyed youngster in 1995. With no doubts about his own talent and no hesitation, he asked for his future employer's autograph while the other boys at the event nervously stood by. 'He looked me square in the face and informed me where he was going in his life,' Dennis recalls. 'Without breaking eye contact, he told me how he was going to go about his career. It impressed the hell out of me.'

Dennis started following his career and a few years later signed him up to McLaren's Driver Development Programme, investing £5million in him over nine years. During that time, Lewis learned the ropes under the master; his natural talent honed with one ultimate aim: to make him World Champion. He would become the best, but never got carried away as his success snowballed over the years. 'Confidence is often coupled with arrogance,' Dennis said, 'but there isn't an ounce of arrogance about Lewis.'

Lewis later admitted that was correct; he put his success down to hard work and his faith. From a devout Catholic family, he would say 'My faith is very important to me. I'm a true believer. I really believe that my talent is God-given and that I've been truly blessed. I guess every driver is talented but some of us are prepared to work harder to make the most of our talent. Some don't possess the talent of someone like Kimi Raikkonen [Ferrari's number one driver and, after Alonso, Lewis' main rival at the time], but they've worked harder to become better than him. I don't know if I have more talent than Fernando Alonso, but I do know I've worked very hard.'

His impact on Formula One was both instant and remarkable, drawing comparisons to Tiger Woods and his success in the world of golf. Like Woods, Lewis was articulate, good-looking and possessed a similar talent. He had this to say on the Tiger comparisons: 'It's obviously nice to be compared to somebody like Tiger Woods but you just have to remember I'm not Tiger Woods, I'm Lewis Hamilton and this is Formula One – it is not golf. Whether or not it can have a similar impact, I'm not sure. It will be good for the sport if it can. I hope my purpose here serves its place.'

Top Formula One journalist Rory Ross maintained Lewis had made a much bigger impact worldwide than he or anyone else had imagined: 'His popularity has spread like morning sunlight. In Brazil, he has eclipsed Felipe Massa, the Brazilian Ferrari driver, especially in the Favelas, where they see in Hamilton one of their own doing well. In Spain, he is more popular than Fernando Alonso, much to the irritation of the Spanish champion.'

And Kevin Eason of *The Times* commented: 'Bernie

Ecclestone is rubbing his hands with glee. Formula One's ringmaster was stuck with a show that was losing fans in increasing numbers. Schumacher was a serial winner, but outside Germany and Italy, home of the retired former champion's Ferrari team, he was a turn-off for millions. Hamilton is pure box office... and the interest is coming from all over the world, with camera crews from places as far afield as Colombia and Russia queuing for interviews.'

Unlike Tiger Woods, Lewis Hamilton has had to rise above a much more talented playing field of rivals. Woods' ascent came at a time of relative mediocrity in golf, but Lewis had to overcome drivers of immeasurable quality and defiance, opponents and team-mates alike. It was a measure of his ability and maturity that he had the double World Champion almost in tears, certainly tears of fury at times during the season.

The duel between the two was another reason why the masses tuned into Formula One in 2007; to see if the young lamb could stave off the aggressive tactics of his older, seemingly less wise team-mate. Alonso had transferred from Renault to McLaren, believing it to be a dream move: he had always wanted a car like the McLaren-Mercedes MP4-22. He believed it his destiny to show just how good he was in that new car, that he was a champion truly worthy of creating his own era after the dominant years of Michael Schumacher.

Alonso niggled at Lewis as the season – and Lewis' remarkable results – unfolded. He claimed he had never been 'completely comfortable' and added that he believed

Lewis was unfairly favoured by McLaren because he was a British driver and they were a British team. He said: 'We knew all the support and help would go his way.' The Spaniard was playing the victim. Later he would try to unnerve Lewis and undermine his confidence by saying his team-mate was 'lucky'.

Ron Dennis has continually refuted Alonso's claims, saying: 'There is a healthy competition between the teams working on each car but I can categorically state that both drivers have equal equipment, support and opportunity to win.' It seemed he was determined not to appear biased towards his protégé in much the same way as the father who employs his son in the family firm and deliberately gives him a harder time than the rest of the staff to prove there is no favouritism. At times, it appeared Lewis was getting a rough deal from the man known in the pit lane as his surrogate father.

To an extent, you could see Big Ron's dilemma. He was paying the world champion £10 million a year and Lewis a basic £340,000. In Alonso he had made a major invest-ment and was therefore keen to see him happy. I don't doubt that in an ideal world Dennis always wanted to see Alonso champion again and Lewis second.

But the script did not run to type in the first nine races. After Silverstone Alonso was 12 points behind Lewis and constantly moaning to the Spanish press about how bad a deal he was getting. He had come to McLaren expecting to be treated as an incoming hero and had thought Lewis would be a willing No. 2 to his own garlanded, victorious warrior. He was a young pup to offer the occasional scrap of advice, a boy he could teach to drive almost as majestically as himself. But for a World Champion with five years' more experience of Formula One than Lewis, Alonso sometimes came across as incredibly insensitive, too earnest and grim. It was hard for the public to take a shine to him and he seemed to allow the young whippersnapper to get under his skin. He lost the all-important psychological battle with a boy on his debut campaign and his behaviour was at best immature, but at times ungracious and some-what unbecoming of a double World Champion.

As the season went on, Lewis appeared perturbed and puzzled by the Spaniard's attitude towards him. In comparison, he was always friendly and approachable, and made time for the people who matter the most – the fans. One Formula One fan, Allison Foster, said 'The way that Hamilton treats his fans separates him from most other drivers. It's great to see a driver who acknowledges the fans' support, and I hope he keeps it up.' She gave the name of one British driver who was supposedly far less personable: 'In his home Grand Prix, with 20 people who just wanted an autograph, he refused to even acknowledge that the crowd was there and left without a word to these people who had been up since 3am to support him. I guess the difference is that Lewis remembers what is was like to be a fan, trying to give the driver you support a bit of encouragement.'

Already the legends of Formula One were queuing up to pay tribute to the young man who could be the greatest driver ever to grace the sport. When Lewis scored a sensational victory in the GP2 race at Silverstone in 2006, Sir Stirling Moss was impressed. His wife Suzy sought to drag him off to an important appointment, but Moss hesitated. 'Just a moment, darling. I must congratulate Lewis.' David Coulthard – who initially urged caution in believing Lewis could achieve much so early on – would then say: 'How good is Lewis? Undoubtedly, the guy is very special. I'd say he is a combination of Senna and Prost. We had Senna and Prost, Mansell and Piquet, then Michael Schumacher. We have now just entered the Lewis Hamilton era.' And three-times World Champion Niki Lauda admitted he had been 'stunned' by Lewis' achievements.

The legendary Formula One commentator Murray Walker also pitched in with his own tribute, saying Lewis would easily live up to the ever-growing hype: 'It's my considered opinion that Lewis Hamilton will go on to be one of the greatest drivers of all time…There aren't enough superlatives for what Lewis Hamilton is doing, race after race… It is unprecedented in the history of Formula One. I've been watching Formula One since it began and I have never seen anything like this in my life; it is quite incredible. It's more than feasible that he could win the Championship this year, which would be incredible.'

Inevitably, there were dissenters, and, perhaps not surprisingly, they were from those who had once been heroes themselves, men who now maybe looked on with a glint of disbelief at the young man who made it all seem so easy. Nigel Mansell was one of the first – although to be fair, later in the season he paid tribute to Lewis. The 1992 champion said, 'We had to win races and challenge for championships before we got the rewards. Now you seem to get the rewards before you achieve... They [McLaren] have been way overdue for success. Timing is everything. When a driver can arrive with a team and an engine coming right, it makes a difference. No disrespect to him... I think it was ordained, my story was a lot harder.'

Eddie Jordan was also a bit of a party pooper, questioning whether Lewis had the required ruthlessness to rule Formula One: 'Lewis is fortunate to have a well-grounded team with a structure he probably wouldn't have got anywhere else. But if he needed to do what Schumacher did to Villeneuve or Hill, would he do that? You need to do that to win. Winning is in the mind, and you have to do it at all costs. Anyone who tells you different is either lying or hasn't achieved what they're capable of. There has to be a steely aspect that we haven't seen, otherwise Hamilton will be swamped. He needs to have that arrogance otherwise he will not succeed. Does Alex Ferguson have it? Yes. Does José Mourinho? Yes. Winners generally are not nice people. They try to be, but they are immensely selfish, immensely arrogant and have a total belief in their own ability. Nothing else matters to them when they are at work.'

When told of the comments Lewis simply shrugged. He was that kind of guy: cool, easy-going, but hard-nosed when necessary. But Jordan's mention of the great Schumacher was interesting. His name and that of Ayrton Senna were to come up again and again when the talk turned to Lewis' style of driving, and Lewis himself would later admit they were his Formula One idols. He admired the German for his coolness and as a boy he had cried when he heard of Senna's tragic death.

Schumacher remained a sort of 'Phantom of The Opera' figure in Formula One during the 2007 season, his name and face haunting the pit lane even after his retirement – a result no doubt of his astonishing years of success and dominance. And it seemed to me that, yes, Lewis' driving had elements of both him and Senna: the cool, measured approach of Schuey mixed in with the heady aggression and risk-taking of the Brazilian. Psychologically; Lewis approached races with Schumacher's deadly intent, aware half the battle was indeed in the head, but he was also not averse to pushing himself to the limit and taking a calculated gamble in the style of Senna if that was required to secure victory.

I asked Formula One insider Darren Simpson about that assessment. He told me: 'Yes, Lewis is calm, consistent and hard-working but also has an edge about him. For example, the way he chooses to drive so close to the wall, allowing him to maintain incredible speed coming out of corners. And the kind of tactics that he used in the US Grand Prix against his team-mate, Alonso, when he used a centre-to-right and then slight right-back-to-centre defensive overtaking manoeuvre that just about avoided punishment.

'Driving so close to the wall is a breathtaking tactic while it pays off, but we must pray he will not one day end up in the wall like Senna. Only once was the wall a problem for Schumacher, when he broke his leg in 1999 at Silverstone.

The rest of the time Schumacher's ruthless "win at any cost" mentality, which on occasions resulted in Formula One driving becoming a contact sport, was the problem. Ask Damon Hill!

'There is an inescapable fact: Hamilton drives like a karter. He loves the edge of the track and takes a late turn in to the hairpin and clips a late apex. In fact, his driving does reflect that of Schuey's early in the German's career. Lots of sharp turn-ins, lots of brake lock-ups.'

Asked which driver from the past he would like to face, Hamilton replied: 'The likes of Juan Manuel Fangio, Alain Prost, Ayrton Senna and Michael Schumacher because I have always wanted to race against him.' He then joked: 'The year I get here, he bails out – I don't know if I had something to do with that!'

By October 2007 there was talk that the German superstar might even come out of retirement – such was the pull and presence of the new kid on the block, who had so comfortably taken on his role as the superstar of Formula One. Lewis' world had changed dramatically: he was now indeed a superstar, but the normal lad remained underneath his elevation to celebrity status. His dad Anthony said: 'Lewis is a feet-on-the-ground kid and as long as I've got anything to do with him, he'll remain that way.' But after his son's first podium finish in Australia he said that he was not naïve enough to think Lewis could still lead a normal life, that he could walk down the street without being recognised. Anthony understood their lives would never be the same: 'The emotions are incredible – it's taken us 10 years to get here. I don't want Lewis to lose focus. We're ordinary people but, yes, we know things are going to change.'

There was another factor keeping Lewis' feet on the ground – the smiling face of his 15-year-old half-brother Nicolas, who suffers from cerebral palsy, but who, along with their father Anthony, accompanies Lewis to every race. The boys are extremely close and Lewis said 'Nicolas is my greatest inspiration. I look at him and that puts my life into perspective. He comes to all my races we are very close – I race for him. He's what keeps me up there and keeps me motivated. I always wanted a brother and I remember when my parents [as he always refers to his father and stepmother Linda] first told me they were going to have a boy, I was well excited. It's quite a cool feeling to watch someone grow up, to see the difficulties and troubles he's had, the experience he's had. To go through them with him and see how he pulls out of them. I think he's just an amazing lad and I really love to do things for him. For instance, we love to race remote-control cars. I bought him a new one, then I bought one as well so we can race together. I've been a couple of times to the site where they race them and I get hassled a little bit now.

'Nicolas loves a challenge and he's got a lot steeper challenges ahead of him. He is seven years younger than me and he's a great character. He might have cerebral palsy, but he definitely wants to do something special with his life – maybe in the wheelchair Olympics or even something around Formula One. I wouldn't put it past him trying to be a commentator. We hang around together a lot and he gives me real perspective. He's the one member of my family who'll keep my feet on the ground, especially in Formula One.'

Keeping those feet on the ground includes regular routines such as a family Chinese takeaway after race meetings and chats with family and close friends in the build-up to races. Lewis says: 'I'm not into all those lucky charms or voodoo routines before a race. I just talk to my family and get into the dressing room, focus and get out there. I'm lucky to have my family and a few good friends supporting me. I can count my friends on one hand and I keep those closest to me. Trust needs to be earned.'

He would certainly need to stay grounded and take heed of what his family and friends told him. By the time of the US Grand Prix, world famous celebrities were queuing up to meet the boy who had taken racing by storm. Yet even the stars of showbiz who had so easily fallen under his spell – including the singer Beyoncé, who was said to have been 'very taken' with Lewis when they were introduced – spoke of his charm and endearing normality.

American rapper Pharrell Williams appeared trackside on several occasions to support Lewis. At the US Grand Prix, he said 'He's a good kid – he represents a lot of humility for all his achievements. It sounds like gibberish but that's what brought us here. It's not in the pocket, but in the heart and the mind.'

He was also being described as a trailblazer, one that would open up Formula One to children who previously would not have presumed they could enter the sport because of its predominantly rich, middle-class, white background. Ash Hussain of the *Mail on Sunday* newspaper, himself a man who had battled to break down barriers in journalism to reach the top, believed Lewis would indeed have a beneficial effect. Himself a Formula One fanatic, Ash told me: 'I strongly believe Lewis will inspire kids from ethnic backgrounds into motor racing. I think what he has already achieved in the last few months has already encouraged a whole generation of young ethnic drivers to compete in motor racing. Certainly I have met many thinking that way, which is in itself a revolutionary change from the past.'

He also admires the way Lewis has no desire to distance himself from the fans and his determination not to play the big star. He believes this endears him to the youth of today, and encourages them to be part of its tomorrows: 'He's just a great guy, absolutely fantastic. At the Goodwood Festival of Speed last summer, for instance, he came out and signed autographs in driving rain. He could have gone off home but he spent the whole day there. That is the difference between him and other drivers – he is such a terrific ambassador for the sport, and the ethnic minorities.

'In many ways, he reminds me of Amir Khan and how he has brought boxing into the young Asian community. They are both decent, down-to-earth young guys despite their talents and fame. I am proud of Lewis and Amir and what they have achieved, and the great things they will no doubt achieve in the future. They are both true heroes and great role models.'

A role model and a worldwide star... this was certainly a

long way from where it all began, back in Stevenage in 1985 when Lewis was born, and even humbler surroundings before that when his paternal grandfather emigrated from Grenada to England. Years of hard work, from his first outings in karts at the age of six through his apprenticeship with McLaren and F3 and GP2, years of dedication had now finally paid off.

So how exactly did Lewis Hamilton become the biggest name in Formula One? Let's first examine the origins of the boy who was to become an idol for a whole new generation, one who would resurrect an ailing Formula One and, at the same time, be hailed its new king...

CHAPTER 2

ROOTS, ROCK, REGGAE

The pretty Caribbean island of Grenada has more spices per square mile than any other in the region and is hence known as The Spice Isle. Indeed, sales of cinnamon, cloves, ginger, mace and, in particular, nutmeg – 20 per cent of the world's supply of nutmeg – are vital exports and, along with tourism, play a key role in the nation's economy.

Now the island is fast becoming as famous for its links to Lewis Hamilton – and his larger-than-life granddad, Davidson Hamilton. Take the tour bus to Grand Roy, time it right – either just before secondary school starts, or just after it finishes for the day – and you can't miss him. He's the guy driving the kids to and from school in the shiny new minibus, the one who will automatically give you a big wave of the hand and a beaming smile if you catch his eye. Failing that, just ask where Lewis Hamilton's grandfather lives and you'll immediately be pointed in the right direction. His grandson's overnight fame has turned Davidson Augustin Hamilton into a celebrity and the old guy just loves it.

A sprightly 77-year-old, he is a man who likes to keep active. 'Busy brain and busy body makes for a longer life,' he says. 'I like to be doing things – I'm not one for sitting around getting old.' Likeable and popular, Davidson is a trusted figure in his local community and that's why, despite his advancing years, they allow him to drive the kids to and from school in his pride-and-joy minibus.

On the back window is a sign that proclaims the belief and moral dictum by which this proud man has lived his life: To God Be Glory. It's a slogan from which his grandson Lewis also operates and he is the first to admit that he believes the good lord is behind his astonishing feats.

The sign also provides a link with his son – and Lewis' father – Anthony. It was Anthony who insisted on upgrading the battered old Mitsubishi his dad used to drive around the island, replacing it with the new £20,000 minibus. That way, he also provided a small income for Davidson, who had previously refused gifts for gifts' sake. When Anthony explained the motive behind the minibus – that it would provide the old man with a few pounds to help out in his retirement years and would also be safer to ferry around the kids – Davidson finally accepted his kind offer.

Of course that's after checking first with his wife Uelisia. He explained what Anthony had told him and how the money would come in handy, little though it was (with him charging just 20p a trip the venture would not make them millionaires), and she had finally given her blessing.

A matron at a nearby retirement home, Uelisia is also a person of high morals and a strong belief 'in living the right way – God's way'. She is a member of the Seventh-day Adventist church in Grenada – in fact, she is on the executive committee of the Grenadian Conference, the organising body for the island's Adventists set up in 1983. Her role within the organisation perhaps goes some way to explaining the work ethic so common in the family as a whole. The Seventh-day Adventists is an evangelical movement which believes strongly in passing on the message via missionaries and recognises the Sabbath as Saturday rather than Sunday.

A spokesman for the movement said: 'The emphasis in our church is on making the most of the gifts that God gives us. We believe in clean healthy living, the importance of the family, hard work and developing our God-given talents for the benefit of our families and the wider community. We believe that the Sabbath is a time to come together as families and as a community to pray together and eat together, but we also believe that we should try to live up to our ideals every day, not just on the Sabbath.'

Lewis' grandparents enjoy a quiet life and Davidson admits he 'gets a great deal of joy and satisfaction' at putting something back into the community in which they live by taking the kids on their daily 15-minute journey from Grand Roy to the nearby St John's Christian Secondary School.

It's all a far cry from the hedonistic world of Formula One, but Davidson says he is proud of his grandson and the impact he has had on motor racing. Indeed, he admits he would not have minded being a racer himself – and gave a hint that racing at high speeds has not just arrived with Lewis... that it has run in the family for generations. He said, 'I used to be a bit of a speed king myself in my younger days! When I was 18 I passed my test and bought a motorbike. I used to tear up and down the roads but I never had an accident. People would say: "Watch out, Davidson's about."' Davidson then got an Austin A40 car and got stopped for speeding – at 40mph in a 30mph limit. 'That was when I learnt my lesson and decided to take things a little slower. Now I just drive the minibus, but I'm a slowcoach now – I only do 15mph!'

To the locals he will always be known as 'Uncle Dave' in reverence to his kindness and warmth. I am told he is renowned for always having the time for people, and if he hasn't got the time, he invariably makes it later. Elvis Glean, a court bailiff and friend, told the *Daily Telegraph*: 'Uncle Dave's' speeding was legendary when he was younger among the 600 residents of Grand Roy. He once rode from Grand Roy to the police station in Gouyave – the next town along the coast, about three miles away – in not much more than five minutes. I think he was riding one of those huge BSA bikes. He rode like the wind and we sometimes worried he would end up dead, but I don't think he even ever had an accident: he is a true survivor.'

Proud Davidson joined up with his famous grandson at Silverstone in July 2007 to watch him in a Formula One grand prix for the first time. It was several years since he had seen him in a race. Lewis was delighted that he had been able to fly over for 'the big one', saying: 'Grandad was at a karting race years and years ago, but he's never been to a grand prix. He's coming over to meet the family, and it's just convenient it is at the same time as this grand prix.

'But a lot of my family have not seen a grand prix – and I've a very big family. You can't always get passes so I'm sure it will take quite a few years for them all to come and see me. I'm just glad Granddad has been able to make it now – it's great to see him again.'

Davidson watched from the paddock with a big smile as his grandson finished third and returned to Grenada and his daily routine the following week a happy man. He admitted the occasion had brought a tear to his eyes. 'He is such a fine young man and a very talented driver,' he said. 'I pray that his good fortune continues and he becomes World Champion. Lewis may live far away from us in England, but we are a close-knit family. He is a very nice young man, who is respectful and thoughtful when it comes to the welfare of others as well as being a competitor.

Talking to the *Sunday Mirror*, Davidson was the picture of a doting grandfather: 'He is a regular guy. He loves to joke, listen to reggae music and go to the beach when he comes here on holiday and he sometimes joins us at church. His father has been so careful about his upbringing that the money won't change him. He will remain kind-hearted and down-to-earth because that is how we are in this family.'

When Davidson was 25, people were more interested in

getting off the island – which is the second-smallest independent country in the Western Hemisphere (after Saint Kitts and Nevis) – than visiting it. He was part of the 1955 exodus to Britain, one of many hoping for a new and better life than the one back home, where poverty and natural disaster were rife. It would be almost another 25 years before he returned to his homeland and his roots.

He decided to make the move after struggling to earn a living in Grenada. In 1955, British Transport were actively encouraging immigrants from the Caribbean. Bosses even visited some of the islands to discuss with interested locals what was on offer in the UK. Davidson was one of those who were keen to try their luck elsewhere. For him, the last straw had been the devastation caused in the year of his departure by Hurricane Janet. Being on the southern edge of the hurricane belt, Grenada has suffered only three hurricanes in the last 60 years. But Hurricane Janet passed over the island in September 1955 with winds of 115 mph, causing severe damage.

While it spelled the end for Davidson, his brother Fleet stayed on in Grenada and became a major success. Nigel Forrester, a teacher in Grenada and Lewis' second cousin, said that Davidson's brother saw an opportunity to thrive after the hurricane destroyed most of the island's nutmeg trees: 'My grandfather – Davidson's brother – replanted, seizing the opportunity to buy the land from people who wanted to sell. He did very well out of it. There's a determination and perseverance in the Hamilton family. They're always trying get to a higher level.'

But Davidson remained convinced that that 'higher level' would not come in Grenada. At about 15 per cent, the island had one of the highest unemployment rates in the Caribbean. Unemployment was particularly high among young people so he clambered aboard the ship that would take him to England, setting in motion a whole train of events.

The immigrants were among the second wave from the Caribbean islands in the twentieth century. The first arrived after the beginning of World War I, working in the war industries and the Merchant Navy. They established themselves in the seaports and major cities and initially they were welcomed as they contributed to the war effort. But as men returned home from the war and the country plunged into depression, resentment grew because the immigrants were seen to be taking 'native' jobs. Ultimately, this sparked off race riots in the years immediately following the war. Despite the trouble, many immigrants considered themselves British nationals and refused to return home. Together they formed the nucleus of Caribbean communities in cities such as Cardiff, Liverpool and London.

The final phase of settlement, which would include Davidson Hamilton, happened after World War II. By that time Britain's labour market was depleted and a quarter of a million Caribbeans settled permanently in Britain between 1955 and 1962. After alighting from boat trains at London stations such as Paddington, Victoria and Waterloo, many dispersed to industrial centres like Liverpool, Manchester and Birmingham. The majority, however, stayed in London – Davidson among them. He settled in west London and worked for the London Underground, initially laying track.

But the new immigrants were not welcomed with open arms by many Britons. Rather than being seen as essential workers – as they had been at the start of World War I – the fresh intake were viewed with suspicion and suggestions that they would be a social problem. It was feared they might take jobs from the locals and put pressure on housing, and that caused resentment within local communities which was later to be fired up by the likes of right-wing agitator Oswald Mosley. Davidson told a family friend: 'It was not the easiest of times. I had just arrived in a new country and some people would point at us newcomers aggressively on the street and shout obscenities. Of course, there were others who were nice to us, but it was difficult to feel at ease.'

A year after his arrival, the tense atmosphere led to the British Caribbean Welfare Service (BCWS) being established to look those who were finding it difficult to integrate. Housing was in short supply as wartime bombing had decimated stock and Davidson and others were met with signs and notices in windows stating 'No Blacks' and 'No Coloureds'. Many migrants ended up in areas where compatriots and friends were already settled and housing was more available. Trinidadians tended to go to Notting Hill and Davidson, who had made friends with some of them on the boat over, also ended up in west London. Historically, Grenadians had friends from Trinidad, their closest neighbour in the Caribbean, and so it was perhaps inevitable that he would follow the trail already mapped out in London.

The west of the capital did not provide an immediate vision of heaven, for some landlords exploited the housing shortage by expelling long-term residents and packing their properties with migrants paying exorbitant rents. Despite all this, Davidson would eventually settle in the area in a small, cramped flat with his sweetheart, Agnes Mitchell, at 12a Broughton Road, Fulham. The couple were married by Catholic priest Maurice Beckett at the nearby Church of Our Lady in Stephendale Road on 26 May 1956. Davidson was 25 and now working as a railway guard, his bride was 23 and unemployed. A couple of years later, they moved a few miles further west to 82 Avenue Road in Acton, and their son Anthony Carl Arthur was born on 31 May 1960 in Hammersmith Hospital.

Anthony had a tough childhood in west London, with his father constantly worried his boy would end up with the wrong crowd. By the time Davidson returned to Grenada in the late seventies, Anthony had moved out to Stevenage, 30 miles north of the capital, with a then population of around 40,000. In 2007 Lewis said Anthony had 'had it tough' because his mother (Agnes) died when Anthony was young. But the family did not wish to talk further about how her death affected the family.

Stevenage seemed an unusual choice of location for a young black man – it was a predominantly white town and had hardly been a magnet for ethnic minorities in previous years. Stevenage became the first of the post-war new towns specifically built to take the overspill from London. By 1961 the UK census showed that a total of 172,877 people moved to Britain from the Caribbean in the previous decade. Antagonism and racism against the newcomers remained rife for another two decades, however, with reports of petty yet persistent incidents well into the mid-1980s.

The situation had calmed down slightly when Anthony Hamilton settled in Stevenage after marrying young, but it was still a testing time for the boy with Grenadian ancestry – particularly when he married a white girl, Carmen Larbalestier, who was five years his senior – at the start of the eighties.

A couple of excellent newspaper articles highlighted the 'loneliness' and 'resentment' blacks like Anthony Hamilton had to overcome when settling in overspill towns such as Stevenage. The influential American journalist Leonard Downie jnr of the *Washington Post* travelled to Britain to report on the country's new towns and how they compared with America. He was keen to learn whether the urban problems experienced in the States were mirrored in Britain. While accepting that the new towns had indeed relieved the pressure on housing, his findings occasionally made grim reading, revealing how immigrants had found 'proper jobs' difficult to come by and how they suffered in 'ghetto-like' conditions.

He wrote: 'The British have successfully used some of their new towns to relieve overcrowded conditions in working-class neighborhoods of the big cities and provide many of their residents with better homes. Planners arrange for the combined transfer of willing businesses and their employees from London to Harlow or Stevenage, for instance... In some places the move of people and industry to the new town was so well co-ordinated that as high as 85 percent of the new town residents – in Harlow, for instance – worked at jobs inside the new town itself and continue to enjoy some of the shared interests and friendships of the old big city neighborhoods from which they came. However, this very success in matching workers and jobs has made many of Britain's new towns single-class communities. To move into most of them, a prospective resident must be assured a job by one of the new town's largely technological or clerical employers; thus the population of each project is disproportionately dominated by white collar and skilled workers. There are few non-skilled workers, non-whites or immigrants of any kind, low-income families, or, at the other end of the spectrum, upper income people. Although this is not particularly disturbing to the British, who readily segregate themselves by social and economic class, the sameness of everyone and everything in each new town bores and disconcerts the visitor, reminding him too much of the economic stratification, and resulting sterility, of too many American suburbs.

'The lack of opportunities for unskilled and lower income workers does leave real problems back in the central cities. In London, for example, from where skilled, middle income, white workers were attracted to new towns like Harlow and Stevenage, mostly low income and jobless

Pakistani, Indian and black immigrants remain today, many trapped in ever worsening, ghetto-like conditions. In this respect, just like U.S. suburbs and new town projects, the British new towns have exacerbated rather than eased a critical urban problem' wrote Downie jnr.

Anthony Davidson was one of those lower income workers, surviving on the meagre wages he earned with British Rail. It was a depressing scenario, but here was a man with a lion's heart and a determination to make something of his life. Just as his father had taken a huge gamble in leaving Grenada for Britain, he too was convinced his destiny lay in another field. Little did he know it would involve nurturing and supporting a brilliant son with a God-given talent.

Anthony would tell friends: 'No, it was not easy. At first it seemed as if I had moved from one nightmare [London] to another. But there was no way I was going to run away – I had had enough, I wanted some stability.' This was to eventually come when Lewis was born in 1985.

In 1999 another fine journalist, Gary Younge, whose hometown is Stevenage and who writes for the *Guardian*, published an outstanding book about his travels through the American south. This also provides insight into the sort of problems that Anthony, and later Lewis, would have had to overcome.

Younge wrote: 'There were three types of reactions a black family could expect in a place like Stevenage. There were those who welcomed us. There were those who tolerated us. And there were those who positively despised us... The despisers, like the Norrises, a scrawny white family who used to stand at the top of the road and shout "Woggy, woggy" at us. Once, when the Norrises had gone too far, she [mum] called the police. The policeman said he wouldn't ask them to stop: "I'm afraid that you are an ethnic minority in this area and you are going to have to put up with that kind of thing from time to time," he said.'

It was powerful stuff. Anthony himself refused to be intimidated and he stood his ground, as did Lewis in later years. Both made it clear to anyone who tried to bully or taunt them that they were there to stay. Lewis even took up karate to look after himself better. First Davidson and then his son Anthony showed a determination and staunch belief that they should be allowed to live and bring up a family in England. It was another example of that fierce Hamilton pride in action. Rooted in strong Catholic faith, throughout time the Hamiltons would always stand their ground and stand up for what they believed in. Yes, the die had been cast for the Hamilton generation and the Lewis Hamilton era. Even now, Stevenage – which one local described to me as 'slightly soulless and nondescript' – only has a 1 per cent black element to its 80,000 population. But, as Gary Younge wrote in the *Guardian* in June 2007, 'Right now, black Stevenage represents 100 per cent of the town's most famous sons.' Yes, that's Lewis Hamilton – and Ashley Young, the promising England football international, who was in the same secondary school class as the Formula One whizzkid. And there was also Albert Campbell, who became the town's first black mayor in 1987.

The hardships his grandfather went through in coming to Britain and staying there in such racially prejudiced times are indelibly carved on the heart of Lewis Hamilton: he knows he owes much to the courage of Davidson Hamilton. He, along with his father Anthony, is the rock on which he has built his success... a rock that originated in the Caribbean.

Nowadays, when Lewis goes to visit his relatives in Grand Roy, he can share a laugh, enjoy some local cuisine cooked up by Uelisia and relax with a cool drink. He also likes listening to some of Bob Marley's tunes on his iPod, as well as some by the reggae legend's sons Ziggy and Damian on the beach. But he will never forget what his family went through to ensure that he and his father had a good start in life; one they would never have enjoyed, had Davidson not taken a gamble by moving to England to start a new life.

Success and fame have their consolations, for in addition to the new minibus Davidson drives around Grand Roy, the Grenadian government has now placed on record its personal pride in its most famous son. After Lewis' fabulous debut grand prix victory in Montreal on 19 June 2007, Edwin Frank, of The Grenada Board of Tourism and the Ministry of Tourism, said: 'We would like to congratulate Mr Lewis Hamilton for the success that he has been achieving as a participant in his first season in Formula One racing. The GBT notes that as a young British driver of Grenadian roots (his grandfather is from Concord in St John), he has placed among the top three in all of the six races that he has participated in for the season. As a member of the McLaren Mercedes team, he has shown and demonstrated to the Formula One racing fraternity that he could indeed become the next big sensation of the sport.

'His recent victory in his first grand prix race in Montreal on Sunday 10 June 2007 has made Grenadians very proud. His achievement has served as an inspiration to the young people of Grenada, who consider him a genuine living example of what hard work and determination can bring to focused individuals.

'The Government and people of Grenada join in applauding his achievements and celebrate the fact that through his excellent performance, people around the world have learnt of his Grenadian ancestry. He is a demonstration of the Grenadian spirit.'

And indeed he is… Let's move on now to fill in some more gaps by taking a look at Lewis' early years.

CHAPTER 3

BOY RACER

Even in the eighties in some quarters, the sight of a black man with a white woman was still met with raised eyebrows by a prejudiced society, which can hardly have helped the union of Anthony Hamilton and Carmen Larbalestier. To be fair, London was much more advanced and liberal in its views, perhaps inevitably given the large black population in districts such as Brixton and Notting Hill.

It was all the more difficult to understand, therefore, why Anthony and Carmen would decide not to base their lives in the capital, instead plumbing for Stevenage, a town which, as we have already noted, even in 2007 has only a small black population. Yet the couple settled in an end-of-terrace at 57 Peartree Way on the Shephall council estate. The couple had married at Stevenage's St Hilda's Catholic

Church on 5 May 1979 when Anthony was 18 and Carmen 23. Anthony was still working for the railways and money was tight; Carmen, who was born miles away in Birmingham and whose father Maurice was a draughtsman, had been working on an assembly line in a factory. It was into this humble, struggling background that Lewis Carl Davidson Hamilton was born on 7 January 1985 in Stevenage's Lister Hospital. That Christmas before the boy's birth had not been easy – a shortage of money, a poorly Carmen and a stressed Anthony made sure of that. But that cold winter's day the couple put their problems aside as they stared at their beautiful son. They had waited long enough to bring him into the world, on some occasions wondering if they were to be denied the child they so wanted. Carmen admitted: 'Lewis is very special for me because we tried for a long time to have him. I didn't think he was ever going to come along.' He was her third child – Lewis has two older half-sisters, Nicola and Samantha.

It was Anthony's idea to name their precious son after US Olympic gold medal winning athlete Carl Lewis. He was something of a hero to him following his remarkable showing at the previous summer's Olympic Games in Los Angeles. Carl Lewis had won an amazing four gold medals – in the 100 metres, the 200 metres, the long jump and the 4 x 100 metres relay. Anthony also added the name Davidson at the last minute, in tribute to his own father. Yet Carmen would also have a say, insisting that her newborn son's Christian names should be turned around so that he was called Lewis Carl. It was the last time the word reverse would be used when talking about Lewis Carl Hamilton – from now on, it was always fast forward...

Carmen admitted to the *Daily Express* that from the very start her son was a motor racing natural: 'Lewis had a love for speed as soon as he cut his first teeth. On his first birthday, he was given a toy steering wheel for his baby buggy. It was a big plastic one you could stick on the buggy and drive it along. He's had his hands on a steering wheel since that day.'

But the couple's joy was short-lived. Within months it was clear their marriage no longer worked and when Lewis was 2, Anthony and Carmen separated. Anthony moved out of the house in Peartree Way and Carmen's new boyfriend, Raymond Lockhart, moved in. Carmen would later wed Raymond and they remain happily married to this day. Back then, Lewis was happy enough to be living with his mother and the man who had become his stepfather. He was a good boy, who spent much of his time reading and playing football on the streets of the council estate with his friends. Easy to get on with and always with a smile on his face, he was well liked in Shephall.

His first school was just 200 yards from home and he fitted in easily at the Peartree Infants School despite the fact that he was the only black boy in his class. The school's deputy head, Carol Hopkins, confirmed he was a popular boy, but said that at that time he had not yet shown any of the competitiveness that would eventually mark him out as a possible racing great: 'I remember him for his bright, smiley face and lovely manners. He enjoyed school to the full, certainly, but in those early years you would not have seen him as a competitive little chap, just very happy. Bright little button, but normal, very normal.'

Naturally enough, he is now a hero at the school. The young pupils set up their own 'Lewis Hamilton Corner' during the 2007 season, where they put up his cuttings and marked off his race wins. 'He is somebody for them to look up to,' says Carol Hopkins. 'He is their hero.'

By the age of 5 Lewis had already shown an interest in cars – Carmen said he spent hours playing with the array of toy cars littered across his bedroom floor and would, inevitably, end up racing them against each other with lavish victory ceremonies for the winners. He also began driving on Dodgems at amusement arcades, and it was then that his father Anthony – now his manager – recognised the remarkable hand-eye coordination his son possessed.

At 6 it was not only his mother who had noted his love of cars: friends and neighbours shook their heads and smiled as he played excitedly in the street with the radio-controlled car he got for Christmas while other boys kicked their footballs about. His first driving victory came, also aged 6, when he raced his radio-controlled car against other youngsters in a competition on the children's TV show *Blue Peter*.

Anthony, by now a motor racing fanatic, would visit regularly and also noted his son's fascination with everything automotive. By the time Lewis progressed to junior school, he decided to take his ever-growing hobby a step further: on some of his visits he would go karting with him.

Lewis had his first drive in a go-kart while on a childhood holiday in Spain. Shortly afterwards, Anthony managed to scrape together £1,000 to buy him his own. Carmen says: 'When his dad bought him a go-kart for Christmas before his eighth birthday, I thought, good grief! He bought him all the kit – the suit, helmet – and popped him in it. Down the street, and he was off. He went from model cars to go-karts, to Formula One.'

She said that by the age of 8 Lewis had started to get interested in Formula One. His hero was Ayrton Senna, who would die tragically in 1994 when his young fan was 9. Carmen, now says: 'He was kart-racing the weekend Ayrton Senna died. The news came through and he was really upset, bless him, but Senna's death didn't sway him. I knew early on that his passion was so big that nothing would stop him.'

Lewis remembers that weekend and admits the death of Senna had a major impact on him: 'Yes, I was 9 when Ayrton Senna died, and he was my hero. I remember racing that weekend in Hoddesdon. My dad had a small Vauxhall Cavalier and a trailer at the back. We'd sit in the Cavalier and wait for my turn to race. And that day I was told Senna had just died. It hit me hard, but I never liked to show emotion in front of my dad. So I went behind the trailer and cried. That was the turning point of my life: because when you're so young, you believe people like Senna are invincible. And then you realise that they're also mortal. It made me understand I need to make the most of my talent.'

When Lewis was 10, his life and that of his father

changed forever after Anthony took him to the Rye House kart track, a few miles south of Stevenage. Lewis had already lapped his father when they raced in karts at other circuits and now he told him that he wanted to be a professional racer. Tony Delahunty was at Rye House on the same day with his son, Andrew, who was a couple of years older than Lewis. Delahunty, a commentator on karting for British Eurosport, said: 'Anthony told me that before this Lewis had been an expert in model-car racing – you know, that remote control stuff – and that Lewis had been winning everything, but that most of the people he was competing against were adults. So they were looking for something more apt for a youngster.' Delahunty was mighty impressed by the young Lewis – so much so, in fact, that within a year, 'I was doing press releases for him.'

Anthony too knew his son meant business and *was* the business. He himself was a strong, determined man, who had made advances in his own life since splitting from Carmen eight years previously, becoming computer savvy and moving up to the job of IT manager. Despite this, he now decided to take a gamble, putting everything he earned on his son's future. He took redundancy from his job so that he could be with Lewis as he advanced, taking on casual work, and at one stage he was doing three jobs at a time to make ends meet, including putting up estate agents' signs. According to Lewis: 'I don't think he ever went into debt but he had quite a few jobs on the go. He had his main job, but I also remember him putting up "For Sale" signs – he'd get £15 a sign.'

This was quite a remarkable show of faith and commitment. Anthony Hamilton was such a winner that eventually the computer firm he set up while dedicating his life to his son also become big-time, employing 20 staff in 2007, but the 47-year-old stressed that his first loyalty remained with his son, who he now manages. Back then, he would also drive Lewis to races all over the country and overseas as part of his duties.

Anthony explained he had done a deal with Lewis over their new commitment. He would only keep to his side if Lewis continued to try his best to achieve academic success at school and dedicated himself to racing: 'From the start I also tried to ensure that Lewis looked after himself and was never in any danger of going off the rails with too much partying and late nights, all the temptations that young kids like to get up to. To be frank, I think that honesty and trust played a big, big role in our relationship as Lewis was climbing up the ladder.

'I think we've always tried to bring Lewis up to do things right and to understand that positive consequences flow from taking an honest approach to things, whether we were talking about his kart racing or his school work. I told him that if he had any doubts then he shouldn't do it. But I was also confident that if he took my advice and listened to what I was telling him, then a few years down the road it would all work out for him the way he wanted.

'I suppose you could say it was tempting to apply the carrot-and-stick approach to Lewis for getting behind with his school work by saying "Right, you're not going to the next race", but in truth Lewis was too good to be penalised in such a way.'

The decision to push Lewis onwards also meant a change of living arrangements. After eight years with his mother, the 10-year-old now moved in with Anthony, his stepmother, Linda, and stepbrother, Nicolas. Carmen and stepfather Raymond also opted for a change of direction, announcing they were to marry and had chosen to settle down in London.

Understandably, Carmen was sad that she would now be apart from the boy she had loved and nurtured, but she still felt it was for the best given that Anthony would do anything within his power to ensure their son reached the very top. Looking back on the initial split from Anthony when Lewis was 2, she said 'It didn't damage Lewis. He is probably better for it than if we had stuck together in an unhappy marriage. Tony wanted to be somebody and he has achieved that. I wanted the quiet life and that put a barrier between us. I couldn't see myself in that busy, hectic lifestyle, but I didn't stop him making sure Lewis got what he wanted.'

And speaking of the time when Lewis left her at the age of 10 she also said, with typical honesty and pride, paying her former husband considerable compliments: 'It was heart-breaking... but I had to let him go and live with his dad for him to be a star. His dad has worked very hard to raise the money for Lewis' career. Without his dad's constant, constant work, he would not have been able to continue, as it's a very expensive sport. It takes millions and a lot of kids have millionaire parents. The parents can't understand quite why their sons are not winning when Lewis is. It's not all about money, it's about talent.'

There have been suggestions Carmen has not been happy at being portrayed in the press as someone Lewis left behind, and she herself has publicly refuted further suggestions that she feels as if 'she has missed the boat' as her son's star rises inexorably upwards. She now lives in a terraced house in Letchworth Garden City, Hertfordshire with her husband Raymond. They bought the property in June 2006 for £197,000. The area is described as one of 'Blue collar enterprise – White van culture' by Experian's neighbourhood classification system, Mosaic.

Lewis, Anthony, Linda and his brother Nicolas, meanwhile, reside in a £1 million-plus detached mansion in Tewin Wood, Hertfordshire. Lewis also has his own luxury £250,000 apartment, near the McLaren HQ in Woking, Surrey. The extent of Anthony's own success with his computer firm is shown by the fact that he paid a cool £630,000 for the house back in March 2001, way before Lewis' success in Formula One. The area is deemed highly sought after and populated by corporate chieftains, usually very wealthy people who have rewarding careers rather than jobs, and who own expensive cars and indulge in the most exotic leisure pursuits.

At the start of the Formula One season in 2007 it was revealed that Carmen Lockhart had entered a TV competition to win a trip to Sydney to see Lewis make his debut in the Australian Grand Prix in Melbourne. The implication being, of course, that she could not afford the trip and that her son had not invited her to Oz, nor offered to pay for her.

A family friend tried to put the whole situation into perspective for me with these words: 'When Lewis went to live with his dad at 10, Carmen really missed him but knew she couldn't have the same input into his karting career as Tony. It has been hard, but both sides have worked hard to maintain family ties. However, there are times Carmen feels left out and, I think, a little jealous – [and] who wouldn't? – of his closeness with Tony.

'It's only natural and like any mum in this type of situation she is a bit wary of the press and their implying she wasn't there for him because he lived with his dad. The truth is in fact it was because she loved him she let him go to become the champion he is. It was actually an act of true selflessness.'

To me, this seems a fair take on the situation and I am assured by others who know the family that it is along the right lines. Both Carmen and Anthony were in attendance when Lewis signed his Formula One contract with McLaren at a London nightclub. And, as the 2007 Formula One season progressed, his parents were hardly at loggerheads, but seemed to be good friends, attending races together. There was even talk of them going away on holiday with their new partners. Lewis himself also admitted he loved it when he and Carmen went on their regular ten-pin bowling trips – they would go at least once a month and 'have great fun, even though she usually beats me!'

Carmen confirmed everything had settled down and that she now enjoyed quality time with Lewis: 'I am his biggest fan. I am so proud of him – how could I not be proud of him? Lewis has got such a magnetism about him. His personality is outstanding and he just makes people get on. Everyone in racing thinks we're an unusual bunch. They're quite amazed when they see us come down the pit lane.

'Lewis now has his racing life with his dad and his normal life when he comes over to my house. Everything Lewis has got, he's worked really hard for. He wasn't born with a silver spoon in his mouth. Lewis has got everything – he has the personality, the looks, the physique and charisma to become a massive, absolutely massive star. I'd like people to see beyond the colour. The fact that he's the first black driver is going to be the cherry on the cake.'

Like any concerned mother, she admits she keeps a wary eye out for gold-digging women near her boy. She had thought he would stick with his college sweetheart Jodia Ma, 21, saying: 'She is the kind of girl that will help him keep his feet on the ground. She is not after the high life. I think he'd rather hang on to somebody he knows than have all these dolly birds in Formula One. You never know what they're after. Jenson Button had a lovely girlfriend and all that finished. Maybe now he wished he had hung onto her.' It turned out that Carmen was wrong on this one: by September 2007, Lewis and Jodia Ma had split up.

Lewis soon settled down into his new life, living with his father, and he and Anthony made a fine team as they pushed for glory in the karting world. It was the first step on the road to their joint ambition: to be the best in Formula One. Lewis proved an immediate sensation. Wearing black plates as a novice kart racer, he was at once competing with the fastest. His obvious talent soon brought attention from enthusiasts. Martin Hines was one such early fan. His kart manufacturing company, Zipkart, was based near to the Rye House track and he approached father and son with an offer of help.

Martin recalled in the *Guardian*: 'I would go round to watch the kart racing. If you are a novice racer you have to wear a black numberplate for your first six races. Normally, that means all the novices are at the back of the grid because they don't have enough experience to get through the field. But one day I saw Lewis Hamilton, with his black plate, and he was battling it out at the front. Someone off the street wouldn't have noticed the difference, but I knew straight away – he stuck out as something a bit special.

'I introduced myself to Lewis and his father, and offered to supply them with kart chassis. It's usually the case in motorsport that you can only go as fast as the amount of money you have. The Hamiltons weren't rich, I wanted to help.'

This would be the start of a 5-year association. Martin is glad to have helped out at such a vital time in Lewis' burgeoning career, but also to have him and Anthony as friends. Lewis, in turn, has never forgotten the faith shown in him. Anthony remains grateful to this day, saying: 'In those early days we were very lucky in finding some very gentlemanly personalities in karting, who really helped us when money was tight early in his career. We had Martin Hines helping us out with the chassis, John Davies and John Button [Jenson's father] helping us out with the engine and an old friend Martin Howells supplying us with tyres. If it wasn't for guys like that, I don't think Lewis would have got off the lowest rung of the karting ladder.'

Bill Sisley, boss of the Buckmore Park circuit, near Chatham in Kent, where Lewis was to dominate races from the start of his karting career and would later admit to it being his favourite track, could also see the genius: 'I have talent-spotted for over 35 years. I always say I can tell within two laps whether a young driver has what it takes, but the sort of raw talent enough to take them all the way to Formula One is rare. In fact, there are only one or two in a generation that good. Lewis was certainly one of them and it showed; his talent shouted out.

Sisley recalled how Lewis just did everything right. The youngster was quick, braked at the right times, overtook at the right times, instinctively took the right line into the corners and, importantly, he didn't crash. Even at that young age, his desire to win was obvious. There have been other drivers as naturally talented, but lacking that aggression and passion to get to the flag first.'

Anthony had taken Lewis to the track, knowing Bill was a famed talent spotter. Bill was quickly bowled over: 'Lewis was a once-in-a-generation talent and very few, if any, will match his achievements, but the interest he has created in a short time is fantastic. He had the three key ingredients that made up the perfect package for a great racing driver: he was packed with natural talent, he subsequently had the financial backing of the McLaren organisation and he had the professionalism and determination.

'He also had a very nice, supportive family, and when you add that to the mix you get the extremely likeable and totally focused young man that Lewis Hamilton is.'

Former Radio 1 DJ David 'Kid' Jensen was covering the kart racing at Buckmore Park for Channel 4 in 1997 when Lewis rode the circuit for the final time. He thought he would be a great, saying 'Even at 11 he was a pleasure to interview, really interesting and amenable. Lewis just had a natural way about him that was always appealing, never arrogant. He was the star of the show. He is a credit to his father.'

Jensen was full of admiration for the way in which Lewis and his father operated, their tremendous sense of respect for each other shining through: 'I saw some awful things. It would be a normal sight where a 6ft-plus guy would be bending over a 3ft-nothing little kid, bellowing insults at the top of his voice.' Anthony was an exception to this type of behaviour, someone the commentator never saw losing it. 'He was one of the ones not living out his own frustrations or vicariously trying to make up for their own failures through his child.

'In fact, the pair were a great father-son combination, which was even more commendable when you discovered that Lewis' parents had split up.'

Looking back, Lewis recalls those karting days with affection. He admits that it was the hard work in practice and testing that kept him from falling by the wayside: 'If I didn't love it, I'm sure I wouldn't be as good as I am today because I'd have put half the effort in and just have done the races. I think you find drivers who just rely on their racing ability and don't do the hard yards. When you're young you don't really understand that philosophy: work hard and see the result. You think, I can't be bothered to work hard now, and when you get there you struggle and complain. But if you really put the effort in, you see the result. Even if you don't do well, you know you've done the work, so next time you can improve on it.'

His headmaster at his junior school, Peartree, John Seal, also feels it is down to Lewis' focus and determination back then that he is the brilliant Formula One driver he is today: 'He stood out at school, and not just because he was winning all these karting trophies. He was popular, he was composed when it came to speaking in public, and he was focused – exceptionally so for someone so young. More than anything, I remember just how much support he got from his father. They were just an ordinary family from a hard-working background, that's why it's so good to see that things have turned out the way they have.'

Lewis was soon crowned Britain's youngest cadet kart champion (aged 10) and it was at the subsequent Autosport Awards ceremony in London that his legendary meeting with McLaren boss Ron Dennis took place. He asked Big Ron for his autograph. The Formula One supremo duly obliged – telling Lewis to 'try me in nine years' when the youngster said he also wanted Ron to let him drive for

McLaren. But it was to be a mere three years down the road when they would meet again. Lewis remembers that first encounter fondly: 'We couldn't afford a suit and so I'd borrowed a dark green silky suit off this guy who had won the same karting championship the year before – I even got his shoes. I went up to Ron and told him I wanted to drive for McLaren and become World Champion. He wrote in my autograph book: "Try me in nine years". But two or three years later he called me.'

Lewis moved up to secondary school, becoming a pupil at the John Henry Newman Roman Catholic School in Stevenage, where he proved himself good at other physical activities. The football he had years previously tossed aside to concentrate on his remote-control car re-emerged as he starred at John Henry Newman with a boy who would go on to become an England under-21 player. He also found the karate he had taken up a couple of years before was a more than adequate deterrent against the unwelcome attentions of another pupil.

One journalist reported: 'He took up karate after he caught the eye of the school bully. By the age of 12, he was a Black Belt. He was also a more-than-useful footballer at John Henry Newman… and played in the same team there as Ashley Young, the midfielder who joined Aston Villa from Watford in January for £9.65 million.'

Lewis told him: 'I was quicker than Ashley Young, stronger than him – so I had that with me. But he was very skilled and very neat, and would dribble the ball round people very nicely. I was very powerful in the team, I was always a midfielder and in my team I was the fittest by far because of my racing and the training I did. I'd run up and down, and up and down, and if someone tackled me I'd get them back. I'd always get them back because I never gave up, whereas a lot of people would get tackled then just leave it for the next stage of the game. I'd never let that happen.'

Meanwhile, his career in karting was to bring more honours. In 1996 he won the Champions of the Future, Sky TV KartMasters and Five Nations karting series and, a year later, moved up to junior Yamaha and won the Champions of the Future series and Super One series. Former Jaguar Racing team boss Tony Purnell was another of his sponsors, via Tony's Pi Research Company. He too was convinced he had seen the future of motor racing, saying Lewis' talent particularly shone through when McLaren took him under their wings. 'Admittedly, ever since he was 12 when I stopped sponsoring him, he's had the very best equipment. That's because he had that most important of assets, an infinitely wealthy "father figure" – McLaren's Ron Dennis. But it's one thing to have the best tools; it's quite another to be gifted enough to use them.

'Perhaps it helps to note that Lewis has always comprehensively blown away his team-mates. Consider his team-mate in Formula A [the top Euro karting class]: one Nico Rosberg. I saw Lewis race a handful of times during this period, and he was fantastic. Nico? Well, ordinary, I'd say. In short, Lewis races like... Michael Schumacher. The boy's a winner.'

At this point it's useful to note the origins of Lewis' now-famous yellow helmet.

The reason why he wears it goes back to the days when he was racing karts. His father Anthony insisted Lewis wore a yellow helmet because it would make him stand out from the crowd; also he would know instantly if his son was involved in a crash if he did not spot the helmet.

It was in 1998 that Lewis signed up with Dennis for the McLaren and Mercedes-Benz Young Drivers Programme. He was 13, still at John Henry Newman, and now he was the youngest driver ever to be contracted to a Formula One team. His father and Big Ron agreed that as he was spending such a large amount of time testing and racing, McLaren should pay for a private tutor to supplement his education. Both were keen for him not to fall behind with his schoolwork. The records were already being broken and Lewis continued his rapid rise by dominating every level in the karting world in the three years that followed. Competing in the junior Intercontinental A section, he was second in McLaren Mercedes Champions of the Future event in 1998 and fourth at the Italian Open. In 1999 he won the Italian 'Industrials' champion at Intercontinental A level, was Vice European champion and lifted the Trophy de Pomposa. He was also fourth at the Italian Open Championship at junior-Intercontinental level. As the new millennium dawned, Lewis won all four rounds in Formula A to become European Champion and also won the World Cup and the Masters at Bercy. It was the icing on the cake after another fabulous season when he was named British

Racing Drivers' Club's 'Rising Star'. Six years had passed since he and Anthony had made their pact to take him to the top of the racing world. He had experienced ups and downs in his home life and had ended up moving away from his mother to live with his father. Along the way, he had also had to sacrifice many things normal kids take for granted in their teens: 'Kids at school would say, "What you doing this weekend?" and I'd say, "Oh, I'm going karting." They'd say, "I might see you up the road then" at the local karting track. I would just nod because I wanted to keep the real extent of my racing quiet. It helped make school feel like an escape if no one knew what I was achieving in racing.

'School was my time to mess about and have a kid's life, to be normal. But at weekends I never had a chance to go to any of those under-18 clubs or parties. And that affects you because your friendships are not so strong. When you say, "I can't go out because I'm racing this weekend" your friends think you're just blowing them off. Even when, near the end, I'd tell people at school I was going to Japan for a week to race, they'd look at me blankly. It just didn't click.'

His time at secondary school passed largely without incident – he was well liked by fellow pupils and teachers. One rather bizarre incident deserves a mention, however. It revolves around him being wrongly expelled in a mix-up in his final year when he was 16, after another boy was attacked and needed hospital treatment.

Lewis was one of six teenage boys excluded in 2001 when 15-year-old classmate Sebastian Webber was attacked in the toilets, suffering two fractured fingers, bruising and an injured arm. But when Anthony Hamilton protested his son's innocence, Lewis was cleared of any wrongdoing and reinstated two months later by a local authority appeals panel. The inquiry concluded that he had been wrongly identified and he received an apology from the education authority. Vincent Hayward, Lewis' form teacher at the time, recalled 'It happened during the lunch hour. Some of them took this lad to the toilets and gave him a bit of a going over.'

Former pupil Michelle Vooght said: 'I remember the incident and it was other boys, not Lewis. He was a nice boy, friends with everyone and genuine. He was self-confident, but he'd never brag about his racing. He'd get dropped off at school in a Mercedes with "Lewis Hamilton" down the side!' Another ex-pupil, Sean Beahan, agreed: 'A lot of people had their names dragged into the attack incident and it was later found that Lewis and a few others had done nothing wrong.'

Hertfordshire County Council spokesman John Ryan said: 'Lewis was cleared of all involvement after an independent review. He was originally accused by one of the teachers. It was basically an administrative cock-up that led to the accusation and it boils down to mistaken identity.'

Perhaps inevitably, Lewis' best friend during those teen years was another racing fanatic: Nico Rosberg, who would go on to race for Williams in 2007. Lewis said: 'We were karting team-mates in Italy for two seasons and were racing to see who would become the youngest ever driver in Formula One. Nico got there first because he had a season in GP2 while I was in Formula Three. GP2 is vital because the set-up of the car is very similar to Formula One and on some tracks we hit the same speed at the end of a straight.

'He's the most competitive person I've ever met and he was really tough – but I won the European Championship and he came second. But we shared the same hotel room and always spoke of how fantastic it would be to compete against each other for the Formula One World Championship.'

Lewis had now won everything there was to win in karting. He had secured his deal with McLaren, winning a place on their prestigious training programme and he was ready to move up another gear. From karts to cars... the next stage of his quest for world domination was about to take shape.

CHAPTER 4

A WINNING FORMULA

The next move on the road to the top came in 2001 when Lewis Hamilton finally stepped into a racing car and, in his debut season, finished fifth overall in the Renault Winter Series. His career was being mapped out and engineered by Ron Dennis and McLaren. Lewis was now 16 and, although he did not know it at the time, just six years away from Formula One.

He was undoubtedly a quick learner and by the end of the following season he finished third in the British Formula Renault series – along the way notching up three wins, three fastest laps and three pole positions. Not only this but he was also fifth in the Formula Renault EuroCup Championship with one win and three podiums after competing in four rounds out of nine.

His learning period in the series was over, and he soon

roared to the 2003 British Formula Renault Championship with 10 victories and 11 pole positions. His 419 points compared dramatically with the 377 points (including just two wins) of his nearest rival, Alex Lloyd. Victory had come in double quick time during the season – he had lifted the title with two rounds to spare – and that comfort zone meant Lewis could debut in the British F3 season, taking part in the last two races of the Championship.

The team boss of Manor Motorsport, John Booth, was the man who guided him during his Formula Renault years after McLaren decided he was ready to move up from karts. John has helped a number of promising drivers in his successful team, and was glad to have been there at the second stage of the Lewis Hamilton racing career story. The wonderboy would race for him in Formula Renault and then in his early F3 days. John told the *Guardian*: 'McLaren asked us to give Lewis a test in our Formula Renault car. He had never driven a racing car before, not even a road car because he was only 16, and he crashed after a couple of laps.' This was hardly surprising, but what really impressed Booth was once the car had been put back together, Lewis went back out and immediately picked up the pace. The accident hadn't fazed him at all.

'He did the 2001 Renault Winter Series with us – and the full UK Championship in 2002 and 2003. There were a few mistakes, what do you expect from a 17-year-old?' What indeed... always a great deal in the case of Hamilton, perhaps too much at times. Stepping away from the racing circuit for a moment, Lewis was also doing well at college, especially considering his other commitments. He had moved on to the Cambridge College of Arts and Science – which, despite its name is located in Stevenage – to study for his A-levels after completing GCSEs at John Henry Newman. The college could offer him a flexible timetable, allowing him to fit his studies around his commitments as a Formula 3 driver.

A college newsletter, produced while he was studying there, revealed a little more about their star pupil: 'Lewis came to CATS after a recommendation from a friend, when he was looking for a place where his studies could be better fitted around his racing schedule. Lewis still finds it hard to concentrate on studies when his mind turns to the weekend's racing, but his studies have gone well.' Written in 2002, the report predicted big things: 'Lewis now races in the UK Formula Renault Single-Seater Championship and plans to become a full-time racing driver and graduate to Formula One when he finishes his studies.'

It was at Cambridge that he met girlfriend, Jodia Ma. Although Lewis refuses to speak publicly about their relationship, it is known that she lived in London for a spell after finishing her studies before moving back to Hong Kong in January 2007. She and Lewis remained an item for five years, with him splashing out £10,000 on a diamond bracelet for her 21st birthday. In stark comparison to his council house upbringing, she comes from a wealthy background. Her parents own a massive house in a gated community in Hong Kong's Clearwater Bay, a seaside village populated by wealthy professionals.

Jodia flew back from Hong Kong to London to be with

Lewis on her 22nd birthday on 28 July 2007. She has admitted to friends that she moved back home six months previously as she had been unsure whether they would remain together – because of Lewis' race commitments and her own uncertainty about what the future held for her. But Lewis refused to give up on her. In March of that year, he went to Hong Kong to see her, and from there, they went on holiday to Bali. Then in July she flew in to the UK to be with him, confirming they were still going steady despite the 6,000 miles between them. Jodia said: 'I think the world of him. I am just so proud of him. He is a lovely, amazing guy and so talented. He is a national hero and I can understand why people are so interested in him.'

A few weeks later she travelled to Hungary to see Lewis in action at the grand prix in Budapest – the first time she had watched him race. A friend of the couple said they had talked about the possibility of Jodia moving to London full-time to be with Lewis, and how she could perhaps develop her career in events management in the UK. But her hopes of a lasting relationship with Lewis would be dashed when they separated during the summer of 2007.

Jodia was only Lewis' second serious girlfriend. His first was Rachel Butterfield, whom he dated a year previous to meeting Jodia, while at secondary school. Rachel, of Biggleswade, in Befordshire, later did a 'kiss and tell', selling the story of their time together to the *News of the World*.

In between college studies and racing commitments, Lewis did a succession of small jobs. When he moved to Tewin, he served at the White Horse gastro pub in Burnham Green and also worked for a car valet firm. It was around this time that he passed his driving test – at the first attempt and after just six hours of lessons – though he had to be cautioned to slow down on the bends. His driving instructor, Stephen Sivell, said he knew at once that the 17-year-old had a special talent, but added: 'I had to warn him to slow down at corners and stop revving the engine of my Nissan Micra so hard.'

Now 53, Stephen's business records show that he was first contacted by Lewis' father Anthony on 10 April 2002 to inquire about driving lessons for his son. And initially the instructor was apprehensive after noting the unusual clothing Lewis wore for his first session: 'He was dressed all in white when I collected him from his home and was wearing Oakley designer sunglasses. He looked stylish, but I thought to myself: we've got a right boy racer here.'

Stephen was also concerned about the skills his learner driver had picked up in karting. He added: 'I had to point out that while he took the racing line, that wasn't what the examiner was going to be looking for when it came to his test. He would swing out to the right before turning left, which might have been acceptable for an advanced test, but not for the basic one.

'And he was taking the bends a bit fast on the country lanes – he was going into a bend so fast it was making me flinch. I think he saw that it was making me a bit nervy and he seemed to be enjoying it in a mischievous sort of way. I told him he could come out of a bend more quickly than he went in, but he had to go into them more slowly. He listened, and he learned very quickly.'

Stephen's old, silver Nissan Micra had never known anything like it: 'At one point I had to say "If you rev any harder, you will propel the engine into orbit!" But he added that Lewis was also tremendously focused. 'He took everything on board very quickly.'

After four 90-minute lessons in little more than a week, at a cost of £18 each, Stephen advised his young client that he was ready to sit his test. He passed with flying colours. Stephen said 'I know he passed first time because he phoned me to tell me. I believe he only had a very few minor faults, but that superb control that he had always had saw him through.' The driving instructor also witnessed Lewis' delight when his father presented him with his first car, a Mini coupé with a checkered flag on the roof. He recalled, 'We got back to his home at the end of one of our last lessons to find that Lewis' father, Anthony, had bought him the car. Lewis was thrilled, and I reckon he deserved it.'

Stephen remembers Lewis talking about racial taunts and snobbery he had encountered on his way to the top: 'I think it was difficult for him because some people weren't being over-pleasant to him at that time. Some parents were throwing everything they had got financially behind their children, getting them all the best equipment, but they were less talented than Lewis, and I think that caused jealousy.

'But Lewis was more talented than the others, and he was still winning. The odd remark, such as "Blacky", was chucked in from time to time. I would love to see him again. I'd just give him a big hug and say "Well done!"'

So, by the time of his second season with Yorkshire-based

Manor Motorsport in 2002, Lewis had passed his 'normal' driving test and was expected to pass the next test in his racing career: he was clear favorite to win the Formula Renault title. 'We'd been quickest in the pre-season test,' recalls John Booth. 'But things went awry at the first race – he got taken off by a backmarker. He went for three races without winning, which was a surprise to us, to say the least.'

Then came the big breakthrough: Lewis' first win in a racing car, at Silverstone. John says, 'He was lying fifth, on slicks, and it rained. He came through and won quite comfortably. That was it. He just clicked, his confidence was up and I don't think he was beaten again for the rest of that season.'

Lewis' debut in F3 at Brands Hatch was a nightmare. In the first race of the day he was forced out with a puncture and in the second he crashed out and was taken to hospital after a collision with team-mate Tor Graves.

Stella-Maria Thomas and Lynne Waite of Motorsport.com reported wryly on his F3 debut on 13 October 2003: 'At the back, life was proving interesting for Lewis Hamilton (Manor Motorsport). Having made his debut in the category in the morning's race, he started this one from the back after making a mistake in qualifying and failing to set anything that vaguely resembled a time...

'Trying to pass his teammate, Tor Graves, the two of them made contact, and the resulting off saw Graves' car almost destroyed, while the driver escaped with a suspected broken thumb. Hamilton wasn't quite so lucky. He was trapped in the car for a while, complaining of back pain. Naturally the marshals at the scene weren't about to take any chances and his extraction would clearly take some time.

'Finally Hamilton was extracted, his neck in a collar, and was taken away in the ambulance to the medical unit and later to hospital. He was declared fit but the doctors wanted to keep him in overnight for observation. He's not likely to forget his F3 debut weekend in a hurry.'

Lewis and Manor then made their debut in the 2004 Formula Three Euroseries. They won just one race and Lewis finished fifth in the Championship. But he did win the Bahrain F3 Superprix. John Booth admitted the problem lay with the car and not the driver: 'When we moved into F3, we didn't have the most competitive car. Lewis won a couple of races, but it was quite difficult for him being in a car that wasn't the best because he has this amazing desire to win. But even when the going is difficult, he didn't have a spat or a tantrum.

Booth admired the natural way Lewis had even then that gets everyone on side, in marked contrast to Ayrton Senna. 'He would have the same aim, but be manipulative. When we were racing together, Ayrton was a very pleasant young man but he'd be quite cold about it. He would say, "I will do this, and I will get the mechanics on my side." But, with Lewis, you would regularly see him bouncing about with a smile on his face. That's the way he's always been.'

By the end of 2004 the writing was on the wall for the link-up between Lewis and Manor – and in mid-December of that year it was announced that he had completed his first test drive for McLaren at Silverstone on 1 December.

There was even speculation he might jump two levels and become their third F1 man. One report said: 'Team McLaren-Mercedes have confirmed that Alexander Wurz will not test the new 2005 car, the MP4-20, in January, as he is too tall to fit into it. Although the team added that the car may be modified to accommodate the Austrian, it is thought this may take some time, and as such Pedro de la Rosa has effectively been promoted to "third driver".

'Jamie Green, Lewis Hamilton and Alex Lloyd are also all rumoured to be in the frame, after testing the MP4-19 recently at Silverstone, and despite McLaren's statement on Monday, that Mika Hakkinen will concentrate solely on the DTM [the Deutsche Tourenwagen Masters] in 2005, he may also be given the opportunity.'

It was not to be, but at least Lewis was in the frame. A good two years before Ron Dennis would make him his new chosen one, he was out testing with more established names. As he entered the second year of the F3 Euroseries, he was given another helping hand by McLaren when they engineered his move to rival team ASM. Yet he would not forget the part John Booth had played in his career. Before the French Formula One Grand Prix at Magny-Cours in 2007 he searched him out to see how he was doing. John, who was that day preparing for action with his Manor Motorsport Formula Three team, was touched by the gesture: 'That was so typical of Lewis. There he was, facing a big weekend, leading the Formula One Championship, and he took time to come and have a chat.'

At the end of the 2004 season there was also talk in the

pit lane that the test drive in the Formula One car at Silverstone may have gone to Lewis' head, that he and Anthony did not agree with Ron Dennis' decision to keep him in F3 for another season. Also, that Lewis and his father wanted to move into GP2 racing straightaway. Sources claimed there was a falling-out, which led Lewis to compete in the Macau F3 Grand Prix without McLaren's backing and that the Hamiltons sought another sponsor to race in GP2.

It is claimed they failed to attract enough support and 'had to go back to Dennis cap in hand'. Lewis, his father and McLaren all refuse to confirm or deny the allegations, but if it was correct then it was a salutary lesson for the young man. Dennis proved to be spot-on – when Lewis moved to ASM in 2005 success was to come easily and quickly, and it enabled him to eventually step up to F2 with even more confidence.

Backed by ASM's plentiful resources, Lewis' second season in F3 began with an emphatic victory at Hockenheim and he went on to become a brilliant champion. His Roll of Honour included 15 wins, 10 fastest laps, 13 pole positions and securing the title with four races remaining. At the same time, he also won the F3 Masters at Zandvoort, notching pole position and the lap record, and triumphed at the Monaco F3 Grand Prix and the Pau F3 Grand Prix in France.

By the time he wrapped up the title with four races to go in August 2005, Formula 3 paid personal tribute, acclaiming Lewis the best-ever driver in F3: 'Lewis Hamilton (ASM F3, Dallara-Mercedes) was regarded as one of the big favourites already at the beginning of the 2005 season – and the 20-year old succeeded in dominating the Formula 3 Euro Series like no other driver in the series' history. In the 16 rounds of the season contested so far, the young Briton has clinched 11 wins, gained 11 poles and set seven fastest race laps, thus securing the title with still four more rounds to go.

'Lewis Hamilton is clearly dominating the 2005 season. He makes nearly no mistakes and is always extremely quick. Hence, his title triumph was the logical consequence.

'When not sitting behind the wheel of his car, Lewis Hamilton is a calm and polite man, whose second passion apart from motor racing is to play guitar.'

It was a nice tribute from F3's bosses, and it would not go unnoticed at McLaren that his feats that season equalled the early achievements of driving legends Jackie Stewart and Alain Prost.

ASM team boss Frederic Vasseur was also full of praise for his driver, admitting it felt like something of a coup when McLaren asked him to take Lewis under his wing: 'My first encounter with Lewis was in the Formula Renault Eurocup at Assen in 2003. ASM won the second race there, with Simon Pagenaud, and Lewis finished second. He had the look of a very good driver, and graduated with Manor to the F3 Euroseries against us in 2004. It was a difficult situation for him, as both he and the team were new to the series, and the Kumho control tyres have particular characteristics that needed to be learned. There was also strong competition in Jamie Green, Nico Rosenberg and

Alexandre Premat. By the end of it, I was very interested in signing Lewis for 2005, but before I got the chance to speak with him, Martin Whitmarsh [the McLaren CEO] phoned me, saying he wanted Lewis to drive for us!'

Lewis' relationship with Vasseur was to continue beyond F3. When McLaren decided the time was right for him to move up to F2 in 2006, he stepped up a level with ASM's sister team, ART Grand Prix. But first he would take a well-earned rest at the end of that successful F3 season in 2005: 'I spent time with my family, my girlfriend and my friends just catching up; I did a bit of travelling. I started off by going to New York with my girlfriend and we went sightseeing. We went to the top of the Empire State Building, on the boat to the Statue of Liberty, and of course we couldn't go to New York without doing some shopping! Then I moved on to Bermuda with some friends for a week – it was their winter, but it was still nice and warm. It is a really beautiful place and very relaxing, which is just what I needed before the start of the season.'

He would move easily and comfortably from being champion in F3 to champion in GP2. As he stormed to the title, his Roll of Honour read like this: five wins, six fastest laps; first double win at the Nürburgring; pole position and winner of Monaco GP2 race; second double win at Silverstone in home race; seven second place and two third place podiums.

Frederic Vasseur remembers with fondness Lewis' domination of F2, not to mention the devotion and professionalism of Lewis' approach to work: 'It was obvious that he was a natural, but also very dedicated. All drivers say that their ambition is to be World Champion but very few actually focus on doing it. Lewis is one of the few. He is able to motivate the team because he is friendly with everyone. And he is completely honest with himself. If he qualified badly, he would say, "I did a poor job. The car is fine. Don't change it, it's my fault."' This was a key attribute of the youngster, because it ensured the most efficient use of the engineers' and technicians' time – you can waste so much time changing the car when in fact it is the driver who is at fault.

Vasseur recalls numerous impressive drives: 'I remember particularly a few from GP2. Silverstone [when Lewis overtook two cars with a single move] was a fantastic moment for me. And in Turkey, when he had spun to the back of the field, his comeback was incredible. And yet he did not take any big risks. Usually when a driver is coming back from something like that, he passes everyone – and then crashes. Lewis was using his brain, thinking of the Championship and picking off the other drivers one by one. At the Nürburgring, when it started raining and everyone was on slicks, Lewis was 2 to 3 seconds a lap faster than the others. I got on the radio and said, "Calm down." He replied, "OK, it's not a problem." It just came so easy to him. At the pit wall during a race, I was never nervous about him.'

Significantly, he was having a great fight with his team-mate, Alexandre Premat, in Barcelona: 'Premat hit Hamilton and sent his car into a spin on the last lap and yet he congratulated Alex on the podium. "Alex is not the problem," he said. "The problem was my start." Meaning that if he had made a better start, the problem would not have arisen. That's Lewis, an incredible guy.'

Nicolas Todt, co-boss of ART Grand Prix with Vasseur, was also delighted Lewis had taken them to a second consecutive GP2 Championship: 'I am very, very happy. Winning the title last year [with Nico Rosberg] was a really good achievement because it was a new series. Winning it again proved that it wasn't a stroke of luck last year. It proves that we really deserved it. Lewis was astonishing. He was very fast and very determined. It was a pleasure to work with a guy like him. The combination of Lewis and Alex Premat, who was with us last year as well, was the best that we could have.'

Lewis paid tribute to Todt and Vasseur and their team for helping him to get to Formula One more quickly than many had expected. 'Yes, I had a great couple of years with both of them. I think I learned a lot from my engineers there because they run a fantastic two teams in F3 and GP2. They really gave me a good understanding technically, because when you get into Formula One you really have to have a great knowledge of the car to be able to communicate with your team. That's what I learned from those teams.'

His GP2 triumphs at Silverstone in June 2006 are considered by many to have been the moment when Ron Dennis decided he could no longer hold back his protégé; this was when he gave the nod for Lewis to become part of the McLaren F1 set-up. Certainly the team's own official comments on that day seem to back up that theory: 'Lewis Hamilton's dazzling victories in the two GP2 races [at Silverstone] supporting the 2006 British Grand Prix stole the spotlight from many of the drivers in the senior race.

'After winning the first race on Saturday, GP2 rules dictated that he start last on the grid for the Sunday morning sprint race. Lewis dodged past both Clivio Piccioni and Nelson Piquet jnr in a brilliant three-abreast lunge through Maggotts and into Becketts. This mind-boggling manoeuvre vaulted him up to second place, after which he worked hard to displace Felix Porteiro and set the seal on his second win in less than 24 hours. Many predicted that the drive would earn him a Formula One ride for 2007.'

On Saturday 9 September 2006, the momentum for him to be given a McLaren drive increased after confirmation of his GP2 title win at Monza. Renowned Formula One blogger Oliver White set the scene in this way: 'Although Hamilton only finished third in the race, winner Giorgio Pantano had his fastest lap taken away from him as it was set under yellow flags. This gave Lewis an extra point and this means he has beaten his rival, Nelson Piquet jnr. Ron Dennis – team director of McLaren F1 – refused to be led into questions on his driver line-up next year but did have praise for his 21-year-old protégé: "The manner of his many outstanding performances this year, such as those at Silverstone and Turkey, has been phenomenal and he is a deserving champion. Lewis has an exceptional talent, which has been demonstrated this year, and his overall performance during the season gives you a definite sense of pride and satisfaction. In due course the team's and Lewis' plans for 2007 will be announced."

'Hamilton is said to be pleased that the season-long battle with Nelson Piquet jnr was finally over, and is jubilant at his success. With Kimi Raikkonen expected to be at Ferrari next year, Ron Dennis has a tough decision to make for his 2007 drivers. McLaren currently have Fernando Alonso, Pedro De La Rosa, Lewis Hamilton and Gary Paffett available for next year, and while it is possible for Kimi to remain at the Woking squad, it is unlikely.

'Ron would do very little wrong in keeping Pedro in the car. The Spaniard has done well since taking over from the departing Juan Pablo Montoya, and has shown the team that he is a safe pair of hands. But the temptation to put a young, motivated charger in the second seat must be strong.'

Indeed it was, and in the end temptation proved too strong. After nine years, Big Ron decided the time was right for Lewis to come out to play with the big boys. On Saturday 30 September 2006, just before the Chinese Grand Prix, he was invited to his house. Lewis himself takes up the story: 'We sat there and he said, "We have decided you are going to be our driver next year." I had to put a professional front on and I had a small smile on me, but inside it was overwhelming.' In taking him into the big-time, Big Ron was also gambling against his own ground rules. He had gone against his normal recruitment demand, that he would only employ drivers already established in Formula One.

Days of learning through the ranks were finally over and Lewis Hamilton had achieved his lifetime ambition. Starting in Melbourne, six months down the road, he would be a Formula One driver. But learning how to be one was just beginning and long, hard days of testing, practice and training were to follow. This would involve much time in the McLaren Technology Centre at Woking, a location Lewis already knew intimately. It was where his motor racing training and education had been evolving since being first signed to McLaren by Dennis.

Let's take a little look at the training programme that helped turn Lewis from a karting hopeful into a Formula One winner in his nine-year McLaren apprenticeship. Commenting in 2007 as the countdown to his F1 start continued, Lewis said 'I am in the McLaren Technology Centre every day. I have relocated to Woking to be close to the team and the facility. I train every day in the gym, meet team members for training and development sessions, and generally get to know the team and watch closely the progress of the new car. It also gives me the chance to work closely with my new engineers and for us to get to know each other like the back of our hands!'

Joseph Dunn of the *Sunday Times* described Lewis' training in this way: 'The intensity of it is astonishing. High-tech telemetric read-outs enable the driver and engineers to refine lap times down by fractions of a second, while racing simulators and 3-D virtual reality cars mean drivers can know a circuit off by heart without having driven it for real. Some reports have claimed Hamilton has spent thousands of hours in such a simulator at the McLaren base in Woking, although Hamilton downplays its influence.'

Rory Ross developed that theme in the *Daily Telegraph* magazine: 'He is 5ft 10in, 10st 10lb, and has a 16.5in neck, broad shoulders and a superbly developed upper body. His forearms are streaked with pulsating veins like brown thunderbolts...

'For six months before the start of the season, Hamilton was groomed for his Formula One debut. Every day, including weekends, he submitted himself to two 3-hour training sessions: he swam 2 kilometres, cycled 50 miles and spent two hours in the gym. "It's all about endurance," he says. "There is nothing worse than getting to mid-race and starting to fatigue, because your mind needs to work doubly hard to give energy to the rest of your body, and then you lose focus and you can crash. It is about your mind being at ease that you are fit enough."'

The *Guardian*'s Richard Williams talked about the word 'robotic' being used in describing how Lewis had been brought up by McLaren and of a 'training period that included thousands of hours in the McLaren team's unique and highly secret simulator' and 'some of the specific training techniques brought to bear on astronauts and fighter pilots.'

He went on: '[Ron] Dennis put at Hamilton's disposal the greatest learning tool that any driver has ever been given. McLaren's simulator, developed over the past eight years at a cost estimated to be above £20m, has been Hamilton's schoolroom, where he sits in a full-size Formula One car, minus wheels and a functioning engine, in a darkened room in front of a large, curved plasma screen. The chassis is suspended on a multi-point hydraulic rig that moves in response to his touches on the steering wheel and pedals as he watches a circuit unfold on the screen, with appropriate sound effects.

'Everything in this grown-up video game is programmed via the simulator's software: the minutest details of the circuit, the response of the engine under different conditions, the type and wear-rate of the tyres, as well as the noise of the engine.'

It was certainly true that Lewis had undergone a nine-year training period, the like of which no other Formula One driver had ever been subjected to. He was, in that sense, the prototype of the new breed of driver; developed from an early age to be a champion although, as Williams also points out, skill and talent are also essential.

Lewis was happy enough to admit before the British Grand Prix in 2007 that he probably could not have got to where he was so quickly without the £5 million training programme: 'I don't think you get to this position without working hard, as they've said. I was given an opportunity. I remember Ron said "You have the opportunity, but I want you to be the fittest guy out there" and so I had to make sure, even in my own self-confidence and self-belief, I wanted to be the fittest out there. Whether I am or not, who knows?

'I had an opportunity to have a training programme, [to] learn as much as I could about the car, so that I got to the first race and I had no problems. And we didn't look back and say "I wish we had done this differently" or "I wish we had worked an extra day." We took every day as it came and really maximised every day. This is what I've been working for so many years so when you get the opportunity, you don't just let it pass by, you get as much out of it as you can.'

He also admitted before the British Grand Prix that the training programme instilled in him the need to continue learning and ploughing through data, books and videos to reach the absolute top: 'I have had my head buried in books for the past nine months. When I'm not looking at books, I am watching DVDs or talking to the McLaren team about the car. The cars have so much software these days – it's not just mechanical. You don't just get into a car and drive it around a track; you have to learn about the aerodynamics. I've been studying from September to March to make sure that I have it in my head. Then I have to study each individual track. The advice I would give to other drivers is never to give up, even if you spin off. I think once I spun off and I got back on and focused, and ended up coming second.'

'You just can't afford to lose focus. When I am driving at 200mph, if I lost focus then I could die, so it kind of puts it into perspective.'

David Coulthard also backed the McLaren way of doing things, conceding that his training with them had been enormously helpful in his own career. At a press conference before the British Grand Prix in July 2007, he was also at pains to add that Lewis' natural skills completed the winning package: 'Having been part of the McLaren system,

I know some of the facilities that they had up to the point that I left, and I would be surprised if any grand prix team has quite as complete a package in simulation devices that the drivers can use. It's obviously a state-of-the-art facility, more modern probably than anyone else's out there.

'But Lewis has had to prove himself, otherwise he wouldn't be sitting here. It's not charity work that McLaren are doing. They invested because they saw the talent and they've helped him develop that over the time. As Lewis inevitably moves offshore and grows into his life, he will inevitably spend less time at the factory because there just won't be the time. He will need energy, recovery time, to maintain the level that he's achieved already over the next 10–15 years.'

There was a suggestion by some pundits that Dennis played Frankenstein to Lewis, that he was merely his Formula One creation. This theory was backed up, they claimed, by the fact that Big Ron had hired Dr Kerry Spackman, a New Zealand-born neuroscientist, apparently to turn the boy into a race-winning machine. Spackman's research had shown that while in Formula One some cars are faster than others, it was ultimately the driver who is the key to better speed.

One writer, Robert Matthews in the online news magazine thefirstpost.co.uk, spoke of the scientific approach in this way: 'A major part of Spackman's approach is the intensive use of computer simulators, which expose Hamilton to every twist, turn and eventuality of a race until dealing with them is utterly instinctive.' It was the same approach NAS had to astronaut training more than 40 years previously. Spackman, however, goes much further, applying insights from Neuroscience and Psychology to create a more comprehensive picture of Hamilton's technique and mindset, and bring his foibles under control. 'The result is a driver who combines the standard skill-set of focus and controlled aggression with relentless consistency.'

Guardian columnist Richard Williams pointed out that it was more the case that Dr Spackman's work complemented the skills of the wonderboy: 'Spackman's use of virtual-reality techniques has enabled Hamilton to exploit his natural talent even further by expanding his mental capacity. In a way, it is like adding an extra litre to his Mercedes engine.'

Ron Dennis himself was keen to play down the idea that Lewis was simply a factory-manufactured Formula One driver: 'First of all, we've done it for several young kartists. We constructed a karting team for both Lewis and Nico Rosberg. Obviously they've both done a great job and Nico – though really more because of his age than anything and the way the licensing system works – I think he just stepped ahead as regards getting into Formula One a little earlier.

'But I was always keen for Lewis to dominate every category in which he raced because that gives you a certain mind-set and obviously we wanted him to follow the right path into Formula One. But it's important to remember, no matter who gives opportunity to young drivers, ultimately it's their own abilities, their commitment, their own dedication and sacrifices, that determines the result. I will never, ever claim to be the reason that Lewis is the great success he is.

'That is his own effort and his own commitment. Yes, he's had opportunity; yes, he hasn't had to worry about money, but the most difficult thing is actually to deliver, given those opportunities, and that's all down to him and obviously the support of his family.' It was a fine tribute to the boy he had treated as a son for almost a decade. Clearly the bond was deep between them.

But before we move on to the start of Lewis' Formula One career, it's time to take a look at the man he described as his ultimate hero – Ayrton Senna – and McLaren, the team he had always wanted to be a part of. Let's find out exactly how McLaren, with the help of the late, great Senna, developed into the legendary motor racing giant it had become by the time it was ready to welcome Lewis Hamilton aboard.

CHAPTER 5

IN SENNA'S FOOTSTEPS

Asked what had been the biggest dream come true of his life before entering the fray in Formula One, Lewis Hamilton answered without hesitation: Joining McLaren. Without that welcome act of faith from Ron Dennis, back in 1998 when he was 13, there would have been none of the glitz he now laps up. His father Anthony summed it up like this: 'McLaren were the catalyst. Lewis' objective is to stay with McLaren.'

Indeed, McLaren and Lewis Hamilton appear the perfect team. The fastest motor racing outfit on the planet – and the fastest and best driver. The car in which Lewis performed so dazzlingly in his remarkable debut season, the Vodafone McLaren Mercedes Mp4-22, went like the proverbial rocket with eight cylinders powering its enormous 95kg Mercedes-Benz FO 108T engine.

It was mooted the car had been specifically designed for the arrival of double champion Alonso at the start of the 2007 campaign but it would be Lewis who felt most at ease with it. Before the first race, he warned: 'Just wait and see, this car will blow the socks off anyone who even looks at it!' And he wasn't far wrong. Alonso had voiced his fears after McLaren's under-performance, even with the superfast Kimi Raikkonen at the wheel the previous year, and is said to have asked for pledges before he left Renault that the new car would be supercompetitive. It certainly was that.

What Alonso had not expected, however, was that he would be upstaged by his young No. 2, whom he had assumed would be playing a supporting role and learning the game from him, the supposedly superior worldly-wise No. 1.

Lewis is a deep thinker and a man who spends whatever time it takes to get things right. That respect for planning and preparation also helps to explain why he wanted to join McLaren in the first place. This was, after all, no run-of-the-mill outfit – along with Ferrari it is the most legendary of the racing set-ups, with a history to match. It had not escaped his attention that not only would he be testing himself against Alonso, but that he would also be compared with the ghosts of McLaren's own glittering past. To some commentators McLaren is known as the 'jinx team'. Three of its greatest drivers died in their prime: founder Bruce McLaren, the Brazilian genius Ayrton Senna (although not in a McLaren car) and Britain's own marvellous maverick, the great James Hunt. Lewis would say of Senna: 'He's my icon. I used to watch the way he diced around the track and overtook the other drivers. I studied his books and videos, and I hope I learned something from him. I am so very proud to be racing for McLaren because that's who Senna raced for. It feels I am continuing his legacy in a way.'

The McLaren Formula One team was formed in 1963 by New Zealander Bruce McLaren. Bruce McLaren Motor Racing Limited, as it was known then, set about building a Formula One car, and three years later the team made its debut at the 1966 Monaco Grand Prix. In many ways, McLaren was like Lewis: he would not take the short cut to success. A devotee to detail, his motto could also have been that of Lewis: 'Success depends on the highest standards.' McLaren, too, was a brilliant driver but it was his vision beyond the grand prix races, again similarly to that of Lewis, which propelled him to greatness.

From an early age Lewis Hamilton would visit the garages and learn about the mechanics and specs of his karts and cars. This gave him an inside knowledge and an edge to his racing skills, as well as the nous to know how to treat the car almost as if he were riding a horse and nurturing it to victory. Bruce McLaren agreed with all that; he would surely have nodded sagely and smiled at Hamilton's insistence on ensuring all was right before he pulled on his helmet.

As founder, McLaren also took seriously his role as inventor, constructor and tester. By July 2007, the team he founded was well on the way to becoming the greatest in history, having won 152 races since its formation. True, Ferrari had won 195 but they had been racing since 1950 – 16 years more than McLaren, and the gap was ever closing with the exploits of Lewis and Alonso. The team has also dominated CamAm events (56 wins between 1967 and 1972) and taken three Indianapolis 500 races.

In his book *McLaren: A Racing History*, Geoffrey Williams writes: 'Just as Jackie Stewart came to personify the increasing professionalism, commercialism and safety consciousness of grand prix racing in the 1970s and similarly so with Ayrton Senna as the dedicated professional of the 1990s, Bruce McLaren typified the happy, often comradely spirit of earlier times. The most universally liked driver of his era, Bruce's background suggested he may have something out of the ordinary to offer the sport.'

Williams was spot-on with his analysis of Bruce McLaren – the founder who, like Lewis, was always destined for motor racing greatness. Born on 30 August 1937, Bruce had a happy upbringing, with fate decreeing he would spend his formative days in the perfect atmosphere: his father's garage. His parents, Ruth and Les, owned a service station and, more often than not, Bruce would be found in the workshop. Les had raced motorcycles before World War II, but after the hostilities ended, he switched his attentions to car racing. His son Bruce was equally fascinated by cars and what made them tick, and how, exactly, to get the best out of them.

We have already noted how Lewis had to battle against certain obstacles as a youngster to ensure his dream kept on track; it was no different for young Bruce. At the age of 9, he was struck down by Perthes Disease, a debilitating hip condition. The illness affects the top of the thighbone, softening and breaking it down. It usually occurs in children and causes a limp and other symptoms, but the one positive aspect of all this is that the affected bone gradually reforms as the child grows.

Only one in 10,000 children are hit by the disease: Bruce McLaren was one of the unlucky ones and for two years he was severely restricted in his movements. This was an unhappy time for the boy who loved to roam and learn around his father's garage. He was forced to live away in traction – at the Wilson Home for Crippled Children in Auckland, New Zealand – his body strapped up with a so-called Bradshaw Frame to help repair his hip. For months on end, he lay there, immobile. Later, he was allowed a wheelchair but at one time there were fears he would never walk again. But like Lewis, this was a boy who would not be beaten. When his father visited they would talk about cars and what was happening back at the garage.

When he returned home, Bruce had a permanent limp – his left leg was 1½ inches shorter than his right – but an even fiercer determination to make up for those lost 24 months. He spent his time helping his father in the garage and learned to drive in the quarter acre of land they owned at the back. The big breakthrough came when, at the age of 13, he and Les put back together an Austin 7 Ulster. It was then that Bruce knew for sure where his destiny lay. He had caught the car bug for ever and would later describe it in this way: 'With a truck full of boxes of spare parts and towing the Austin Ulster arriving at 8 Upland Road, my motor racing career had started. How Mum put up with Dad and me with her kitchen table covered in bits and pieces of the engine during meals I will never know. She used to say, "If I gave them dry bread and water they wouldn't have noticed."'

By the age of 14, he had persuaded his father to let him race the aging Austin 7 Ulster, which they had now fully restored in his first event, a hillclimb – a competition in which drivers compete against the clock to complete an uphill course. Two years later he took part in his first real race and performed well. He moved up from the Austin to a Ford 10 special and an Austin-Healey, then on to a F2 Cooper-Climax sports. The latter was his opening to the big time. Working on it all hours to improve its performance, he did such a good job that by 1957 he finished runner-up in the New Zealand Championship series.

His plucky displays that season brought him to the attention of motor racing legend Jack Brabham, conjuring up a similarity to Lewis Hamilton. Just as Lewis would profit from the mentoring provided by Ron Dennis, so McLaren himself got his big break courtesy of Brabham. Bruce's performances in the domestic campaign earned him an entry into that season's New Zealand Grand Prix and although he did not win the main race, his skills caught the eye of the big Aussie, who would one day invite Bruce to drive for him.

Ironically and tragically, given that this book is about a new British hero, another would die that day at the Grand Prix at Ardmore: Smethwick-born driver Ken Wharton. He was no Lewis Hamilton – his best result ever was a fourth place finish in Berne, Switzerland, in 1952 – but having been captivated by the same motor racing bug since childhood, his hopes and dreams had been the same.

Brabham encouraged the New Zealand International Grand Prix organisation to select Bruce McLaren for the 'Driver in Europe' scheme. Its aim was to provide a promising Kiwi driver with a year's experience at one of the best teams in the world. In 1958 McLaren was the first recipient. As Ron Dennis and McLaren would later take Lewis Hamilton under their wing from an even earlier age as an apprentice, so Bruce McLaren ended up learning his trade at the sharp end with the Cooper team in the UK. He made a name for himself in F2, but the big time arrived when he took part in the 1958 German Grand Prix at the Nürburgring. Featuring drivers from Formula One and F2, Bruce only earned a starting place from the reserve list, but showed his mettle, finishing fifth overall and first in the F2 lot.

The days of scrapping around and begging for a chance were over. He was promoted to Cooper's Formula One team for the 1959 season, with Brabham as his team-mate. Bruce would enjoy a fine 6-year spell with Cooper, that first season winning the final grand prix of the year at Sebring. At 22 this made him the youngest ever winner of a grand prix, and to ice the cake, Brabham won the World Championship. Bruce's record would stand until the 2003 Hungarian Grand Prix when Fernando Alonso superseded him as the youngest driver ever to win a grand prix at the age of 22 years, 26 days.

By 1960 Cooper was the top team: Jack Brabham finished the year as the world's No. 1, Bruce McLaren was No. 2 and Sterling Moss, also with the Cooper team, came third. That year Bruce won the Argentinian Grand Prix and he would remain in the top 10 drivers in the world for the next 10 years. It was a remarkable rise to fame for the boy from Auckland, and typical of the fierce winning mentality of the McLaren team and the determined character trait of McLaren himself and all those who would follow in his legendary footsteps.

By 1963 he had become disillusioned with the Cooper team and formed his own outfit. But he did not believe their cars were progressing enough technically and registered the name Bruce McLaren Motor Racing Ltd. Until 1966, he continued to race for Cooper, designing and developing his own car in his spare time until the day he was convinced it was finally ready for action. In 1966 he announced his own grand prix racing team, with co-driver and fellow Kiwi Chris Amon. That year they won the 24-hour race at Le Mans in a Ford GT40. A year later Amon was to leave to drive for Ferrari. By 1968, McLaren designer Robin Herd had introduced the Ford Cosworth engine to their car and Bruce signed up fellow New Zealander, World Champion Denny Hulme, as his co-driver. Hulme had won the world title in 1967, in a Brabham. For the developing team, these were heady, exciting times.

Bruce won his first grand prix in his own McLaren car at Spa in 1968, while Hulme won twice in the McLaren-Ford. In tribute to his homeland, McLaren's cars always featured the 'speedy Kiwi' logo. Bruce actually won in Belgium without knowing it. He admitted: 'It's about the nicest thing I've ever been told! Jackie [Stewart] had stopped at the pits for fuel, starting the last lap and I hadn't seen him as he went by. I had won without realising it...'

Yet all the glory would be forgotten when the tears fell on 2 June 1970 at 12.22pm, the day when Bruce McLaren was killed at Goodwood in England. He was just 32. His mother Ruth, in bed in Auckland, later told how she awoke suddenly at the very moment of the crash, sensing her adored boy was dead. Bruce died when his own CanAm car crashed during testing. He had been putting his new M8D through its paces when the rear bodywork came adrift at speed. The loss of aerodynamic downforce destabilised the car, which spun, left the track and hit a concrete bunker used as a flag station. He was killed instantly.

In *McLaren: The Man and His Racing Team*, Eoin S. Young summed up the sense of loss felt after the tragedy: 'In the dark days that followed it was realized that Bruce, the complete man, had virtually penned his own epitaph in the closing paragraph of his book, *From the Cockpit*, written in 1964. He had put down on paper the grief he felt at the death of his teammate Timmy Mayer, killed in a practice crash in Tasmania, but he had also recorded his justification for going racing and those last few sentences in his book are a fitting beginning for this one:

'"The news that he had died instantly was a terrible shock to all of us, but who is to say that he had not seen more, done more and learned more in his few years than many people do in a lifetime? To do something well is so worthwhile that to die trying to do it better cannot be foolhardy. It would be a waste of life to do nothing with one's ability, for I feel that life is measured in achievement, not in years alone."'

In 1991 Bruce McLaren was inducted into the

International Motorsports Hall of Fame, and into the Motorsports Hall of Fame of America in 1995. In the latter, his entry is commemorated with perceptive words that go some way towards defining the man who founded the McLaren legend. They say he was 'universally well liked and remarkably self-effacing. He never claimed to be the world's fastest driver and often smilingly discounted his own engineering ability. "Make it simple enough so even I can understand it," he'd tell his team. But his own work at the drawing board and in the cockpit resulted in racing machines that vanquished all comers.'

By the time of his death McLaren had won four of the 101 grands prix he had started, scoring a total of 196.5 points. But his legacy is much richer than those figures alone, for it extends to the massive enterprise of McLaren International today. Located in Woking, England, with a 325-strong team of designers, engineers and skilled staff, complemented by advanced computer-aided design and manufacturing facilities, it represents everything stunning about modern-day motor racing.

And the team continues to carry the name McLaren as Lewis Hamilton leads it into a new generation of glory, just as it did back in 1974 when Brazilian Emerson Fittipaldi became McLaren's first World Champion. Fittipaldi, once Formula One's youngest champion, took his second crown with the team in 1974 after a first with Lotus as a 25-year-old in 1972. Then in June 2007 the first Brazilian world champion, and the youngest until Alonso won with Renault in 2005 at the age of 24, showed his loyalties remain with his old team when he spoke of his excitement at the development of Lewis Hamilton: 'For the Championship I would go for Lewis now, for sure. When you are so young and suddenly you are leading and winning, it is a tremendous pressure and he [Hamilton] is taking the pressure in a positive way.'

Likening Lewis to golf's Tiger Woods or football's Pelé for his ability to take the sport to a broader public, Fittipaldi outlined his belief that Lewis was opening up an exciting new era: 'I see we are going to reach beyond the borders of motor racing with Lewis Hamilton like we never have before. If you look at all the World Champions before, even the best that we had never reached the public that Lewis can reach.'

Fittipaldi was in Montreal for Lewis' first grand prix victory in May 2007 and was struck by how relaxed the youngster appeared off the track and how in control he was behind the wheel in comparison to his team-mate Alonso: 'Lewis talks to the car and the car talks to him. They understand each other very well, and Fernando, I think, was screaming to the car. He was not having a conversation.'

Fittipaldi will always be a McLaren idol for bringing the world title to Britain. But he will never own the same place in the hearts of the fans as Ayrton Senna or James Hunt, who would also die young. Like Bruce McLaren they too were also fast and furious at the wheel. Two years after Fittipaldi's triumph, James Hunt won the title for McLaren. 'Flamboyant' and 'Privileged' are terms often associated with Hunt... and some also dub him 'lucky'. Let me explain... James Simon Wallis Hunt was born on 29 August

1947, in Belmont, Surrey. He did not have to struggle to make it through life – far from it, in fact. He was the son of a successful stockbroker and educated at Wellington College, Berkshire. In his early teens his ambition was to become a doctor. But at 18 he went to see his first motor race and instantly caught the bug, so much so that he abandoned plans of becoming a medical GP, instead turning to the prospect of racing GPs for his salvation. Moving up quickly through the ranks of Formula Ford and Formula 3, he was landed with the nickname of 'Hunt the Shunt' after he was involved in a series of crashes.

He built up a reputation for wild driving but his big break came at the grand old age of 26, when his rich friend Lord Alexander Hesketh hired him as a driver with his fledgling Hesketh team in Formula One in 1973. His first win came in 1975 in the Dutch Grand Prix at Zandvoort. The following year Hesketh ran out of money, his team folded and Hunt joined the McLaren team for the 1976 season. It was a debut season that ended in glory as he roared to the world title, winning six races. But, for some that achievement was not enough. Certain pundits would belittle him, saying he had only triumphed because of his main rival Niki Lauda's near fatal accident at the Nürburgring on 1 August 1976.

The Austrian-born driver became trapped inside his Ferrari after it swerved off the track before bouncing back into the path of the oncoming cars and catching fire. Eventually the 27-year-old – who had been leading the Drivers' Championship since the beginning of the season –

was pulled from his vehicle. Within six weeks of the accident Lauda was back, but Hunt pipped him to the title by just one point. My view is that, yes, Lauda had been well on course to win the crown, but Hunt still had much to do after the accident, and kept his nerve, driving with confidence and style. I do not think he earned the plaudits that should have gone his way. Nonetheless, the title win made him a hero in the eyes of those who really mattered in the sport... British Formula One fans.

That year proved to be the peak of Hunt's career. In 1977 he only won three grands prix races and the following year he scored hardly any points. In his personal life, he was rapidly heading for skid row too. Stories abound of him turning up at black tie events in shorts and a filthy T-shirt, and his drinking and womanising were legendary. One female journalist seduced him and wrote about his performance in a Dutch magazine. In 1979, he turned out for the Wolf team in what was to be his final season in Formula One. He then set about establishing a career in the commentary box as back-up to the great Murray Walker. It started badly when he arrived late and drunk to his first commentating job at Monaco. Barefoot, with a cast on his left leg from a skiing injury (also incurred while drunk), he plonked his leg on Murray Walker's lap and began his commentary, pausing only to open a bottle of wine.

But the partnership between the two developed and prospered, thanks in no part to Murray's desire to see James get well. Ultimately, his life was tragically cut short just when he seemed to be getting it back on track after years of abuse and financial mismanagement left him close to broke. Yet it was not the hard-living and playboy lifestyle that did for him when he died of a heart attack, aged 45 in 1993. No, this was simply a congenital defect. Just hours before his death he had asked his girlfriend Helen, who was half his age, to be his third wife – and she had accepted his proposal.

He had remained friends with Niki Lauda right up until his death, and one of the most telling quotes about the real James Hunt would come from the Austrian when he was told he was dead: 'Shit. James was one of the really great guys.'

McLaren had to wait until 1984 for their next world title, courtesy of Lauda. In 1980, Marlboro brokered a merger between McLaren and Project Four headed by Ron Dennis. This revitalised McLaren, leading to Lauda's triumph by a half point from team-mate Alain Prost. The Frenchman then lifted the crown from Lauda, winning in 1985, 1986 and 1989, but now there was a new face in the team, and arguably the most legendary of all.

Ayrton Senna da Silva is still believed by many to be the greatest talent ever to grace a Formula One car. He joined McLaren in 1988 and his rivalry with Prost became legendary. The duo was total opposites: Prost, a reflective, measured operator, while Senna was an instinctively brilliant but uncompromising driver who verged on the dangerous. Their duels, as they battled for supremacy and the prize of the world title, would never be forgotten and their rivalry grew into the most bitter the sport has ever seen. Both won three crowns for McLaren (Senna's coming in 1988, 1990 and 1991), but Senna would edge Prost in terms of grands prix wins: 35 to 30.

Andrew Benson, the BBC's motorsport editor, summed up Senna's mastery of the sport like this: 'Michael Schumacher may statistically be the greatest grand prix driver who ever lived, but to many who watched Ayrton Senna's career no one can equal the brilliant Brazilian. Senna's greatness does not lie in statistics, impressive though his career record is. It is embodied in the irresistible force with which he dominated an era of Formula One.'

The Brazilian's potential, like that of Lewis Hamilton, was apparent even before he made it to Formula One. Born on 21 March 1960, he was the second child of Milton da Silva, a successful businessman and landowner. Ayrton was brought up in the middle-class area of Santana in São Paulo. He first drove a kart – a gift from his father – at the age of 4 and by 8 he was driving the family car. As soon as he turned 13 he was racing competitively. His drive to Formula One had ringing similarities to Lewis' progress. Just as he graduated from karts, so too, in 1977, Senna would win the South American Kart Championship.

He was invited to Europe for speed trials and swiftly adopted his mother's maiden name, Senna, as da Silva was a very common Brazilian name. Senna went on to win the Formula Ford and Formula 3 Championships. In 1983, the Williams' team gave the then up-and-coming F3 driver a test in their grand prix car, and within 40 laps he had taken it around Donington Park faster than its regular drivers, including reigning World Champion Keke Rosberg. Inexplicably, Williams did not sign him; instead Senna was picked up by Formula One minnow Toleman.

In 1984, his debut year, Senna should have won at Monaco. In driving rain he overtook Prost's McLaren to lead on Lap 31 but the race was red-flagged a lap later. Prost triumphed under the rule that should a race be stopped, the classification would go back to two laps previous, but the boy from Brazil had laid down a marker. Senna had secretly been negotiating with Lotus and joined the former greats in 1985, winning his first grand prix in more treacherous conditions at Estoril. Five more wins followed in three years at Lotus, but Senna slowly realised this was not the dream team he had imagined. No longer the Lotus of Jim Clark, it was an outfit in decline. In 1988, he jumped ship. His time had finally come... at McLaren.

They were the team he had always been looking for, the one that would finally give him a car worthy of his talent and ambitions. In his first season he was welcomed by Prost, but the warmth did not last long. This could have been the prototype of the frosty way Alonso treated Hamilton after Lewis won his first grand prix. Senna won eight races as he took his co-driver's world title away from him. The following campaign the duo's battles became increasingly bitter as Prost regained the title with Senna runner-up. The Brazilian had lost the Championship to Prost after the pair collided at the final race in Suzuka. Prost blamed Senna and it was effectively the end of their relationship.

The BBC's Andrew Benson remarked: 'Senna did sometimes appear to be putting his ambition ahead of his instinct for survival, most notably at the Japanese Grand Prix in 1990, when Senna secured the second of his three titles by driving into the back of Prost's Ferrari at 160mph, taking them both out of the race.'

Senna, for all his outward propensity to shock, was an inwardly deep, religious man, who thought long and hard about his role in racing and life itself. He admitted his fears that he would not always be on top of the game, revealing how that edge to be the best kept him going: 'You are doing something that nobody else is able to do. [But] the same moment that you are seen as the best, the fastest and somebody that cannot be touched, you are enormously fragile because in a split second it's gone. These two extremes are feelings that you don't get every day. These are all things that contribute to, how can I say, knowing yourself deeper and deeper. These are the things that keep me going.'

With those motivational sentiments in mind, in 1994 Senna joined Williams for a new challenge: to prove himself all over again at a new team. Williams had dominated the sport in 1992 and 1993, and it was anticipated Senna would easily win back the Championship he had last won (for the third time) at McLaren in 1991. But it did not work out that way. The Williams' car had a serious design flaw and by the time of the San Marino GP at Imola on 1 May 1994, Senna was struggling to keep up with Michael Schumacher (in the superior Benetton) in the title race. Yet as he headed into the Tamburello corner at 192mph, he was a second ahead of the German when the Williams' FW16 crashed into a concrete wall. A front wheel was knocked back towards the cockpit and Senna's helmet visor pierced by a suspension arm. If it had missed him, he would have stepped from the wreck unhurt. Ayrton Senna – the genius of McLaren and Formula One – was dead at just 34.

Murray Walker reflected the mood of the day, saying: 'This is the blackest day for grand prix racing that I can remember.' Senna's body was flown home, and 4 days later, an estimated crowd of half a million people watched the coffin pass by in a state funeral in São Paolo.

It was the end of a dream, and McLaren would also be plunged into mourning. It would be four years before the team finally emerged from the darkness of the Brazilian's death, when Mika Hakkinen brought them back to the top with his world title win. The legendary team that Bruce McLaren had formed and died for had suffered its share of anguish as well as glory.

Ironically, as Hakkinen raced to that title during 1997–98, Lewis was just beginning his apprenticeship at McLaren. After the unforgettable glitz and tragedy of Bruce McLaren, James Hunt and Ayrton Senna, a new era was unfolding, the era of the boy who was born to be its new king at the start of Formula One in the twenty-first century. But Lewis would be the first to admit that none of this would have been possible without the help of his father Anthony and the man whom many called his surrogate father, Ron Dennis. For this was the man who brought Lewis into Formula One and upon whom we shall now turn the spotlight, examining his role in the development of the wonderboy...

CHAPTER 6

BIG RON MANAGER

He may not be the most popular guy in the pit lane, but Ron Dennis, 'Big Ron', as he is known universally on the circuit, couldn't give a proverbial monkeys – brash, confident, looking a bit like the man who owns the joint. Of course, he doesn't: that sobriquet would have to go to Formula One ringmaster Bernie Ecclestone. Yet, as head of one of the era's two most powerful racing team (along with Ferrari), the Big Man carries a definite clout – and, for our purposes, he is the man responsible for the irresistible rise and rise of Lewis Hamilton.

Lewis is the first to admit the debt he owes to Dennis. He said: 'Ron and my father have been the biggest influences on my career. Without them I wouldn't be where I am today. I owe them both a deep gratitude for their faith in me. Ron gave me my big break and I will always be grateful to him for that. He is also my friend, someone I can talk to about anything, someone who always has time for me. He is a great man.'

More of Dennis as surrogate father and mentor – he is directing Lewis' progress in much the same way as football manager Sir Alex Ferguson looked out for his Manchester United stalwart Ryan Giggs in his younger days – later in this chapter. First, let's look at Dennis the man, his background and how he resurrected McLaren after they were struggling to stay on top in the eighties.

Former McLaren No. 1 Kimi Raikkonen echoed the feelings of many in the paddock when he derided his former boss Dennis as a 'control freak' early in 2007. But Dennis, typically managed to turn the tables by declaring that, well, yes, Kimi was absolutely correct: 'I smiled when I heard he said I was a control freak because I am – I don't mind fine attention to detail.'

He is certainly known for that perfectionist streak and for not wanting to have a laugh around the pits. Some think him humourless, but that is only a face value assessment. Get him on his own and he has a dry wit and can laugh at himself. Why, he even admitted that, like Britain's new Prime Minister Gordon Brown in 2007, he had worked a little on becoming more approachable in public. That he did not dislike people; that it was only his commitment to the job that made him appear a dour introvert.

Look at the changes within the McLaren team since the 2006 season if you want the proof of Dennis' attempt to 'spin' himself and his team in a more favourable light. He got rid of the brilliant, but fairly dull Raikkonen and brought in the fierce young reigning double World Champion Alonso as his replacement and then pulled another rabbit out of the hat by giving a relatively unknown rookie – Lewis Hamilton – his head in Formula One. Upon leaving McLaren, Raikkonen, known as 'The Iceman', illustrated that dourness with these few flat words: 'I have been five years with McLaren, but I wanted something else.' He didn't help his own cause while at McLaren by the simple fact that during his final campaign, McLaren failed to win a race for the first time in 10 years. That stark fact made Dennis all the more determined he would get his team back on top of the file – and bring back their first title since Mika Hakkinen last lifted it in 1999.

As the winds of change blew through the team, Dennis also decided that McLaren would begin the 2007 campaign with new title sponsors – only their third in the last 30 years – in communications giant Vodafone. And to cap it all, he laid on a PR extravaganza when he launched his new car, the MP4-22, in Spain. Alonso and Hamilton took to the streets of Valencia on a special circuit in front of 100,000 fans for a few parade laps in a launch estimated to have cost upwards of £4 million. Dennis wanted to show he could put on a launch with style and it went some way towards convincing a sceptical media that maybe he was mellowing a little. The blasts he would give them later in the season for their 'intrusions' into Hamilton's life would make them think twice, but there was little doubt that at the start of the campaign Ron Dennis was working hard to shake off his 'dull, boring, robot' tag. He admitted as much during the Valencia show, saying: 'Before we signed Vodafone over a year ago we had time to conduct an analysis of how people perceive the team. There were positives: integrity, honesty, sporting, cutting-edge, modern… But then came the negatives: cold, not particularly user-friendly, slightly aloof… We were surprised at that because at the circuit we do "meet the team" and we try to be co-operative with the media.

'But however the media might perceive us, we weren't perceived that way by the public, so we said "Let's do something about it". We wanted to make ourselves more human.'

He also spoke of his commitment to revitalise Formula One, which had fallen out of favour with many aficionados during the years of Schumacher dominance: 'Today is really about not just showing the car and the drivers, but more about our effort to practically demonstrate the commitment to Formula One. Don't see it as just a glitzy way to reveal a car. People wanted a dynamic Formula One that reached out – this is our effort to satisfy that need.'

Yet, at the same time in Valencia, he could not hide the more pragmatic side of his nature. Certainly, it had not deserted him when he spoke about his hopes for the new season, although he would enthuse about Lewis Hamilton, the boy he had been nurturing for nine years: 'It's important not to be optimistic or pessimistic, but realistic. So far, everything has led me to believe we are going to have a better car this year, although only time will tell if we're going to be competitive.

'Many people have said Lewis should be in a less competitive team in order that not so much is expected of him, but he's handling it. We've put a lot of work in over the last five months to bring him up to speed, to try to make him the fittest driver, the most knowledgeable driver about the rules. He understands things about the racing car that very few drivers have ever taken the effort to learn.

'He might not be the most experienced driver when he starts the season, but he will be a lot more knowledgeable than most of them about many, many subjects, and superfit as well.' With those words Ron Dennis proved why we Brits are glad to have him on our side in the Formula One battle. Depending on your stance, dull or not, he knows what he is talking about and his decision to blood Lewis Hamilton in F1, when probably no one else would have done so at the time, speaks volumes.

Ron Dennis was born on 1 June 1947 in Woking, the Surrey town in which he also grew up and would one day work as boss of McLaren. At 16 he left school and became an apprentice mechanic for the Thomson & Taylor garage at Weybridge (near the disused Brooklands circuit). He did a part-time Vehicle Technology course at Guildford Technical College. When Thomson & Taylor was taken over by the Chipstead Motor Group, Dennis transferred to another arm of the business: the Cooper Car Company. It was his first big break for they manufactured racing cars. In 1966, aged 19, he became a mechanic for the Cooper Formula One team, whose lead driver was Jochen Rindt. By 1968 Rindt had decided to move to Brabham. It was testament to the skills of Dennis that the ace German driver insisted he move with him. A year later, Rindt was on the move again, this time to Lotus. But now Dennis decided his loyalty was with Brabham and he became his chief mechanic. Tragically, a year later in 1970, Rindt – with whom he maintained a close friendship – would be killed in practice at the Italian Grand Prix in Monza.

The news left him devastated and he was hit by another blow in 1971 when Jack Brabham decided that he would call it a day. At the age of 44, the legendary Aussie had tied with Jackie Stewart for fifth in the points standings in the season. Upon retiring, he explained that he was making a complete break from racing, selling his interest in the team to Ron Tauranac and returning to Australia.

As one door closed another opened for Ron Dennis. Aged 25, he founded his own team in the same year with fellow mechanic Neil Trundle. Called Rondel, it would be based in Ron's stamping ground of Woking. They found sponsors in French oil company Motul and acquired two Brabham BT38s chassis from Tauranac. The team made its first appearance at Hockenheim with drivers Graham Hill and Tim Schenken. Hill won one of the two heats but was beaten to overall victory by François Cevert in his Tecno. A week later, on Easter Monday, Hill gave the team its first outright victory at Thruxton. Later that year the team expanded to a third car with Bob Wollek driving. That winter the same trio went to South America, where Schenken scored the team's second victory at Cordoba.

But trouble loomed. Ron was working all hours and, one

night, driving home late he was involved in a serious road accident. It forced him into a rethink: he decided he would no longer test the cars, turning his skills instead to managing the firm and planning his own cars. This was to be his destiny and soon he would develop his own chassis. A year later he commissioned Ray Jessop to design a F2 car for the 1973 season, to be called a Motul after the team's principal sponsor. The Motul chassis appeared at the start of the year. Henri Pescarolo won the second F2 race of the season and Tim Schenken added a second victory in the autumn. By then Dennis was planning for a Rondel Formula One programme, but his first attempt at the big time was to be spiked by outside sources.

In October 1973 the OPEC (Organisation of the Petroleum Exporting Countries) oil producers created an oil crisis and that winter Motul's sponsorship dried up. Dennis and Trundle had to abandon their dream. The project was sold to businessmen Tony Vlassopoulo and Ken Grob, who established the Token Formula One team. For the rest of that decade Ron Dennis concentrated on F2, quickly setting out the stall of discipline to his staff he demands even today. He explained that he expected cleanliness and orderliness in the traditionally messy garage and paddock, and total devotion and dedication to the job of ensuring the cars were in tip-top condition.

In 1975 he founded the Project Three team and soon he was churning out race winners as he became involved in running the BMW Junior Team F2 cars. By the end of the decade he had set up another new outfit, called Project Four.

The team chalked up success in Formula 2 and Formula 3, taking the British title in 1979 and 1980 with the backing of Philip Morris (Marlboro). They also took the 1980 Procar title with Niki Lauda on board.

Later that year, Dennis stepped up to the role for which he had surely been destined: boss of McLaren. The team's sponsors, who also backed his Project Four via Philip Morris, engineered a merger between the two and the new team was to be called McLaren International.

One of his first key decisions to turn round the flagging McLaren empire was to bring in designer John Barnard, who began work on the team's revolutionary new car, the MP4/1. It was used during the 1981, 1982 and 1983 seasons, and was the first Formula One car to use a carbon fibre composite shell. In 1982 he pulled off another master-stroke as he brought in massive finance by convincing Williams' backer Mansour Ojjeh to support his new set-up with hard cash. Ojjeh, a Syrian-born Saudi Arabian entrepreneur, had a passion for motor racing and did not need much persuading. For Dennis, the beauty of his arrival was that he could now use the $5 million Ojjeh was injecting into the firm for engine development. The new great era of McLaren was imminent as he ploughed cash into a Porsche-built turbo engine. Ojjeh and Dennis established TAG Turbo Engines and in September 1982 announced their first one. It was unveiled at the Geneva Motor Show in early 1983 and raced for the first time at the Dutch Grand Prix in August of that year.

The following year McLaren-TAG drivers Niki Lauda

and Alain Prost dominated the World Championship, scoring 12 wins in 16 races. Dennis was rewarded for all his efforts to turn the firm around as Lauda took the title by a half point from Prost, with both drivers scoring more than double the tally of third placed Elio de Angelis. However, the next year the tables were turned and Prost beat Lauda to the Driver's title with McLaren finishing eight points clear of second-placed Ferrari.

In five years Dennis had turned McLaren from an also-ran into the new kings, a remarkable achievement. At the end of 1984 Ojjeh became the majority shareholder in McLaren, although the deal was not made public until March 1985. It was a fair reward for his investment that had revitalised a company struggling to maintain its seat at the top of the racing world.

The TAG/McLaren empire continued to grow steadily in the late 1980s as more successes followed with Honda engines and they diversified into TAG Electronics and TAG/McLaren Marketing and McLaren Cars. Dennis, who had started out his career as a humble apprentice mechanic in Woking, was literally on top of the world. In 1988 his McLaren team took 15 of the 16 races and both titles, but he had a problem behind the scenes – keeping Prost and Senna from throttling each other. He did a good job, somehow massaging each of their massive egos, but by mid-1989 even he could not keep them at bay. After a controversial collision at the Japanese Grand Prix, which handed the title over to Prost, the Frenchman left the team for Ferrari and was replaced by Gerhard Berger the following season.

Senna continued the victory parade alone and went on to win the title in 1990 and 1991, to add to the one he won for the team in 1988. But by 1993 he too was gone and it would be five years before Mika Hakkinen and David Coulthard took them back to the very top of the sport, with the Finn taking the title.

As he had done so since taking command in 1980, Dennis looked carefully at his team's situation in that mid-90s barren period. He decided what was needed was an injection of new blood and he knew just the man to provide it. In 1996 he approached Williams' brilliant designer Adrian Newey to become technical director of McLaren. Newey agreed and by 1998 McLaren was once more in possession of the Drivers' and Constructors' titles. A second Drivers' title followed in 1999.

Dennis, who lives in Surrey with his wife and three children, was also honoured in his private life when he was awarded an Hon DTech from De Montford University in 1996 and an Hon DSc from City University, London, in 1997. Then, the man who put McLaren back on its feet once more would begin the new millennium in grand style as he received the CBE in 2000. Since taking over the team in 1980, he had guided it to 11 drivers' and eight Constructors' Championships. He had also led McLaren to victory at the first attempt in the Le Mans 24-hour race. At the end of 2000 he earned another notable award when he was presented with the honorary degree of Doctor of the University of Surrey. His citation read: 'Ron Dennis is being honoured for his significant contribution to the automotive engineering industry and for being a supreme ambassador for the UK and Surrey. Through the performance of the McLaren Formula One team, which has been under his direction since the 1980s, he has established a world-class company that continues to push forward the frontiers of technical design and application in many fields.'

Asked how he felt about the award, Dennis said: 'Extremely privileged and fortunate, which I'm sure are feelings everybody who receives a degree can relate to because degrees are a valued acknowledgement of the achievements a person has made.

'The TAG McLaren Group is attached to Surrey in general and Woking in particular. Many of our employees, including myself, are from the local area and have strong ties here. In addition, I am a believer that the working environment is crucial if you are to get the optimum performance from your employees, and the TAG McLaren employees work well in Surrey.'

He also expanded on his core belief that passion is the key to success from the top of the trade down: 'Being a success in industry is to truly care about what you are doing, to be passionate about it. This attitude then filters down through the company as a whole, and ensures that everybody does their utmost to ensure the company succeeds.' In 2001 he was also presented with a BRDC (British Racing Drivers' Club) Gold Medal in recognition for his contribution to motorsport.

As an aside: in June 2007, after the remarkable debut wins by Lewis Hamilton, some members of the public were asking why Dennis had not yet been knighted, that he deserved that recognition after unearthing such a gem. Motoring pundit Steve Robson put it this way: 'I'm pretty sure that the Queen's Birthday Honours are due to be announced sometime in the next week. With everything that he has achieved, isn't it about time Ron Dennis (CBE) was knighted? Frank Williams seems to have been Sir Frank for ages.'

Yet the years from 2000 to 2006 had not been as kind on the track. At least Dennis had the satisfaction of seeing his protégé develop and prosper during that barren spell. His relationship with Lewis Hamilton has always been close since they first met when Lewis was 13, but it has developed over the years into something special. Many trackside pundits refer to him being Hamilton's surrogate father, and it is easy to see why. I know for a fact that he sees Lewis as the greatest find and achievement of his career; there is a special bond between them that will surely never be broken. Ron has said 'You wait all your life for a lad like Lewis to come along. I feel lucky and honoured that I was the one to be with him in his career during his formative years.'

He has certainly become his professional mentor –once even describing Lewis as his '*My Fair Lady* experiment', a comment that may at first seem offhand and patronising. Anyone familiar with the film, though, will know that the protégé outstrips all expectations and the relationship eventually moves on to one of equality rather than mentor and student. That, I am told by a friend of Ron, is what he actually meant by the off-the-cuff remark. In turn, Lewis makes no bones about the fact that his wonderful story may not have happened without his mentor's faith in him: 'I first met Ron when I was 10 years old at an Autosport Awards ceremony. Listening to how he remembers the first time we met is special, and the faith, confidence and loyalty he's had in me over the years since has been key. I think it's a nice story – or the end of one story and the beginning of a new chapter.'

In almost a decade Dennis spent hour after hour with Lewis – teaching him, cajoling him and finally letting him lose on the Formula One track when the majority questioned that decision. Some felt he should have turned to the more experienced Gary Paffett or Pedro de la Rosa. But Dennis would have none of it, saying: 'Since 1998 Lewis has formed an important part of our long-term strategy and we are pleased that we are able to help him take another step and achieve his dream of becoming a Formula One racing driver. Pedro has done an outstanding job for us this season but we felt it was the right time to provide Lewis with this opportunity. It's obviously going to be the biggest challenge of Lewis' career so far but it's one that we are sure he will be able to meet. He is coming into the paddock for the first time as a Formula One racing driver and will have to familiarise himself with the pressures of a grand prix weekend. However, the confidence we have in Lewis' abilities and talent is clear from our decision to give him the chance.'

He also went on to say, with tongue firmly in cheek: 'I'm distinctly unimpressed by the majority of drivers in Formula One. Lewis is well equipped to deal with the drivers who fall into that category. Of course we have reservations – Lewis is an unproven product. But having the World Champion in one of our cars means that we can be less conservative and take the opportunity to give Lewis his chance.'

It was akin to a young lad of 17 being thrown into a Premiership football match for a daunting debut, as was the case with Ryan Giggs when he came on as a substitute for Manchester United against Everton at Old Trafford on 2 March 1991. I was at the match and still remember the gangly lad who was so thin and fragile he looked as if he would collapse if tackled. Until, that was, he danced merrily around the visitors' left-back...

As mentioned, there are strong similarities between the way Giggs' boss Sir Alex Ferguson looked after him and how Dennis has taken care of Hamilton. Both boys were prodigies, potential geniuses, and both had that cool head and fierce determination to make it. That in itself has made it easier for their managers. Both men are level-headed and modest, that is an important part of their appeal, particularly Lewis' as he comes from a sport that is infamous for its pit side arrogance, riches and lack of any humility whatsoever. As pointed out earlier, Lewis is similar in his coolness to his idol Michael Schumacher, but thankfully he does not have the iceman's legendary arrogance and aloofness.

Lewis has, of course, been brought up within the confines of the McLaren training academy for almost a decade. Ron Dennis would point that out to those who implied he had found the boy in the street and thrown him into a racing car. He would also stress, rather modestly, that he had worked with Lewis' father Anthony to keep him on track: 'Lewis gets his basic character from his family values, and we have just supplemented them. He is a well-rounded individual who appreciates not just what McLaren-Mercedes have done for him, but also what his family have done for him.'

British racing legend Nigel Mansell said he was convinced Lewis would not have made such an immediate impact were it not for the cosseting of Dennis and the resources he laid open to his protégé at McLaren: 'McLaren have been way overdue for success. Timing is everything. When a driver can arrive with a team and an engine coming right, it makes a difference. No disrespect to him – I think it was ordained. My story was a lot harder.'

Damon Hill is now convinced, after his initial worries that he would not last the season, that this boy has the lot – and that it is down to Lewis as much as Dennis. Lewis had the receptive abilities to take in what he was being told; he had the sense to listen and learn. Britain's last World Champion back in 1996, said that it was clear that he had also been helped by an excellent McLaren car. Not only this, but he has also consistently shown a maturity beyond his years to keep his cool in the toughest environment in motorsport: 'People should not under-estimate what he has achieved in an incredibly short space of time,' said Hill after Lewis' Canadian victory. 'Yes, he's with a good team, and yes, he's got a good car, but to be winning grands prix, and be putting in performances like that, race after race, takes something special. He may be young and in his first season, but this guy is the real deal. If you're good enough in this sport, you're old enough – and, boy, is Lewis good enough!'

Martin Whitmarsh, McLaren's chief executive, gives an insider's view, agreeing that Lewis deserves credit for listening to Dennis. He confirmed that he has the talent and determination that separates him from the average circuit driver: 'Since I joined McLaren in 1989 I've worked with a lot of great drivers, including Alain Prost, Ayrton Senna, Mika Hakkinen and now Fernando Alonso with Lewis. I think it's pretty clear Lewis ticks all the necessary boxes. We set out to ensure that he arrived at Formula One, not only in a competitive organisation, but also as prepared as possible. Lewis has made a great start to his career: it is our continued job to help him cope with the enormous attention in the British media.

'We are sure that it won't negatively impact on Lewis, but we are keen to make sure that in the early stages of his career nothing occurs that detracts him from his focus of getting the job done.'

However, former grand prix driver Martin Brundle believes there is no chance of him struggling under the weight of explanation: 'No doubt, it's going to be a long haul for Lewis and there are a number of things he has to face – his first big shunt, for instance, and all the travel, which can be pretty wearying. But all the ingredients are there. He excites me. Will he be up there one day with the likes of Prost, Senna and Schumacher? He's got a chance, definitely.'

Ron Dennis' decision to hold his boy back from the hordes of press, as Sir Alex Ferguson did with Ryan Giggs, was also a measured move. It meant he did not have extra pressures to cope with; he could continue his burgeoning career and concentrate on improving his driving skills and awareness. Only when he started his grand prix career – and by then he was 22 – did Dennis give him the green light for interviews. By then he had spent those nine years in the McLaren version of the *Big Brother* house and was well aware of what to expect and how to handle himself. He knew how to avoid leading questions and to keep to the script, a tactic that won the admiration of bloggers: Motoring journalist Adam Spurr summed up the success of keeping the youngster back until he was definitely ready for the inevitable blanket exposure in this perceptive way: 'Formula One's newest star is being kept at arm's length from the media and PR agencies. This will hopefully enable the 22-year-old to concentrate on winning races... Time and time again, British sport has appeared to have found a figurehead. Tim Henman (mummy's little soldier), Greg Rusedski (that well-known Canadian – I mean British – superstar) and Jenson Button (rather left out in the cold now) have all failed to impress the most British of solo sports. Hamilton, however, was quietly ushered in to McLaren, and ridiculed the highest hopes and dreams of those of us who watched him enter Bernie Ecclestone's circuit.

'I think that this is a very important part of his success. He has been kept under the wing of Ron Dennis and guarded from the media hype that now surrounds him, so that he can concentrate on his driving. Even ITV F1, that bastion of drivers' interviews, have respected the request from Mr Dennis to respect his privacy. Everybody at ITV F1 seems to be willing Lewis to win, and doing everything in their power not to cause the slightest bit of disruption.'

Let's leave the final word in this chapter to Ron Dennis, the man who built up the McLaren legend into the glory story that young Lewis Hamilton desperately wanted to be a part of, the man who had enough faith in Lewis to push him to the threshold of greatness. Dennis said: 'He now has enough brownie points that he can lose some without getting severe criticism. Confidence is often coupled with arrogance, but there isn't an ounce of arrogance in Lewis. He listened, which frequently young people don't, and progressively built his career...'

CHAPTER 7

WIZARD
IN OZ

After all the hype and anticipation finally the time had come for the talk to stop and for Lewis to walk the walk. Or, more precisely, drive the drive. Almost 10 years under the auspices of Ron Dennis and McLaren in Woking had passed and now the world would see whether Lewis could really cut it, or whether he was merely the planet's first 'engineered' Formula One driver, who failed because he was simply a prototype without soul.

Of course, those who had been following his development with interest and hope over that learning decade knew beforehand that he had all the right attributes in abundance. And after 18 March 2007, the secret would be shared by the whole world. Lewis Hamilton arrived at Melbourne on the Thursday before the race and the McLaren team noticed how cool and calm he was. One mechanic remarked: 'We knew he was a lad with composure and self-confidence, but we had not seen anything like the level of his calmness before. He seemed to have no nerves; he was certainly a lot different than Fernando Alonso, who was fidgety and kept asking us if everything was all right, if the car was really ready to go. Lewis acted as if he was out on a Sunday race around a go-kart track – you would never have guessed it was his debut in Formula One.'

The track, at Albert Park in the city of Melbourne, is hardly one of the most exciting on the circuit. If anything, it invites a fairly dull day's racing. There are few opportunities to overtake and David Coulthard once admitted it was far from being the most challenging of circuits. The track, which has been part of the Formula One circuit since 1996, lies within the city's park and its layout is smooth and flowing, with no 90-degree street corners to break the speed. It runs clockwise around a lake, and the scenery and atmosphere is relaxed and peaceful – one of the reasons why it is well liked by the drivers. For Lewis Hamilton, there could hardly have been a better setting for his opening.

One of the other features of Albert Park on a Formula One weekend is its intimacy; drivers tend to sit out and chat with each other behind the garages. Maybe because it's the traditional curtain-raiser, there is a friendliness and empathy between the teams that certainly evaporates by the time the Formula One circus hits Europe three months later, when rivalries have been established and the whole business is much more cutthroat.

At the opener, it's not the end of the world if you don't

win – there are another 16 races on which to stake your claim for glory. Sure, it's a chance to set down a marker, but it's only the aperitif to the main course. For the boy from Britain this was another plus factor: already he could relax without the pressure of being expected to win, being a rookie. But he could also unwind with his father Anthony, having a chat and a glass of soda in a deckchair in between practice and qualifying.

That suited Lewis perfectly. All the limelight, all the attention, was on his co-driver Alonso, the double World Champion, who was soaking up all the interest before his debut for his new team. This was the man who had won at Melbourne the previous season and who was expected to win again, this time for a new team at the start of the 2007 campaign.

It was certainly an unusual scenario: two men making their debut in the same team. Usually, one would be a seasoned pro who had worked for the team for a few seasons. Who knew the team inside out and knew the mechanics and the tech man, and how they worked; was aware of their idiosyncrasies and demands. Ron Dennis was not renowned for being a gambler – he would later contend there was no gamble. That he knew full well what Lewis was capable of, and that Alonso was, after all, a World Champion, who should hardly have needed nursing into a new team.

Typically, he was right on both points although Alonso's questions did surprise the team. He was to settle down after a couple of practice sessions when the car handled well and he knew everything would be OK. Dennis later admitted the Spaniard's previous nerves and doubts were a good sign. Alonso was also a perfectionist, and there was nothing wrong with that – on the contrary it showed the professionalism of the man he was willing to pay £10 million a year to be his No. 1 driver.

In the build-up to the race, Big Ron allowed Lewis to speak a little to the press, to open up a bit and show who he was. Here are some of the more interesting points from a question and answer section.

Asked what drove him on, Lewis replied: 'I am motivated by a desire to be the best at whatever I decide to put my mind to. Once I have decided to take up a challenge, my inner self will not let me give up unless I have achieved my goal. I love motor racing and I have done so since I first watched it on TV when I was about 5. The key element in all of this is that I am not here to take part, I am here to win, and I will do whatever mentally and physically it takes to achieve that in due course. I do not plan to waste this opportunity.'

When asked about Alonso he was Mr Tactful: 'It is truly an honour for me to be given this opportunity to work alongside Fernando in my first year as a Formula One driver. I have a tremendous amount of respect for what he has achieved. The sheer size of the challenge of working with him and competing against him is what is most exciting. All of my former team-mates have been hugely competitive and the challenge and excitement comes from having to find the answers to the most important question, "Just how far do I need to push myself to beat that person and just how far can I go?" With Fernando being a two-times World Champion, I know I have to dig deeper than ever before which is what I love about being a racing driver.'

He admitted it was his dream come true to make his debut for McLaren: 'The feeling is indescribable. Growing up I always dreamed of racing for McLaren and now I am. The thought of racing and working with my team-mates is a great feeling, to be driving a Vodafone McLaren Mercedes is literally surreal.' Ever thankful to his immediate family, whose support he readily acknowledges as playing a key role in his success, Lewis also praised his professional family – specifically Ron Dennis, Martin Whitmarsh and Norbert Haug – for the long-term support and guidance, and of course for the initial opportunity to succeed in a field he loves more than any other.

He also recalled how the history of McLaren was a big attraction: 'Like most kids, I am sure I dreamt of one day racing with Ayrton Senna and Alain Prost. Now my dream has literally turned into a reality and I am driving not only in Formula One but also for the same team as Ayrton and Alain did. I worked hard to make it to Formula One but never imagined it would actually be with a team such as McLaren and in my first year!

Asked if he could possibly emulate his success in GP2 2006 in 2007 in Formula One, his response was typically modest: '2006 was a fantastic year, a year in which everything I had learned through karting, Formula Renault and Formula 3 all came together in GP2. I learned a great deal in GP2 and thank Frederic Vasseur and everyone at

ART for their support. At the end of each year, I sit down with my manager and we review and evaluate the year and come up with a plan for the following year. 2007 will be no different to any other year. Once I have a plan, I always follow it to the end. I know I have to work harder to be stronger, mentally and physically, and to prepare myself for whatever may come my way in Formula One, but I am ready and relishing the challenge.'

And what made him tick – what was his ambition now that he had finally made it into Formula One? He replied: 'If you want to be the best at whatever career you choose in life, then you have to compete at the very top. Formula One is the pinnacle of motorsport. From the time I started my racing career in Cadet Karts in 1994, right the way through to Formula Renault, Formula 3 and GP2, I have dedicated my life to achieving my goal of becoming a Formula One World Champion. I am now another huge step closer to reaching my ultimate dream.'

Unashamedly, Lewis stated that his aim is always to win but, aware that it was still his debut season, he recognized there was work to do to learn as much as possible from Alonso and the whole team: 'I aim to do a steady job for the team and help them progress towards both Constructor's and Driver's Championships.'

He then revealed a little more about his personal life, his ambitions, loves and hopes in a Q-and-A session with the Formula One Complete website team. Asked what he would wish for if he were granted three wishes, Lewis replied that the first one would be for more, and then for the health and security of his family. 'Finally, I would wish that I could do something positive for others less fortunate. I am not sure what or how just yet, but I'm sure the answer will come to me in time.'

The journalist enquired what items he couldn't live without if stranded on a remote island; the reply being music ('My MP3 player as I couldn't cope without having any music'), his girlfriend, and unsurprisingly, a super-fast form of transport: 'A speedboat with a full tank of fuel would be useful.'

If he weren't a racing driver, Lewis identified music as the field he's be most interested in working in. He plays the guitar and when he was younger he tried to set up his own band. A lot of his friends are involved in music so it is a big part of his life. Failing that, he would have probably pursued another sport.

The questioning quickly returned to Formula One, and gave Lewis the opportunity to talk about what he liked about his job: 'The feeling you get when you are really driving on the edge and pushing beyond the limit. The rush you get, the feeling of speed, the force that your body is under, all of that coming together gives the biggest adrenaline buzz and it's something that you can't experience anywhere else.'

At the time of the interview he was driving a Smart Forfour Brabus, which he described as great fun to drive. But he was keen to extend his collection and getting a Mercedes-Benz was a high priority. His ultimate dream car would be the orange McLaren Formula One LM housed at the McLaren Technology Centre.

Lewis' dream holiday destination would undoubtedly be somewhere in the Caribbean. With family in Grenada he had the developed a love for visiting the island. 'Maybe someday I'll visit some of the other beautiful islands of the Caribbean, but for now Grenada is the place.

'I have a fairly extensive training programme that takes up a lot of my time away from the track. When I do have some downtime,' continued Lewis, 'I like to spend it relaxing with my family and friends, in particular catching up with my younger brother Nicolas.' Away from work, Lewis named golf and basketball as two sports he liked to play to keep in shape.

The website team ended by asking Lewis about his favourite track (Monaco) and whether he had a hero: 'I would say that I haven't really had a hero since I was very young as a hero is someone that seems invincible. There are people that I greatly admire, though. In Formula One Ayrton Senna was really inspirational to me and I didn't think Michael Schumacher would ever be counted as a hero, but I really do look up to him for what he has achieved and what he has done for the sport.' Outside of racing, he named his Dad foremost, then hip hop star P. Diddy, whom Lewis cites as a motivational role model for he way in which he has built up his empire. 'Finally, Martin Luther King who was just a great person and continues to inspire many people, including me.'

Then, this unassuming, eminently likeable boy went out for practice in his first grand prix weekend. During the first and second sessions both he and Alonso turned in fine performances, proving McLaren were in fine fettle and that the team was well on the pace. After practice, Lewis was buzzing with adrenaline, his first taste of Formula One action had left him wanting more. He said: 'I was so excited when I drove out of the garage for the first time this morning; it was an incredible feeling as I have wanted to be a Formula One driver since I started karting, and now I am and enjoying every single moment. The track is good, particularly as I love street circuits and the whole atmosphere is amazing. Back at the McLaren Technology Centre we have done a lot of simulation work to prepare me for this weekend but it was good to actually drive it for real. The car feels good and the two sessions today were really useful.'

He would also do well in his first ever grand prix qualifying sessions, ending up fourth on the grid. Eventual race winner Kimi Raikkonen, in the Ferrari, took pole position in a time of 1:26.072, Alonso came second in 1:26.493 and BMW's Nick Heidfeld third in 1:26.556. Lewis clocked 1:26.755.

After qualifying he said: 'I'm overwhelmed to be on the second row for my first grand prix – a huge thank you to the team who have worked so hard, both here at the track and back at base. This weekend is what I have been preparing myself for during the past 13 years and I'm enjoying every moment. I think we are in with a good chance in the race. Basically I want to get a good start and then work hard to score as many points for the team and myself. I'm not going to make any predictions because anything can happen, but so far, so good.'

The race itself would see the same four who finished top in qualifying finish in the top four, but with Lewis and Heidfeld changing places. A crowd of 105,000 people flocked to Albert Park for the season's opener – and the first race of the 'post-Schumacher' era; the German's final race being the Brazilian Grand Prix on 22 October 2006.

Beforehand, a nervy Ron Dennis had asked that TV companies refrain from conducting pre-race interviews with his boy. Instead, the TV scenes during those vital last few minutes before the start would show Lewis and Ron, student and mentor for the previous decade, together in the pits. Lewis is all ears as the Big Man gives him some last words, some final encouragement as the moment for which they had been building so long edges ever closer.

This was a poignant moment. It could also, conceivably, have been the moment when Fernando Alonso first questioned whether he had made the right decision in joining McLaren. The Spanish boy who loved, nay demanded, the limelight and all the fuss and minute attention of his team saw his boss spending those last key seconds before what was, after all, his big debut too, with a rookie. The rookie he had imagined would be his easy No. 2 on the way to an easy third world crown.

Afterwards Big Ron revealed he had been using those last few minutes to advise his protégé that the start was the key to the race and success: 'I told him to hold his position at the start and not do anything stupid.' Lewis certainly took in the advice, indeed, he even improved on it, taking a calculated gamble to head past Alonso into third place in the early seconds. The *Guardian*'s Paul Kelso explained it in this way: 'What Hamilton did announced the nature of his prodigious gift. As a declaration of intent and talent it has rarely been matched.'

Throughout the race, the youngster never looked out of his depth. Ice-cool, decisive and brilliant, he even matched the fierce pace of Raikkonen's Ferrari, while driving with a fine judgment and maturity to keep Alonso at bay for the best part of the 58-lap race. He would only drop to third when Alonso pulled off a short second pit stop to come out in front after Lewis had been previously been held up on his own in-lap.

For Raikkonen, this was the perfect start in his role as Michael Schumacher's replacement. The Finnish driver led from start to finish and lived up to his pre-season label as title favourite. Kimi said: 'We didn't need to really push as hard as we could have. My biggest problem was the radio – it stopped working just before the start. It is special moment with a new team, everything is new, to win in the first race. I am really happy with the team and the way things are going. It couldn't be any better than it is now.'

But his glory was short-lived for his win was overshadowed by Lewis Hamilton's display as the world's press quickly woke up to the fact that Formula One finally had a new hero, a new phenomenon after the era of Schumacher. Quite simply, it had been an incredible result by Lewis to finish on the podium in his debut race. It also continued the sequence of glory for British drivers at the circuit since its opening in 1996. Damon Hill won the inaugural event that year in the Williams and the following year Britain struck gold again – this time David Coulthard triumphed for McLaren, their first, incidentally, with a Mercedes' engine.

Colourful Eddie Irvine was to win in 1999 – his first Formula One win for Ferrari – and four years later Coulthard notched up his second victory at Melbourne in the McLaren. As this book went to press, that remained David's last Formula One win, and will probably turn out to be his final one.

Damon Hill summed it up: 'Lewis qualified well, and he raced brilliantly. He was at the sharp end in his first grand prix and was competitive with his team-mate – really, really good.' Hill was, of course, Britain's last Formula One World Champion, and he admitted he had seen some fine driving by Lewis; enough to convince even him that the boy had what it took to follow him. He was particularly impressed by his brilliant start: 'The weight of expectation was massive on Lewis and it seemed to me he didn't really show any sign of weakness at all. He was on it right from the word go. His start was just a classic, fantastic, pulling that move on the first corner. It was a brave, but committed overtaking manoeuvre.

'It's very, very easy for someone in their first grand prix to make a hash of that, but he never looked like he was fazed by what he was doing – he just did it and it came off. And when he was in front of Fernando [Alonso], you could see he was really using the entire road. He was right up against the wall going into the switchback at the back of Melbourne and he was using all the road on the exit.

'He was pushing, he was confident, and he never looked ragged. It was good. He looked very happy on the podium. I think he knew he'd done a bloody good job. He was in the race at the sharp end in his first ever grand prix and competitive with his team-mate. Tremendous – really, really good!'

Former Great Britain hope Jenson Button suffered a frustrating weekend in his Honda, finishing 15th in Melbourne. At least he had the good grace to congratulate the man who had taken his place as the nation's new Formula One idol: 'He did a fantastic job. Lewis had a great first race and was lucky enough to be in a good car, but there is no getting away from the fact that he did a great job.'

Lewis was pleased with his weekend's work in Australia and the result enthused him with new confidence – he now felt able to predict that he would one day become Formula One Champion, although modesty forbade him from saying it would be in his first season. He admitted he had enjoyed every moment of the big debut: 'Formula One is the highest challenge I've ever had. I am very competitive and winning is what I want to do. My dream is to win and become a World Champion. Three years is a good time to put on my goal to win a world title.'

His third-place finish proved to be the best debut performance by a British racer in 41 years since Mike Parkes took second place in the French Grand Prix. Lewis finished 11.3 seconds behind Alonso who, in turn, was 7.2 seconds behind the flying Finn. His result meant that he had also become the first Formula One rookie to claim a podium finish since Jacques Villeneuve in 1996, but don't forget that the Canadian already had previous motor racing pedigree in America's Indy Car series. To be fair, Raikkonen also claimed a record: becoming the first driver to win in their first race for Ferrari since Nigel Mansell in 1989. It was also the first race in World Championship history (obviously apart from the all-time opener in 1950) when all three podium finishers were making their debut for their team.

The Finn took the maximum 10 points to lead the Driver's title with Alonso close behind on eight. Lewis had picked up his first grand prix points in his first race, yet very few would have backed him to be third in the race for the Championship with those six points.

Mark Sharman, head of ITV Sport, was understandably also delighted with Hamilton's performance in Melbourne. He knew this would mean increased viewing figures during the season if Lewis could maintain his excellent start and said it had convinced him that the 22-year-old was surely destined to become the next British sporting icon: 'If Lewis begins to win races he will become the biggest sports star in Britain in no time. He's one of a new breed of young sportsmen like Theo Walcott and Amir Khan, who are a breath of fresh air, and he's hugely exciting.'

Former Formula One driver Mark Blundell, now working as ITV's main analyst, agreed and also voiced the opinion that Lewis was on the way to becoming a superstar with McLaren: 'This is a multi-million pound outfit... All their work and all the expectations of the sponsors rest on Lewis' shoulders. He's the first black driver, he came with a lot of expectation, having won the support series GP2 last year, but all we're talking about is a great new driver. This is a sport that lost a superstar in Michael Schumacher last year, and people are wondering if we might have found the replacement.'

Lewis said how much he had enjoyed the race and paid tribute to the effort of his mechanics and technical support: 'I'm absolutely ecstatic – today's result is more than I ever dreamed of achieving on my grand prix debut. A big thank you to the team who have worked so hard during the winter to make sure I was as prepared as I could possibly be. I made a good start, but the BMWs were quick off the line and Kubica managed to get past. There was no room on the inside so I got on the left and managed to outbrake both Kubica and Fernando coming into the first corner to take third. The race was intense, and I was working very hard. I made a few mistakes, but nothing major and really enjoyed myself. It was great to lead the race for a few laps, but I knew it was only a temporary thing. Fernando got past me at the second pit stop as he was able to stay out a bit longer and I lost some time behind backmarkers. We now have a lot of work ahead of us with the Malaysia test and the rest of the season, but there is no doubt that we can build from what has been achieved today.'

Fernando Alonso claimed to be delighted with his McLaren debut, saying it had set down a marker: 'What a great way to start the season and my career as a McLaren Mercedes driver! Of course it's always better to win, but

Kimi Raikkonen was a little bit quicker than us today. However, I'm really pleased. My start was a bit strange, with both BMWs being very quick off the line and I was so busy defending my line from Heidfeld on the outside that it was not possible for me to stay ahead of him. I was then behind Lewis for a while and was just focusing on keeping up with him and sometimes dropping back to allow the car to cool down. I took second after the second pit stop as I was able to stay out for an additional two laps.

'Originally it was meant to be one lap, but because I was behind Lewis I managed to save enough fuel for 1 more lap. We will now continue to work hard to give us the best opportunity to beat Ferrari at the Malaysian Grand Prix.'

Ron Dennis admitted he was pleased with the showing of his two drivers, but typically of his perfectionist zeal, was disappointed not to have won: 'Of course as always we came to Australia to win, but a somewhat unexpected strategy adopted by BMW was very disruptive to our race. Following Heidfeld's first pit stop the gap was just too big to realistically close it and the additional range from our strategy was subsequently wasted.

'Both drivers did an excellent job giving us a narrow lead in the Constructors' Championship. A special thank you to the test team and the workforce back at the McLaren Technology Centre, who have worked so hard during the winter and contributed so much to the faultless reliability that we have enjoyed throughout the weekend. The coming Malaysian test should give us every opportunity to further improve the competitiveness of our cars.'

Norbert Haug, competition chief for McLaren's engine partner Mercedes-Benz, took time out to give both Alonso and Lewis a vote of confidence, saying: 'The season started well with Fernando and Lewis scoring 14 points on their debut race. Fernando showed with his performance exactly why he is the double World Champion whilst Lewis made a perfect start to his grand prix career and proved absolutely worthy of the confidence we have had in him for the past 10 years.'

An interesting sidebar to the Australian Grand Prix of 2007 is that two other drivers were making their Formula One debuts – Heikki Kovalainen and Adrian Sutil. Sutil is considered one of the drivers who could push Lewis in years to come if he gets the right car – he was to finish 17th in Melbourne. But Kovalainen's experiences there sum up just how brilliantly Lewis did to finish third, and just how competitive and unforgiving relative failure is received within Formula One.

The 25-year-old Finn had been promoted from test driver to replace Fernando Alonso at Renault after the Spaniard's move to McLaren. But he spun at the Jones Chicane on his 40th lap, which led to him losing a place to Felipe Massa. He then ran wide on several occasions during the early part of the race, finishing tenth, and received a public wind-up from Renault team chief Flavio Briatore, with the unforgiving Italian describing his debut as 'rubbish'.

Meanwhile, phone-ins and website forums in the UK were buzzing after Lewis' dazzling debut. The BBC prompted a flurry of responses on the 606 site after proclaiming: 'Given that the McLaren was comfortably the second quickest car in Melbourne – and only one of the faster Ferraris was in with a shout at the front following Felipe Massa's problems in qualifying – third is about where Hamilton should have finished. Far, far more remarkable was his performance in comparison with team-mate Fernando Alonso.

'This is the finest all-round driver in the world, a double World Champion. Someone who last year took on and beat in a straight fight Michael Schumacher – who some consider to be the greatest ever and who was certainly the greatest of his generation.

'And yet Hamilton had the temerity to pass the illustrious Spaniard around the outside at the start, and make him work hard for the rest of the race. You could count on one hand the number of drivers who could do that to Alonso in the same car, let alone on their grand prix debut. He made his mark in quite emphatic style and there is no doubt that Alonso, and the rest of the Formula One field, will have taken notice.'

The remarks prompted Formula One fan Graham Parkin to say: 'I was fortunate enough to be able to watch Lewis in GP2 at Silverstone last year and remember a manoeuvre that was surprisingly reminiscent of the one he did at the start in Melbourne as he went past Alonso. The only difference at Silverstone was that he managed to pass *three* cars on a corner you supposedly cannot overtake on. For the rest of the race, he then received a standing ovation for every single lap he completed.

'I don't think I have ever seen a situation where there has been more interest in the "warm-up" race than the actual main event, the Formula One. Everyone was talking about Hamilton and how that if he wasn't in a Formula One car within two years, someone was missing out on a great talent. He is the UK's greatest hope of another Championship winner.'

Karting fanatic Alan Dove said it was about time Lewis received his rightful acclaim: 'It is nice to see that finally everyone is witnessing just how good Lewis Hamilton is! The UK karting scene has been singing his praises for over 10 years. I raced the kid when I was 10 and he was an absolute genius. I would go as far as to say he hasn't really improved much since he was 10.... he has *always* been that good!'

The excellent website, grandprix.com, summed up Lewis' display in fine style by comparing it to a Hollywood movie debut: 'Lewis Hamilton's start was straight out of Hollywood. He edged away off the line and was aware that Robert Kubica, a career-long rival of Lewis', who looks like one of those Nordic villains that Bruce Willis would have shot in the 94th minute of the movie, was alongside him. Worse still (cut to slow motion), Kubica was getting ahead and switching across in front of our hero.

'Lewis did what Sylvester Stallone would have done and jinked the wheel to the left and swooped around the outside in an elegant arc, passing not only the evil Polish villain (who actually seems like a very nice chap) but also the double World Champion Fernando Alonso to grab third place. (Cue stirring music).

'We were watching the birth of a new star as Lewis Hamilton kept Fernando Alonso at bay in the finest traditions of comic books heroes of yesteryear. The double World Champion was being held back by the plucky young chap on his grand prix debut. People in newspaper offices across the world with no interest in Formula One were perking up. This was a news story. Lewis was on his way to the front cover of *Sports Illustrated*, following the path cut recently through the media jungle by Danica Patrick.

'It was the most impressive debut in Formula One for more than 10 years. Hell, that's rubbish! This was much more impressive than what Jacques Villeneuve did back in 1996 because he had much more experience with big powerful cars when he took the Williams to second place in Melbourne.'

Great stuff... Now all Lewis had to do was continue to prove he was worthy of the growing adulation and hype, that his third place finish in Melbourne was no fluke – he was the real thing. Here was the new cool-headed Schumacher mixed with a liberal sprinkling of the adventure of that legendary daredevil Senna. He now had three weeks to contemplate his initial success and rev himself up for another test on the other side of the world. Sepang, in Malaysia, eagerly awaited the young star, but would he survive unscathed and retain his cool in the heat and humidity of a circuit built on land that was formerly a jungle?

CHAPTER 8

THE RUMBLE IN THE JUNGLE

As he approached the second Formula One grand prix of his life at Sepang on 8 April 2007, the heat was on for Lewis Hamilton. If Melbourne had been a relatively easy-going introduction to the high-stress of top-level motor racing, and given that little was expected of him in his debut race, it was now a different story altogether in the humidity of Malaysia. Now the whole wide world knew Ron Dennis and McLaren had been hiding away and cultivating a phenomenon, and that Lewis Hamilton was no traditional young man thrown into the Formula One inferno. No, here was someone who was the virtual finished article before he had even properly started. A one-off who could not only live up to the hype, but exceed it.

Sepang was a prime example of how Formula One ring-master Bernie Ecclestone envisaged the sport developing.

The track had been specially built in 1999 on land that had been jungle. It was a shimmering, shining circuit – the first of Formula One's new generation of ultra-modern, high-tech circuits. It was also part of the Malaysian government's attempt to bring riches to the country: in the mid-1990s the Prime Minister, Dr Mahathir Mohamad, determined that by 2020 Malaysia would be a fully industrialised nation. He decided that the best way to achieve this would be through the auto trade.

The nation's biggest oil company, Petronas, began investing heavily in Formula One when Sauber and Malaysia's national car company, Proton, bought Lotus Engineering. Dr Mohamad ordered a grand prix track to be constructed as part of the vision and not just any track either. In conjunction with Bernie Ecclestone, he wanted to create a new-style circuit that would be the envy of the world in terms of facilities and technology. Just 2 miles from Kuala Lumpur, the circuit did not disappoint – its combination of long, high-speed straights and tight, twisting corners made it a challenge for drivers. Overtaking was possible but you had to be top-notch to master the circuit.

That humid Sunday the circuit of the future would welcome the driver of the future. Lewis Hamilton arrived in sweltering heat on the Thursday before the race and was taken aback by the level of interest in him. His incognito lifestyle was now a thing of the past; everyone in Sepang was asking about him. Interest was not just from the UK – the Americans and the Germans were also keen to learn all they could, as were his Far Eastern hosts. He was in big demand. His third place finish in Melbourne ensured this would be the case, but his personality and easy-going charm was also a massive lure for a press and Formula One following that had found itself distanced from the drivers during the heyday of Schumacher.

The young black British wunderkind provided a welcome antithesis to the ice-cool arrogance, some might say lack of soul, of the German. In contrast, Lewis was very approachable and full of smiles; he was welcoming and, most of all, down-to-earth. It was a remarkable landshift in the world of Formula One and it was clear as early as the second grand prix of the season.

Lewis was asked how he felt on his arrival: could he emulate his success in Melbourne, or did he concede that it had maybe been a mere fluke? His reply was telling: he said that he was not in Sepang to make up the numbers, no, he was here to win: 'There's no rush as there are 16 races left. But I'm here to win and whether it's the first weekend or the last, as long as I get one in, then I'll be happy. From what I had seen of the track before arriving for the test I thought it looked like a great circuit and I was not disappointed. Its layout means you can build up a great rhythm, with all the corners running into each other. It is also really wide, which I imagine will lead to exciting racing.'

And how was he coping with his new fame? He admitted: 'I'm still relaxed about it all but it is a bit like an out-of-body experience. It's like I'm sitting out there watching myself. Just yesterday in town, I saw a big poster of myself. It is a bit strange with all the attention.'

Of course, he was at a natural disadvantage to Alonso and most of the other drivers at Sepang: apart from testing the previous week, he had never driven around the track. It would be the same story when they finally arrived in America. Sure, he had an idea what it would be like from his time in the McLaren simulator at Woking, but his only first-hand experience had been during testing, whereas Alonso, for example, had won in Malaysia in 2005 and was second behind Giancarlo Fisichella in 2006. Yes, he was at a distinct disadvantage but was he concerned? By Sunday night he finished runner-up to his team-mate, with another 8 points in the bag in the title race. As Murray Walker might say... remarkable.

Lewis was pleased with the way things went during practice and felt he had acclimatised well: 'This is my first Malaysian Grand Prix, but I got to know the circuit well during last week's test. The heat and humidity are as I expected and have trained for. The practice today was pretty straightforward and we made further steps. The circuit conditions are constantly changing, which makes it challenging to find the right balance. I'm looking forward to qualifying tomorrow.'

In qualifying, Ferrari's Felipe Massa had taken pole after a brilliant final lap. The Brazilian made amends for his qualifying failure in Melbourne by clocking 1:35.043, 0.267 secs ahead of Alonso. Raikkonen was third in 1:35.479 and Hamilton fourth in 1:36.045. As an illustration of just how superbly Lewis was driving, his vastly more experienced fellow Brits David Coulthard and

Jenson Button were thirteenth and fifteenth respectively on the grid, come Sunday.

After qualifying he admitted he had eased off a little as the rain had started to fall; that he could possibly have done even better, but did not want to gamble on a wet circuit. He said: 'It went pretty smoothly. I think the car performed well and we look forward to the race. I'm optimistic about the race and I'm on the clean side of the track. The car is working well and I think we could have had two cars on the front row. However, when I came to Turn 7 it had started spitting with rain a little bit. I had experienced this at the test last week and knew it could be slippery, so I eased off a small amount.'

In the race he delivered another fine display of measured, mature driving, finishing in 17.5 seconds and runner-up to Alonso. This was the Spanish ace's first victory for McLaren and elevated him above Kimi Raikkonen in the title race; it was also the team's first win since Japan in 2005. Hamilton held off a late challenge from Raikkonen to confirm his second successive podium appearance. After going from fourth to second on the first lap, Lewis also saw off a determined Felipe Masa. The Brazilian had tried to charge past Lewis on lap six but overshot the corner, slid off the track and finished in fifth position.

The McLaren 1–2 finish was an emphatic declaration of intent to Ferrari after their triumph in Melbourne. Ferrari themselves conceded they had a faster car, but their drivers had not matched Alonso and Lewis. Afterwards, perhaps predictably, given the heat and humidity, Lewis was drained but still coherent and making a lot of sense in what he said. It had been, he admitted, easily the toughest race and challenge he had ever faced: 'I was defending my position for a lot of the time and I'm so pleased that I managed to keep both Felipe and Kimi behind me. However, it was hard work and it was just so hot inside the cockpit. I made a good start and was able to get past Felipe and Kimi to take second. At one point Felipe was attacking and ended up going slightly off the track, and I was able to keep second. Kimi was catching towards the end as I was struggling with the balance a bit, but what a race! I now have experience of racing in these conditions and will be even better prepared next year.

'To see two Ferraris behind you, two red blobs in the mirror, knowing that they had started lighter than you and were quicker than you... I had to keep pushing all the way to the last lap and not make any mistakes. I had to bite my tongue and dig as deep as I could, and yet preserve the energy I had and pull the car to the end. Defending is 10 times harder than trying to overtake someone when you have two guys lighter on fuel and perhaps slightly faster. I'm now looking forward to Bahrain. Congratulations to Fernando, very well done.'

Even before the cars had been packed away in the trucks, Ron Dennis was also planning ahead for Bahrain. He took time out to say a few words about Hamilton's second place finish: 'Lewis continues to demonstrate why he has warranted the enthusiasm of all of us who have worked with him over the years.'

Bahrain was just a week after Sepang, giving Lewis little time to recover from the ordeal of Malaysia. Another new, hi-tech circuit, the Manama – located in desert land in Sakhir – was designed by Formula One's in-house architect with the aim of opening up the sport to the Middle East. In 2004 Bahrain became the first country in the region to host a Formula One grand prix and it did not take Lewis long to acclimatise. Then again, he was no stranger to it: indeed, this had been the circuit where he had achieved one of his best ever results prior to joining Formula One. In December 2004 he won the first ever Bahrain F3 Superprix after starting eleventh on the grid. In a superb drive, he moved up to fourth by the end of the opening lap, and on the final lap sped past his two main rivals, Nico Rosberg and Jamie Green, to take victory.

The memory of that race gave him hope that he could repeat his glory run. As in Malaysia, he showed an incredible coolness in searing heat. Those months of fitness training back in Woking had clearly paid off – his body had shown a remarkable recovery rate from a week previous when he had clearly been exhausted after finishing his work in Sepang.

As they got down to business back in Bahrain, his father Anthony expressed his own excitement and apprehension over Lewis' start to his grand prix career. That second place in Malaysia had also made him the first man to finish in the top three in his first two races since another Brit, Peter Arundell, did so in 1964. And that prompted Anthony to say: 'I'm frightened what's going to happen next. It's crazy.'

Once again, Lewis was the focus of attention for the world's media who had gathered in the desert. And he did not let them down – giving a confident soundbite when asked what they could expect of him: he was out to make history by becoming the first man ever to record three straight podium finishes in Formula One. And, no, he wasn't ruling out the possibility of winning his third race. Jenson Button, the previous blue-eyed British boy, had needed 113 starts to earn his first win, but Lewis was quietly confident: 'I'm pushing and working as hard as I can. It may be this weekend, it may be the last race of the year; it may be next year.

'So far I haven't made a mistake. But we all make mistakes trying to put the car through everything and trying to better ourselves. It is inevitable when you are pushing the car to the limit that you are going to make mistakes and it will happen at some point.'

Practice went well as Lewis' uncanny knack of adapting swiftly to any circuit continued apace. After a steady few laps getting to grips with the Sakhir circuit, he said: 'It has been a positive session today. In the first practice the track was very dirty and slippery so there was no point spending too much time looking at the set-up. In the second session we began our fine tuning and completed a couple of long runs. I think I was quicker and more consistent than previously in the long runs, which is positive and there is definitely more to come. We now have quite a bit of data to look at, but so far, so good.'

So far, so good indeed! Lewis was third in the drivers' standings, four points behind Alonso and Raikkonen, and

McLaren headed the team standings with 32 points, nine ahead of Ferrari. Could he maintain his dynamic start? Qualifying suggested yes, he could. Massa would once again take pole, but Lewis also qualified on the front row of the grid for the first time in his career. Significantly, there were also heavy brows and mutterings from Alonso – the rookie had outpaced the double World Champion, his senior co-driver, for the first time, and he had done so in the same car. This was a watershed in his relationship with Alonso. While the Spaniard had been happy to go along with his less experienced team-mate, now, for the first time, he looked at him through different eyes – of grudging respect and, possibly, fear.

After qualifying, Lewis was, inevitably, on a high: 'To go into my third race in Formula One and get a front row is amazing. But the lap was not that great. Earlier in the session I had better laps. Qualifying is tough, really intense, and you need to pull out absolutely everything in that final flying lap. The wind is always changing – sometimes there is a tailwind, sometimes a crosswind. I feel pretty relaxed about what has happened so far. It feels natural. I am happy to be where I am. But the race is going to be tough. The first corner here is always tricky; it is such a tight corner.

'But I have been here before and feel a bit more comfortable with the circuit. I am sure we'll have a strong race tomorrow.'

But he did better than that. By the end of Sunday's race, he was joint leader in the battle for the Driver's title. Massa took first place from pole in his Ferrari for the third win of his career, but Lewis was runner-up, just 2.3 seconds behind the Brazilian, with Raikkonen third, 8.5 seconds behind Lewis. A distraught Alonso finished fifth. The result meant that he, Raikkonen and Lewis were all now on 22 points, locked together at the head of the Championship.

Lewis acknowledged his place in the record books: 'I'm very pleased with today's result. To have finished on the podium three times out of three is fantastic. We have definitely closed the gap to Ferrari and I know everybody will continue to push hard to improve even more in time for the Spanish Grand Prix.

'I was able to keep up with Felipe in the first stint but I really struggled with the balance of the car in the second. I had a lot of understeer and wasn't able to brake as late as I would have liked. However, after the second pit stop – when I changed to hard tyres – I was able to push again. I really enjoyed the race today and with a few more laps I might have been able to challenge Felipe for the lead.'

Alonso tried to put a brave face on what had been a poor result for him, blaming the car and saying he would make things right when they reached the next stop on the tour: Barcelona in his Spanish homeland: 'In a way I feel happy as I came away with four points and I am still leading the Championship, which is what is important. This was not a great race for me but these things happen. I was struggling for pace and overall grip, which means that you can't drive the car as well as you would like. You always start the race believing you can win, but after six or seven laps I knew that it would be tough. I couldn't keep up with the Ferraris and Lewis, and in the end had to settle for fifth.

'I now look forward to the next couple of weeks where we will all work hard to further improve the car in time for my home grand prix in Barcelona.'

Ron Dennis tried to take the heat off by not making too much of Lewis' brilliant achievement: 'Even though it was not a perfect day, we can leave Bahrain leading both Championships, which is a great achievement for the team. Fernando struggled a bit with the balance of his car and we never really managed to perfect his set-up. Lewis was more comfortable with his car and had a great race.'

It was time for a break in the hectic schedule. Lewis and the McLaren team flew out of Bahrain soon after the race on 15 April and headed back to England. He now had almost a month away from the circuit until the Barcelona race on 13 May. But this was not a month off by any stretch of the imagination. It was time to go home and unwind for a couple of days, and then go back to Woking for more training and testing on the car.

Alonso was also busy – recovering from the shock of being beaten by his No. 2. He returned to Spain to lick his wounds and determined that he would once again be top dog when battle resumed at the Circuit de Catalunya.

Half an hour north of the city of Barcelona, the track had opened in 1991 and already held a fond place in Alonso's heart. It was there, in 2006 that he had won the race in his Renault and he approached the 2007 event with much confidence. He also applauded changes made to the circuit for 2007: a tight chicane had been added to help overtaking by slowing cars through the last corner: 'I will miss the final two corners, because as a driver I prefer the high-speed turns, which are more fun to drive. However, it should enable us to get a good slipstream onto the main straight and have a go at overtaking on to Turn One, which is always a good thing.

'One of the downsides of Barcelona is that overtaking has always been very difficult as the two corners that led onto the main straight were always very high speed, and it was difficult to get a tow and get close to the guy in front. This will now change.'

He also made it clear that he did not expect Lewis Hamilton to get one over on him on his home territory, claiming the near month away had helped him get over the disappointment of Sakhir. He said: 'The race in Bahrain was not great for me but we had a strong test at this track earlier this week, and we got to understand how the car performs at the Circuit de Catalunya and the changes to the layout.'

When Lewis arrived for work in Barcelona, it seemed he could not have cared less what Alonso was thinking or saying in public. The years of training under the McLaren regime had taught him that the only focus that mattered was on oneself. As practice began he was his usual approachable self, although he admitted the fame game had surprised him. The change in his own fortunes had become clear when he spent some time during the break between Bahrain and Barcelona at his family home in Tewin, Hertfordshire. He admitted: 'It was strange going back as what people describe as a "celebrity". When I got home there were photographers outside my house. They are there from eight in the morning until six at night, just sitting in their cars. It's really weird but there's not much you can do about it.

'Fortunately for me I've not just shot to the top, and I've not got hundreds of people coming up to me every day. It's bit by bit that people are noticing me in the streets.'

Here was a young man you could take to your heart. There was none of the usual moaning about the drawbacks of being a star, simply a comfortable acceptance that if you are in the public eye in a big way, it is acceptable. It was an example some 'stars' would certainly do well to follow: Piers Morgan once told me that the thing he most detested about celebrities was when they whined on about being photographed and questioned about their lives. It was all part and parcel of the celebrity package. If they couldn't stand the heat, they should get out of the kitchen – and sharp. And it's a view I endorse totally.

Talking of stars, the Formula One mega names of the past were queuing up to salute the youngster as practice loomed in Barcelona. Motor racing legend Sir Jackie Stewart led the way: 'He is, of course, driving for one of the best teams in the world at the present time, with a competitive car, but nevertheless he's been able to accomplish more in a shorter time than any driver I've ever seen enter Formula One.

'It's no easy matter, getting into Formula One and attacking the great talents that are out there. For a new driver to do that with such consistency and not to be making the kind of mistakes that new drivers usually make is in itself a remarkable achievement.

'It's not unusual for a driver to do very well in his first year and have a bit of a dip in the second year – that's par for the course. But I think within the next three years, Lewis Hamilton will certainly be in contention and could easily win the World Championship.'

And Michael Schumacher – in Spain to watch his first Formula One grand prix since his retirement – joined in the chorus of approval. He admitted he had been keeping an eye on Lewis even when he was racing and winning in GP2: 'He's doing a very good job – he's well prepared and he's quick. It's not a surprise to me after seeing his races last year. Maybe it's a surprise that he's so consistent, but there you go.'

Schumacher certainly was correct in that last statement: in the first practice session Lewis was the star man, recording a lap four-tenths of a second faster than Alonso. Yet another sign of the times came when you saw Jenson Button celebrating after he had posted his best showing for a while – with the tenth best time.

Lewis knew he had thrown down a gauntlet to the Spaniard and said, with a big smile on his face: 'We completed our pre-planned programme focusing on tyres and set-up work. Everything went well. I set my fastest time early in the session and was able to be consistent throughout, so I'm fairly confident for the rest of the weekend.'

By the end of the qualifying session the next day he was brought down to earth a little. Massa gained yet another pole by finishing in 1:21.421, while Alono secured second position on the grid with a time of 1:21.451. Raikkonen was third in 1:21.723 and Lewis finished fourth in 1:21.785.

The Spanish crowd seemed disappointed Alonso had not taken pole but he himself was surprisingly upbeat. Had that anything to do with the fact that he had reclaimed the limelight from his No. 2, whom he was increasingly seeing as a potential rival rather than the lapdog he had expected? Alonso said: 'It is a good weekend for us so far. The car is performing really well and the first row is confirmation of the competitive pace we have had all weekend. Hopefully we can see a very good race. It was a really close fight and that is confirmation of how tight things are. There was nothing more I could get from the car. Both my qualifying laps were pretty good so we will see tomorrow.'

Once again, he appeared to be blaming the car, not himself for going faster or doing better. There were no comments from Lewis; he just went back to his motorhome and planned how he would improve the next day. From him there were no words of remorse or blame, just a gritty determination to show his worth when it really mattered. And didn't he do just that on the Sunday? Belying his fourth spot in qualifying, he beat Alonso on his home turf, another brilliant landmark. Massa clocked up another win, roaring home in 1hr 31m 36.230s. Lewis was runner-up, 6.79 seconds behind the Brazilian, and Alonso came third, trailing Lewis by almost 11 seconds.

This was hardly the victorious homecoming Alonso had envisaged. Worse still, was the fact that Lewis' fourth consecutive podium finish – and his third second place in succession – meant that he was not only the clear Championship leader but also the youngest ever. More bad news followed at the McLaren inquest as they confirmed that the Spaniard had only himself to blame for losing out to Lewis: his brush with Massa at the first corner on the first lap had caused him to run wide on to the gravel. The mistake pushed him down to fourth and left one of the aerodynamic deflectors on the right-hand side of his chassis damaged.

Lewis' elevation to clear title leader was a moving moment for all at McLaren. He was, of course, taking a record formerly held by the team's founder, Bruce McLaren. Lewis was just one month and two days younger than the New Zealander had been when he won his legendary grand prix in Argentina back in 1960. Though it was hard to play down the sense of euphoria he felt at the situation, Lewis did his best to try to pour some calm on to what had by now became a frenzied widespread belief that he would be World Champion in his first season. He said: 'I wouldn't really say it fuels my belief that I can win the World Championship in my first year but it is a positive development. This is only my first season and there will obviously be some ups and downs. If we can keep scoring podium finishes, we can do well.'

He had made a fine start, swiftly banishing the blues from his qualifying result and roaring past Raikkonen on the way to the first corner to move into second place as Alonso and Massa blundered together. Lewis admitted getting off to a flyer had been instrumental in his plans to finish higher than his qualifying fourth: 'The key was to get the best position at the first corner. It was very close when he [Alonso] came back on the track but we got through it. In the early stages I was struggling to get heat into the tyres and had a bit of oversteer, but things improved considerably a few laps into the race – however, the gap to Felipe was already too big.

'In the second stint I was a bit unlucky with the traffic but that happens sometimes. We certainly had the pace in the closing stages. Things just keep getting better and I continue living my dream. To come into my fourth grand prix and come out leading the World Championship against all these great drivers is unbelievable. The team has worked really hard since Bahrain and while we didn't win, I still think we can take some satisfaction as we are leading both Championships.'

Alonso found something else to blame for his defeat: the tyres. Although he did accept that he made a mistake on the first corner, he had no words of encouragement or praise for his young team-mate: 'My chance for victory disappeared after the incident at the first corner. I got off the line OK at the start, and was able to get a tow from Felipe and challenge into the first corner, as I was already half a car length in front. But we touched, and I had to go on the gravel to avoid an accident. We were both lucky to finish the race. As a result by the second corner I was fourth. I also sustained a bit of damage to my car, which upset the balance for the rest of the race. I lost additional time in the second stint as the tyres were not working as well.'

Once again Ron Dennis was in a situation he could have hardly envisaged, with his young 'upstart' once more beating the man he had brought into the team at a cost of millions. Again, he showed his tactical skills by refusing to blame Alonso for that first lap mistake. He kept the praise of Lewis to a measured: 'Coming into the Monaco Grand Prix being first and second in the Drivers' Championship and leading the Constructors' battle is a good achievement for the entire team. Our pace was a little weak in the middle sector. Fernando's race was hampered by having damaged his deflector during his efforts to get past Massa in the first corner.

'Another solid performance from Lewis. As you would expect, we will continue to push hard in our development programme to put the team in the best possible position to win as many of the remaining races as possible.'

'Another solid performance from Lewis'... If you hadn't known the result, you might have thought he had finished something like fifteenth! Norbert Haug, Mercedes Motorsport boss, was a little more liberal in his praise: 'It's great that Lewis and Fernando are at the top of the list in the Drivers' Championship after the fourth race here in Barcelona. Well done and thank you to all the team members for leading the Constructors' rankings too. Lewis again did a great job – we will keep pushing and will increase our performance further. We are now looking forward to the next race in Monaco in two weeks' time.'

An editorial on the F1 Pit Box pointed out that Hamilton could now win the title in the opposite way to Alonso in

2005: 'Lewis Hamilton leads the Championship. His astounding rookie year continues with another fabulous race; even when his tyre choice looked to be hurting him in the final leg he refused to let up, keeping Alonso way behind, regardless of his increased pace on harder tyres. I seem to remember Alonso cementing his first Championship win with a string of second places after punching in a few wins – I see no reason why Hamilton couldn't do it the other way around.'

An interesting point: yes, Lewis Hamilton was already looking forward to Monaco. He was leading the Drivers' title race with 30 points, ahead of Alonso on 28, Massa on 27 and Raikkonen – who had retired on the tenth lap with a mechanical problem – on 22. Not only this but in the past Monte Carlo had always turned up trumps for him: the previous year he had won in Monaco in the GP2 race and triumphed in the Monaco Formula Three Grand Prix in 2005. Now he was aiming for the hat trick. Yet what started out as a dream was to turn into something much more disturbing; something neither he, Alonso nor Ron Dennis could have anticipated in his first season by the end of a contravesial race in the gamblers' paradise. As Monaco loomed, there was another, more positive element to Lewis' first season, however. It was becoming clear he had changed the landscape of Formula One for the better. In fact, some even claimed he had *saved* it...

CHAPTER 9

THE BOY WHO SAVED FORMULA ONE

As the season progressed, it became clear that Lewis Hamilton had done much more than make an enormous personal impact on the sport: his exploits also transformed the fortunes of motor racing. From a sport that had been struggling, it suddenly became trendy. For the first time in many years it was once more compelling viewing and Lewis' daring brought in new fans that would hardly have been dreamed of in the predictable days of Michael Schumacher. I myself experienced the jaw-dropping impact Lewis had made when my mother phoned me out of the blue to ask me how he was doing during the Italian Grand Prix in Monza in September! Even my young sons Frankie, 9, and Jude, 7, had been captured by the magnetic charm of Britain's latest hero, tuning in to ITV1 on Sundays to see what was unfolding during the second stage of the season.

Lewis Hamilton had magically turned motor racing from a peripheral viewing sport for the few into a must-see for the masses. And some people, motor experts among them, would even argue that the Stevenage Rocket had emerged as an unlikely saviour for Formula One and the British leg of the season at Silverstone, which had been under threat for a couple of seasons. Put simply, Lewis has sparked a level of interest in Formula One unseen in the UK since the mid-1990s when Damon Hill won Britain's last World Championship. Even at grassroots events the Lewis ripple had its effect: karting tracks, for instance, reported a surge in the number of kids turning up.

A spokesman for ITV, which has the contract for Formula One racing, summed up the Lewis effect in this way: 'Lewis Hamilton appeals not just to the core petrolheads, but to the average Joe Bloggs on the street. He has attracted a new demographic to the audience because he is young and black.' As the season progressed, ITV grand prix viewing figures almost doubled and Autosport magazine reported its best sales for many years... admitting this was also down to Lewis Hamilton.

With all that in mind, I asked Chris Hockley, an F1 expert and journalist at the *Sun* newspaper, to investigate how Lewis had changed the landscape of Formula One and opened it up to a much wider audience. He came up with some interesting explanations and revelations: 'It's no coincidence that in the stressed-out, information-overloaded twenty-first century, fairytales have once again become big box-office. And as Harry Potter and the Hobbits' mythical quest have captured our imagination at the cinema, so young adventurer Lewis Carl Hamilton, named after one of the great Olympic heroes, has us glued to the small screen to watch the latest episode of his incredible journey.

'Not only has Lewis single-handedly restored Formula One to the pinnacle of world sport, he has set it on fire... and thrown petrol on the flames for good measure. With the heat has come cool, Hamilton style. He's calm, conscientious and collected, despite the pressure cooker lifestyle he has been hurled into. After taking the Formula One grid by storm in the space of a few weeks, he has gone showbiz by appearing on the star-spangled pages of newspapers. When the *Sun*'s pace-making *Bizarre* column pictured him out on the town with rappers P. Diddy and Pharrell Williams, Lewis knew he had arrived not just as a racing driver but as a celeb-britt-tee.

'Now girls want to kiss him, mums want to cuddle him, dads admire him and boys want to be him. His rocket-ship rise to fame has bumped up British TV audiences for grands prix by a whopping 50 per cent. And enthusiasm for Formula One is soaring across the world – even in the stock-car domain of America, they were forced to sit up and take notice when this upstart rookie kid beat off the reigning World Champ to win the US Grand Prix.

'It's a fairytale, you see, enacted across the globe.

'And all of a sudden everyone, from barmaids to vicars, from paperboys to company directors has an opinion on Lewis, and asks after his progress. No more is Formula One the preserve of anoraks, petrolheads and techno-junkies who salivate at the prospect of a 0.63 per cent increase in front aerofoil downforce eked out by Ferrari's engineers.

'Now, wives who decades ago gave up trying to understand their husbands' weird obsession with "watching cars go round in circles" are dallying at the telly and asking: "How's Lewis doing?" Surely it won't be long before traffic cops tell speeding motorists: "Who do you think you are? Lewis Hamilton?"

'In a nutshell, Lewis has returned motorsport to the masses. But it's not as if he has changed its physical make-up, or intrinsic excitement value. Formula One racing, for years mired in aerodynamic über-technology that makes overtaking all but impossible, is still largely comprised of a dash to the first corner followed by a high-speed procession and the odd change of order through pit stops. Superhero or not, Lewis can't change much about that.

'So what is it about him that is pulling in the crowds – and saving the skins of TV commentators who were beginning to splutter on empty as another drone-a-thon unfolded before them?

'The answers, of course, are many and varied – each contributing to what Formula One folk like to call "the package". Like a state-of-the-art grand prix car, it's possible to break it down to its components. But be warned, the list is growing longer by the day...

'*The Charm*. Fast becoming legendary as looker Lewis fields yet another barrage of questions with a polite, easy-going manner way beyond his 22 years. "How do you explain your brilliance?" he is asked. "I'm just doing the best that I can," comes the reply. Guaranteed to make him a favourite of mums and grandmas. What a nice young man!

'*The Modesty*. The shy smile as he is interviewed in the run-up to the British Grand Prix by a hard-nosed TV news anchorman, more used to dealing with terrorist atrocities, who describes him as a "global phenomenon" and compares him to the superlative Tiger Woods.

'*The Belief*. An unshakeable and fearless conviction in his own ability to drive cars as fast as they can be driven, and to dive through gaps that lesser mortals would not dare. It would be a cliché to say this belief is "hidden" behind his self-effacing attitude. It would also be untrue. For all his humility, Lewis constantly emanates an aura akin to what toothpaste ad makers would call "the glow of confidence".

'I remember meeting him at last year's *Autosport* Awards show, the Oscars of motor racing, at which Lewis, recently announced as a 2007 McLaren Mercedes Formula One driver, picked up yet another gong. McLaren chief Ron Dennis made a bizarre speech in which he warned Lewis that the British media would likely build him up with the sinister long-term aim of knocking him down again. As a tabloid hack myself, I felt duty-bound to tell Lewis this was paranoid rubbish, and that he would have our 110 per cent support.

'I waited while Dennis introduced Lewis to the evening's guest of honour, former Ferrari Formula One star Carlos Reutemann, now a leading politician in his native Argentina, then stepped in to voice my reassurance in the manner of kind uncle to naïve nephew. Lewis listened patiently and thanked me with an understanding nod. Yet, although he didn't say it, the calm look in his eyes left me in no doubt that having the support of the media was all very well and good, but he didn't really need it to achieve what he wanted to achieve. That would be done on the track, thank you very much. He was far too polite to accuse me of being patronising but that's how I felt, guiltily, as I left his side.

'*The Family*. The support Lewis has received from his family has been well chronicled – and his dad Anthony is as familiar a sight at the circuits as his son. Lewis' long-time mentor Ron Dennis is widely regarded as a second father figure, though it did not stop paddock gossip suggesting the determined Hamiltons would walk to another team, had Dennis not put Lewis in a McLaren for 2007. The devotion from family and team seems to have given Lewis a sense of obligation admired by millions of parents more accustomed to ungrateful children who habitually throw their toys out of the pram.

'Lewis' upbringing and nurturing has also resulted in a refreshing lack of ego and disarming honesty. Asked how he keeps his snowballing fame in perspective, he replied: "You've just got to be yourself. That's the best advice I could give anyone. It doesn't matter who you meet – the Queen, anybody."

'*The Attitude*. It has come to be a dirty word used to describe sneering youth. But it doesn't have to be so. Lewis has attitude – but in a positive way. He discovered his remarkable talent soon after his father bought him a go-kart when he was 6. But though he raced hard, he continued to study hard at school, too. He was 12 when Dennis signed him up to McLaren's young driver programme. And ever since, you get the feeling he has been dedicated to achieving success because so many people were supporting him, and he felt duty-bound to try his hardest to pay them back.

'*The Rookie*. Part of Lewis' attraction emanates from him "coming from nowhere" to take on the giants of grand prix. It's not really the case. Despite his youth, Lewis has had a long and illustrious career in the lower reaches of motor racing, and his speed and daring have come as no surprise to keen followers of the sport. Yet although motor racing is a massive global industry with countless categories, it's also true that the vast majority of the population know nothing of it apart from Formula One. And therefore they were barely aware of Lewis' existence until his startling grand prix debut in Australia. So, even though under the patronage of McLaren he is the best-prepared rookie in Formula One's history, he is still perceived as a newcomer – an incredibly exciting one at that. And what timing! He is following in the tyre smoke of one Michael Schumacher, a peerless driver who was never able to capture the public imagination like a Senna, a Mansell – or a Hamilton. Formula One fans wish – oh, how they wish – that Schuey had delayed his retirement by a year so Lewis could go up against him; I reckon the pair of them feel the same. And who knows, Schumacher may yet take it on. Wouldn't put it past him.

'Look, also, at the contrast between Lewis and his team-mate Fernando Alonso – a fantastic racer, a double World Champion, universally admired by Formula aficionados, yet unable to command a wider audience beyond his native Spain.

'*The Normality*. Matt Bishop, editor-in-chief of the respected *F1 Racing* magazine, reckons the hoo-ha about Lewis is down to him being "so damn normal". An unprivileged lad from the Home Counties with "an engaging humility as unforced as his astonishingly natural driving style" – I'd go along with that ... with one rider, which is that Lewis has the true superstar quality of making the abnormal seem normal.

'I take you back to the comparison with Tiger Woods. Wins golf tourneys effortlessly, doesn't he? He doesn't, of course. There are hundreds of brilliant golfers out there on the fairways ready to put one over on him – and he has to try like hell to overcome them. He just makes it look like the work of a moment, then shrugs his shoulders afterwards. Recognise the trait?

'*The Tributes*. It's not just Ordinary Joes who have been gobsmacked by Lewis' astonishing arrival in Formula One. Past greats of the sport have been even more impressed. And they have said so, too, which in turn feeds back into the public consciousness. Take, for example, the astonishing assessment by Stirling Moss, who said: "I'm flattered people are comparing me with Lewis."

'Nigel Mansell calls Lewis "the Chosen One". Damon Hill says: "I've never seen a rookie as good as he is." And

Niki Lauda reckons he is "the best guy around with even more potential than the British media expect." And that's saying something!

'Fortunately, through pure ability, Lewis was quickly able to shake off the monicker as "the first black grand prix driver". But former team boss Eddie Jordan put it succinctly when he said of him: "All the indications border on the sensational. He's black, he's attractive, he's rock'n'roll."

'Which, in a roundabout way after all the analysis, brings us back to Lewis as Mr Cool. He even uses the word a lot, which makes him, well, cool! For instance, talking about his party night with P. Diddy & Co, he said: "The weird thing was, there were all these celebrities there – and yet I seemed to be the main attraction. I expected to be the big nobody, the guy they didn't know all that much about.

'But people were coming up and asking me for my number – and asking if I wanted theirs. How cool was that?'

'Very cool, Lewis, is the answer. Cool enough for David and Victoria Beckham to wish you well on the British Grand Prix starting grid. It seems as if the man himself cannot quite believe what's happening to him. And he admits as much in all his post-race interviews and TV appearances.

"I'm living my dream," he repeats, again and again.

'It's a theme vigorously exploited by McLaren's main sponsor Vodafone, whose TV adverts show a young Lewis piloting a spaceship as he chases his wildest wish. And as other kids crash out, one by one, Lewis remains stoically at the helm of the craft as it morphs into a McLaren Formula One car.

'But, heck, we lesser beings know we can't all make it. We know our limitations – we're just glad *someone* can do it. To prove that, yes, by crikey, it *can* be done! And by someone so "damn normal" and pleasant... So we join Lewis in the fairytale and it goes on for us all. We're living the dream, too. And it feels good.'

Indeed it does, Chris... indeed it does. As I have followed Lewis' fortunes in Formula One over the last year, I have also noticed how he has caught the imagination of many youngsters. In June 2007, for instance, pupils at a Norfolk school enjoyed a motorsport day as a direct result of the influence Lewis was having in Formula One. They had seen him roar to the top of the Driver's title on TV and the school's headmaster had been only too happy to invite along a local motor racing company to show them a real racing car.

Pupils at Spooner Row Primary were spellbound at the sight of Comtec Racing's 175mph World Series single-seat car. Based near Attleborough, Comtec won the Drivers' Championship at their first attempt in the World Series in 2006. Jonathan Lewis, owner of the Norfolk-based team, talked of how motorsport had played a major role in his life – and let them sit in his £250,000 pride and joy. He also spoke of how Lewis Hamilton had fired the imagination of the youngsters – and encouraged their interest in his visit. He said: 'It was surprising how knowledgeable they were about motorsport. All of them knew Lewis Hamilton – he's done great things for the sport. The reception class loved it and were just in awe, but the older ones asked some really difficult questions. They were proper little switched-on individuals. The best question was "Why do you do it?" How do you answer *that*?'

Headteacher Simon Wakeman said: 'The children thought it was fantastic, very exciting, particularly the younger children, who were thrilled to get the opportunity to sit inside the car and pretend they were racing drivers. They all want to be Lewis Hamilton when they grow up!'

Lewis' father Anthony is also delighted at how youngsters are jumping on his son's bandwagon – and how he is opening up the sport to a new generation. He says this particular spin-off of his son's success is making both him and Lewis 'very happy indeed': 'I remember when I was a kid I didn't have anything. When Lewis was a boy we still had nothing. We got this opportunity to do something and now we're here. Every day is a dream and is something to enjoy and cherish.

'I want Lewis' story to be an inspiration to other kids that if you do have a dream, and you work hard at it, then you could make it happen. He made a lot of sacrifices as a kid to follow his dream. But his success hasn't changed him – he's the same guy now he's on top of the world and he will stay like that forever.

'It is important that he keeps focused and keeps winning for the good of the other young guys and girls who have nothing and want to achieve something. I want them to look at Lewis and see that if you work hard, you make sacrifices, your dreams could come true.

'Lewis says he doesn't feel like a superstar. At the end of

the day he's just Lewis and it's important for him to stay like that. He still lives with the family. There's no yachts or wild parties – it's all about hard work and his dream to win the Drivers' World Championship.

'He is a fully committed Formula One racing driver, not a half-hearted "I'm there now – I am going to live the lifestyle and be a playboy racing driver". His view is "I'm here to race and that's all I want to do". He has said it himself, "I'm not here to come second." If he was here to do that then he could live the lifestyle, afford to go partying, enjoy the sun, then think, oh I'm racing this weekend, am I? I will be there in five minutes'. No way!

'It was his dream to get to Formula One and the next dream was to win. The ultimate dream is to win the World Championship. We have been blessed. We have been given some great opportunities and Lewis is making the best possible use of them.

'It's not like winning the Lottery, buying the ticket and hoping your numbers come up – it's about having the dream and staying the course. We are really lucky to be here: we're not going to be arrogant and waste the opportunity. That is why I want kids with hopes and aspirations to look at Lewis and see him as an inspiration.'

Just a couple of weeks into the season, before Lewis' impact had been truly realised and had taken hold of the sport, Renault boss Flavio Briatore voiced the feeling even from within the sport that it had become a dull spectacle. He said: 'Normally it's boring.' It was certainly a demoralising view.

A couple of months later, the Italian would have reason to feel grateful to Lewis Hamilton, but at the start of the campaign Briatore went on: 'A 1-hour 30-minute race is too long because the last 30 minutes – 90 per cent of the time – is really boring. Every time there's excitement it's because something's happened outside or because it's heavy rain, or there's some accident or stuff like that. I still don't understand why we don't try to make excitement in every race.'

Mark Sharman, head of ITV Sport, naturally disagreed with the idea that motor racing had become boring although he also had reason to be grateful to Lewis Hamilton – particularly for the way he had drummed up an avalanche of new interest and, consequently, increased viewing figures for the independent network. By the time of the British Grand Prix, ITV's viewing figures were significantly up on the previous year, with 7.7 million watching the United States Grand Prix compared to 5.4 million in 2006. And figures for Silverstone proved just how much of an effect Lewis was having: the ITV1 audience peaked at 5.1 million for the British Grand Prix, while over on BBC1 the men's singles final at Wimbledon drew in just 2.2 million when the two events clashed.

Former Formula One driver Mark Blundell, now working as ITV's main analyst, agreed that Lewis was the superstar the sport urgently needed to take it forward. He said: 'He's the first black driver, he came with a lot of expectation, having won the support series GP2 last year, but all we're talking about is a great new driver.' The *Independent*'s TV columnist Chris Maume summed up Lewis' impact after the

US Grand Prix: 'As the camera panned across the serried ranks of petrolheads at Indianapolis in the minutes before the US Grand Prix, Mark Blundell remarked to Steve Ryder that Lewis Hamilton has brought a whole new audience to Formula One. Quite right: in 10 years of this column I don't recall writing a single sentence about it (unless that sentence was "Christ, I'm bored!"). And until the Saturday before last I'm sure I'd never watched a second of qualifying. Which, for a male of the species born five days after Fangio's last grand prix, is just weird. So the Hamilton kid has got me hooked...'

Damon Hill was in no doubt that Lewis Hamilton would play a major part in guaranteeing the future of the British Grand Prix at Silverstone for years to come. The Lewis effect led to a record 42,000 fans attending on the Friday, followed by a Saturday best of 80,000, with race day an 85,000 sell-out. Ticket prices that day ranged from £99 to £260. It was also reported that online retailers had been inundated with customers buying £19.95 Lewis baseball caps and replica T-shirts at £27.95. Hill said the ticket sales – a direct consequence of Lewis' impact in the run-up to the 2007 race at the Northamptonshire site – proved just how vital and relevant the British leg remained.

Damon said: 'I am as excited as everyone by his proven potential and promise, and for the first time since I did it in 1996, a British driver will arrive at Silverstone leading the World Championship... Sorry if I'm banging on about Lewis too much, but as president of the British Racing Driver's Club (BRDC), it's my job to bang on a bit...

'The extension of the grand prix contract beyond 2009 will require a development programme of the facilities to keep pace with the kind of venue sports fans are getting used to expecting around the world. This is a crucial time for the British Grand Prix. Failure to achieve our goals and to reach a viable, sustainable agreement with Formula One's management could mean the event will be lost. I am not in any doubt that Formula One will move on without us, just as a driver would lose the pack and never look back – but we also have a duty to protect our venue for all motorsport. It's a tough call.

'Little wonder then that I am excited by the arrival of Lewis Hamilton. I would be lying if I did not regard his appearance as somewhat timely. But he just goes to prove the power of an individual in the world of organisations.'

BRDC chairman Robert Brooks echoed those views: 'Members like Lewis are helping us. The Hamilton factor is very positive and helpful in keeping the British Grand Prix.'

Business analyst Alan Switzer backed both men in their belief that Hamilton's success could propel Silverstone to new heights of popularity. Switzer, a director of the Sports Business Group at Deloitte, said: 'Local heroes can have a huge impact on the financial health of a sport. Lewis Hamilton's success has helped lift the British Grand Prix to become the third highest attended event in the UK's sporting calendar after Wimbledon and Royal Ascot.

'Should Lewis consolidate his success, motor racing can expect a significant revenue boost, particularly once existing broadcasting and sponsorship contracts expire. Broadcasters and corporates will compete to be associated with such a potentially attractive global sporting icon.

'ITV's current Formula One television rights contract is reportedly worth around £25 million a year. But the success of Lewis means that could increase substantially when it expires at the end of the 2010 season.'

He also believes Silverstone will benefit as circuit owners, the BRDC, look to secure a new contract once the present deal expires in 2009: 'At a more local level, the increased ticketing revenue and secondary spend will form an important part of the funding mix for the redevelopment of Silverstone. This is almost certainly necessary for Silverstone to retain its grand prix in 2010 and beyond. Indeed, if extra capacity could be added to Silverstone, Lewis' success suggests it would be matched by demand.

'Fernando Alonso's success has been the main factor for the Spanish Grand Prix now attracting more than 340,000 spectators over the extended weekend, the highest of the Formula One races.'

The Hamilton effect was also apparent in a sustained betting spree in the run-up to Silverstone. Bookies reported that in the same race the year previously there was not half so much interest because of the lack of a genuine British title challenger and competitive action in races. According to Ladbrokes' spokesman, David Williams: 'Even before Hamilton's first race there was little to suggest a betting boom but his first podium finish saw a huge upsurge. Betting on race two increased by 75 per cent across all channels and this year has broken all previous records on turnover.

Already on the British Grand Prix we have seen more money bet on Hamilton than on all the other drivers combined.'

There were a series of other bets you could have made on the brilliant young Briton before Silverstone. Again, this all showed the enormously positive influence he was having on the sport in so many different ways. The odds on him winning the Drivers' title were now 8–13 as against a pre-season 25–1, for example. You could also find odds of 9–2 that he would finish on the podium in every grand prix. Also, 11–10 that he would win more races than any British driver (Nigel Mansell held the record with 31) and 10–1 that he would go on to break Michael Schumacher's record 91 grand prix wins. Everywhere you looked was Lewis Hamilton. He was the main man and the man to whom a whole host of workers within the Formula One 'industry' owed a mighty debt.

It was boom time again for Formula One – and the public was not slow in admitting their interest was all down to one man. Already a Formula One fan, Neil Adamson of London admitted Lewis had taken things to a new level: 'None of my friends like Formula One so I got into it by accident. I started watching it on TV and I got a passion for it. I've tried getting friends to watch it with me, but they say they haven't got time for it. Maybe it's a different buzz for them. I watch it all the time on TV, even if it's on at 2am. My daughter is into it too. I wish I could go to all the meets, but I have a family and a shop to run, so I don't have the time. I went to Silverstone years ago in Nigel Mansell's time. It was absolutely marvellous – not even the race, just the spectacle. I was walking around, admiring the people and the vibes.'

Julian Phillips, of Bury, near Manchester, said: 'Whether you like the sport or not, you have to admit it is incredible what Lewis has done. The sport itself is boring, but you cannot take anything away from him. Would you say that Tiger Woods has done "OK", only because you don't like the sport? Nobody – however good they are – comes in, wins and finishes on the podium so many times. It takes someone special to break the win barrier that soon.

'Jenson Button is not as good as Lewis – because he does not have his mental strength. Hamilton just wants to win. And don't tell me it's just down to him being in a McLaren. Even in a Honda he would do better than *their* current drivers! He is, without doubt, set to become the greatest sportsmen *ever*. He will have more of an impact than Tiger Woods, and I'm saying that as a golf fan.'

Finally, Louis Graham, of St Ives, Cornwall, summed up the remarkable effect Lewis has had on motor racing: 'Lewis Hamilton is great news for British motorsport – in fact, he is the saviour of it. He has raised the profile of a sport that lags massively behind in the viewing ratings when compared with the likes of football, bringing in thousands of new converts, and making it fresh and new.

'And he is a nice guy too, which is unusual among today's usual prima donnas. Lewis Hamilton is the living proof that good guys do sometimes win. We are proud of you, Lewis, and will follow you for years to come – now go and win more titles than Schumacher!'

Sentiments certainly echoed, Lewis...

CHAPTER 10

MONTE CARLO – AND BUST

'Mugged in the streets of Monte Carlo' – that's one way to describe what happened to Lewis Hamilton in Monaco on the weekend of 27 May 2007.

Yet it had all started so differently when they arrived at the so-called playboy paradise the previous Wednesday. As already noted, Lewis loved it there: indeed, later in the season he admitted that he could easily live in the principality. The sun was shining, the atmosphere relaxed and the race around the streets is one that every Formula One driver I have ever spoken to admits to enjoying. They thrive on the challenge of the tight and twisty streets and the specific demands of road racing. Lewis had his own views on the circuit: 'Well, there is no room for error and it's all about knowing your braking zones, knowing where the bumps are...'

And how was he getting along with Alonso? Had he noticed any change in their relationship as they got down to business again? 'I don't think it's changed. I think with the team, the relationship grows constantly. I've been at McLaren for a long, long time and it just gets better and better – we're very much working extremely hard together to succeed and it's going extremely well. As you can see, it's getting better and better. I think with me and Fernando the relationship is growing. We're sort of starting to understand each other. Obviously we've got a huge amount of respect for each other as we always have. But it's doing fine.'

But was Alonso still top dog; was he the pupil to Alonso's master? 'I never actually thought it was a master-pupil thing, to be honest. I think that as in every team, there's a little bit of rivalry there but that's only on the track. We're professionals. Off the track we're friends – we can talk, we're relaxed, there's no tension there.' And how was he adjusting to his newfound fame? 'Well, it has been a roller coaster, the whole journey. One, getting to Formula One, and then having four podiums in my first four races – it is unknown, but it is difficult. You know, I don't think it has kicked in really. You look at the races and you think wow, I finished second to Felipe Massa! It is just that these last few years, I have been watching these guys racing and I was admiring them. And now I am amongst them. It is really difficult to come to terms with...

'I don't read much about what is going on back in the UK in terms of what is being written about me. I think it is the way I deal with it. I don't feel I particularly need to read it.

The hype is growing, but that is the way I control it. It is nice to see your face in a magazine or a newspaper. It is good to see that you have the support, but I hear they are very good stories so that keeps me happy.'

'Good stories' they certainly were. The boy was a clean-shaven hero of our times and what would surely become known as The Hamilton Brand – in the same way as the Beckham Brand – was already taking shape. He was different; a nice, normal, steady sort of guy in a sport more used to excess and hedonism. To his credit, he also laughed off the suggestion made a few days earlier by Eddie Jordan that he perhaps did not have the necessary aggressive side of a World Champion to his character. Jordan said 'Lewis is fortunate to have a well-grounded team with a structure he probably wouldn't have got anywhere else. But if he needed to do what Schumacher did to Villeneuve or Hill, would he do that? You need to do that to win. Winning is in the mind, and you have to do it at all costs.

'Anyone who tells you different is either lying, or hasn't achieved what they're capable of. There has to be a steely aspect that we haven't seen, otherwise Hamilton will be swamped. He needs to have that arrogance otherwise he will not succeed. Does Alex Ferguson have it? Yes. Does José Mourinho? Yes.

'Winners generally are not nice people. They try to be, but they are immensely selfish, immensely arrogant and have a total belief in their own ability. Nothing else matters to them when they are at work.'

Lewis just shrugged his shoulders when told of Jordan's

words: 'I don't know if I particularly believe that "win at all costs" is the way forward. Yes, we are here to win, so you prepare yourself and you work as hard as you can, but I don't particularly agree with win at all costs. Sure, every driver has a different way to look at it.' It was a brilliant putdown of the Irishman whom over the years had sometimes seemed to believe his own publicity that he was the oracle and saviour of Formula One.

Ron Dennis also waded into the row, saying 'There are drivers who are prepared to do anything to win. They've been in Formula One and left, but Lewis isn't one of them. People relate to the fact that good guys can win. For us, he is not just a great racing driver snapping at the heels of a double World Champion, but he is also, along with Fernando Alonso, a great human being. These guys are fun to have in the team, with the popularity of Lewis very much about living the dream.'

Confident and assured, Lewis then joined his father for a light supper and a little rest before the business of practice. In the first session he was second to Alonso – the Spaniard setting the fastest time with a lap of 1:16.973. Earlier in the day, Lewis had actually been ahead but a problem with the starter motor meant he could only complete 14 out of 32 laps. The gap between the two men was six-tenths of a second.

In the second session the McLaren team were thrown into a panic when Lewis, trying desperately to overhaul Alonso's time, crashed. Almost an hour on, he ran into trouble as he raced too close to the barriers, losing control as he braked on the approach to the first corner – the Sainte Devote right-hander – and crashed into the tyre barrier. Clearly concerned, Ron Dennis was observed looking grimly at the scene and his relief was tangible as his boy jumped out of his car and signalled he was not hurt.

Lewis, shaken by the incident, said 'Today was the first time I have ever driven a Formula One car around Monaco and it was awesome. I have obviously had experience of the circuit from Formula Three and grand prix two, but in a Formula One car it's very different.

'Everyone makes mistakes, and I'm only human – these small things happen. I was pushing and right on the limit, which is something you always have to do at Monaco. I then found the limit – at the mid-point of the second session – and found out how unforgiving this track can be. I just locked the rear wheels, and as it came before the apex, I lost the back end, tried to brake too quick and went off into the wall. There is just no room for error in Monaco. To be honest, it was a light impact, even if it looked quite quick. I'm obviously sorry as there will be a bit of work for the guys.'

The colour had also returned to Ron Dennis' face after practice was complete – with Lewis third behind Alonso and Raikkonen. Big Ron said 'This is a mistake all drivers make of all standards. It's not something I will level any criticism at. I'd obviously rather not have a bent racing car but, under the circumstances, we're pretty comfortable with his contribution to this season.' And with tongue in cheek, a big smile on his face and a wink, the paternal McLaren boss added in a conspiratorial whisper: 'He still has a few Brownie points in hand!'

By the end of qualifying, Lewis had proved just how mentally tough he was. The crash had no impact on his performance as he finished second only to Alonso in determining his place on the grid for the race itself. For the first time in the season Alonso took pole after rocketing to a time of 1:15.726. Lewis was second in 1:15.905, but had been ahead of his team-mate with just 4 minutes left on the clock. Alonso pipped him at the last after being delayed in traffic by Mark Webber. Massa was third.

It was the first time McLaren had claimed a clean sweep of the front row in the season and Alonso's first pole since the China Grand Prix the previous October. Lewis was glad to have made that front row but conceded he could even have snatched pole: 'To start my first Formula One race in Monaco from the front row is amazing and for the team to have a 1–2 is just fantastic. I have really enjoyed my weekend and qualifying was no exception. It's hard to explain, but around this circuit you are just constantly on the limit. My last flying lap was affected by traffic and I lost a lot of time but that is just the challenge of this place.

'I was three-tenths up on my previous best but I was held up by Webber. I don't know if he saw me. I lost half a second behind him but I managed to pull it back to within a tenth, but after that the tyres were gone. The car felt great. It was exactly the same time I did on heavy fuel. So we did a good job and I am happy with that. It will be interesting to see what happens tomorrow. We want to finish the race in the points and continue as we have been going this season.

'The car has been super all the way through, and I believe we have a strong strategy. I think it will be a great race, and hopefully Fernando and I can provide the team with a 1–2 finish.'

Alonso was more delighted than usual with his pole position – he was now in the unlikely position of having to chase for the title with Lewis out in front in the standings, and he was determined to hunt down and conquer his young rival. He admitted 'This is a very important pole position. There was a little bit of everything going on. We were expecting rain at the start but that only affected 1 lap and then we were at normal speeds as usual. Monaco is very stressful for everyone.

'All weekend has been good for us and the car seems very competitive, but you know Monaco is a very special race. It could be very difficult. Starting from pole is good, but it is a very long race. And the weather is changing so much. Obviously pole position gives you the best possible start to the race but there are 78 laps, and as it's Monaco anything can happen.' Clearly the master was feeling the pressure. He needed a win if he was to reel in Hamilton; even the weather was starting to worry him.

By the end of Sunday night, the Spanish driver was feeling more at ease with himself as he once again led the drivers' standings. Both he and Lewis were now on 38 points after Alonso won his second successive Monaco Grand Prix, at the same time notching up McLaren's 150th success. He took the lead in the standings courtesy of his two wins in the season so far, as opposed to none by Lewis.

It was also the fourteenth time that the team had won in Monte Carlo and McLaren's first 1–2 finish at the race since 1989, the heyday of Ayrton Senna, who won in that year, and Alain Prost, who was second. The stark facts of May 2007 show Alonso beat Lewis into second place. For Lewis, consolation was found in his fourth successive second place in his maiden season, and in that he beat Massa into third. But the youngster was clearly upset that McLaren's unusual strategic requirements – requesting their drivers maintain their positions so as not put each other at risk on the notoriously demanding and dangerous track – had meant Alonso took first place.

For Alonso, it was a seventeenth career win as he came home in a time of 1 hr 40m 29.329s, 4 seconds in front of Lewis. The lead had yo-yoed between the two McLaren men in a thrilling contest in front of a crowd estimated at more than 120,000. Among them were Hollywood actors Jude Law and Jonny Lee Miller, Juventus and Czech Republic soccer star Pavel Nedved and the German tennis legend, and now sports commentator, Boris Becker. But on Lap 58, with 20 to go, the two men were told to conserve their equipment and settle for McLaren's second 1–2 finish of the season.

Alonso also set the fastest lap on Lap 44 in 1:15.284 and at the end of the race he was beaming. Top cat once again: 'It has been a fantastic weekend, no doubt, and to score this hat-trick of pole, fastest lap and win is something very special and even more here in Monaco.

'I enjoyed very much today's race, with a perfect car all through the race. It was so good to drive such a nice car for 78 laps and win at the end. This win means a lot to me – I have never had the experience of being more than 1 minute ahead of the competition, which probably makes this one of my best victories.

'I didn't get off the line brilliantly from pole position, but as there is such a short run to the first corner I was pretty sure that I would be able to keep the lead. However, as I was able to save fuel in my first stint I was able to stay out for two more laps than originally planned. After that the race was pretty quiet with only the backmarkers causing a few problems, especially shortly before my second pit stop when I lost a lot of time. I will enjoy this victory and look forward to the races in north America.'

In public at least, Lewis put a brave face on it, saying: 'I knew we were both extremely quick, so I could only apply pressure, but he's a two-time World Champion and he doesn't really make mistakes.

'I tried to attack him and wanted to win if I could, but I have to accept that I am in my rookie season and he has number one on his car and I have number two. I am the second driver and so I must accept that and respect that for the team.

'I had good pace at the start, but then I had some graining on my front tyres which didn't help. It was an exciting race which also saw me tapping the guardrails a couple of times, fortunately without influencing the handling of the car.'

These were stoical, resigned words that hid an inner hurt.

The decision by McLaren to rein him in would cause a public storm. Alonso benefited on this occasion but it would have the effect of denying him the same opportunity again. Public disquiet told McLaren they had dropped a clanger and it was a mistake they were keen not to repeat. Ever the diplomat, Ron Dennis tried to play down the possibility of any resentment: 'Both Fernando and Lewis drove so well and responded excellently to the team's wishes of bringing both cars home safely in what was a memorable 1–2 result and our fourteenth victory in the principality. However, there is some disappointment because of the different strategies we needed to follow to cope with a potential deployment of the safety car – which has happened four times in the last five years. Consequently you virtually have to decide in advance which one of the team's two drivers will claim the victory.'

Team orders that interfere with a race result were outlawed in October 2002. Dennis cited safety issues as the reason for keeping Lewis behind Fernando. 'Once the first round of pit stops had taken place we reverted Lewis from a one-stop strategy to the faster two-stop strategy and at the same time slowed both cars down to conserve the brakes. As a team we would like to race but this circuit requires a disciplined approach and as a result we can leave Monte Carlo with the maximum amount of points.'

Massa paid tribute to the blistering pace of Alonso and Hamilton: 'McLaren showed really an incredible pace – even if I'd pushed like 150 per cent on the limit it would have stayed the same. There was nothing to do. I was just thinking about finishing third and scoring points. Five points [deficit] is nothing in the Championship, so let's work hard for the next race and try to be in front there.'

A plethora of fine words and plaudits but the fact remained that Lewis was disappointed at having to play second fiddle to Alonso. At the end of the race he even handed his trophy to his brother, Nicolas. Asked whether there was any significance in that – did it perhaps mean he thought it was small reward in light of what could have been? – Lewis again stonewalled the suggestion that he felt hard done by 'My brother supports me in every race and it is good to have him there and he loves to be a part of it. I am proud to have him with me and it is great when he comes up and I can give him the trophy to make him feel important – and just show him that he is.'

The British public remained unconvinced. They felt that from now on Lewis and Alonso should be given equal billing and equal opportunities. We had been told they both had the same car so let the fastest man, and the better driver win. Then there could be no questions of favouring one against the other, could there?

Radio 5 Live presenter David Croft started a fevered debate on the rights and wrongs of Ron's tinkering, saying: 'Now I know how much regard and respect Ron Dennis has for Fernando Alonso, and I know how hard he's trying to make the double World Champion welcome at his team.' But Croft believed that this tactic, 'Demoralises Hamilton for one thing, and secondly sets a precedent that Alonso may expect to be repeated in the future… Hamilton wasn't happy after the race and I didn't expect him to be. His flying start in the sport has increased his and the media's expectations. He wanted to win, to make his mark and become the first rookie to do so in Monte Carlo.'

Racing fan Paul Hurley, of Burton in Staffordshire, responded by saying Dennis was well out of order: 'It just wasn't a fair thing to do. We all know he has got to protect his investment, but surely he can see that Lewis deserves to be set free? He's lucky that Lewis didn't give him a right earful, prodigy for 10 years or not!'

And Karen Pugh of Birmingham was similarly scathing 'He spends all those years bringing him through. He should have allowed them both the same rights. Why does Alonso need nursing if he is so good? I thought he was the man who said he wasn't scared of anything, or anyone? Well, little ol' Lewis seems to be scaring the living daylights out of him!'

Dave Butler of Romford spoke for those who believed Big Ron had made the right decision in putting the team first: 'Sure, Lewis had a chance of winning this weekend, and he's proved he is just as quick as Alonso, but to have allowed them to race to the end and push each other to the limit would have been suicide for a team. They would have been getting hammered in the press if they had allowed that and the drivers had taken each other off of the circuit. Monaco is not an easy place to pass, so if Lewis had caught Alonso it would have taken a brave move to stick your car where it was at risk of being chopped.

'Well done RD and everyone at McLaren.... A silver car looks better than a red one at the front.'

Rony, a Brazilian Formula One fan, claimed the furore showed Lewis was getting too big for his boots: 'Your daring Hamilton has started to show some new colours, hasn't he? He not only wanted to go for the win, he also felt he was entitled to rant over the radio when his team told him to stop being foolish. Furthermore, his attitude and noise brought about the Fédération Internationale de l'Automobile (FIA) investigation that could have cost his team dear. And then, when asked if he was surprised with Ferrari's lack of performance, he sported a smile and said "Not really, no." One could not but feel a hint of arrogance in his answer. He is starting to believe in his own myth – the first step towards a fall.'

The debate raged on and Formula One bosses entered the fray. They were also unhappy with McLaren's strategic decision to hold back Hamilton and launched an investigation into a possible breach of their rules after learning that Ron Dennis had admitted he prevented Lewis from challenging Alonso after their first pit stops. But Dennis then denied favouring Alonso, and the FIA subsequently vindicated the team, stating that: 'McLaren were able to pursue an optimum team strategy because they had a substantial advantage over all other cars. They did nothing which could be described as interfering with the race result.' The FIA had examined radio communications between McLaren and their drivers, data from the team and a report from the official observer.

Big Ron breathed a sigh of relief at the verdict and declared it to be the end of the matter as far as he was concerned. He said: 'The entire team was understandably disappointed that outstanding drives from both Fernando and Lewis, resulting in a great 1–2 victory and McLaren's 150th win, was temporarily tarnished.

'The efficient intervention and subsequent inquiry of the FIA into the allegations of the last three days has removed any doubt about the manner in which the team ran its cars during the 2007 Monaco Grand Prix.'

He was glad to be able to turn his back on what had been an unpleasant interlude but the one major plus to come from it was that hopefully Lewis Hamilton would never again be ordered to play second fiddle to Fernando Alonso. From now on the double World Champion would have to beat his arch-rival in a really convincing way, starting at the next race on the calendar... in Montreal on 10 June 2007.

CHAPTER 11

CANADA HIGH

It was make or break as Lewis Hamilton arrived in Canada for the sixth grand prix of what was becoming a thrilling Formula One season. A fortnight on from Monte Carlo and his dismay at being brought to heel by McLaren as he contemplated taking on Alonso, the boy dubbed 'the Stevenage Rocket' in the pit lane now had to put up or shut up.

Although his clear annoyance at being made to play second fiddle to the Spaniard resulted in a FIA inquiry into Ron Dennis' tactics as previously noted, it also created a situation where he would now no longer be expected to handle the car for McLaren's tactical advantage. That was the unexpected bonus of Monaco, but in another sense it put him in an unenviable position. Now, there could be no excuses if Alonso beat him; they were both in the same car and so it would be down to driver quality. Also, there were mutterings from the Alonso camp that maybe he was getting too big for his boots – what had he actually done to warrant equal billing? How many races had he won?

In some quarters, he was labelled with another nickname: the bridesmaid. Second best, never the No. 1. By 10 June in Montreal and for the first time in his short F1 career, the pressure was truly on for him. But his magnificent, and now typical, response was to turn up on the Thursday to 'bed himself in'. There, he met and greeted both press and fans as though he was about to take a gentle stroll in the park rather than hurtle round a circuit at death-defying speeds of up to 203mph in front of a crowd pushing 105,000 on 70 punishing laps. And, at the end of it all on the Sunday afternoon, he was to stand on the podium once again; for the sixth consecutive time, but this time would be the first as the winner. The 'bridesmaid' had eventually reached the altar. For Lewis Hamilton, genius rookie driver, it was the end of a long hard road: he was the No. 1 driver in the world that day, no question about it.

The Circuit Gilles Villeneuve, named after the late, great Ferrari star, is one most of the Formula One drivers can take or leave. No great test, it is, however, a favourite with the fans – its combination of straights and slow corners making for fast, furious, action-packed racing.

Lewis also arrived in Montreal with yet more criticism of his style ringing in his ears. But whereas prior to Monaco Eddie Jordan had knocked him for not being sufficiently aggressive, another 'name' from the past – former World

Champion Jacques Villeneuve – now accused him of being... not aggressive enough! It just went to show how unreliable some of the pundits were.

For Lewis Hamilton was becoming big business. Merely being associated with his name could bring benefits aplenty. Jordan talked about Lewis at the launch of his auto-biography, which helped to gain vital column inches of publicity in the following days' newspapers. The onset of his native Canadian Grand Prix saw Villeneuve appear in a rare public outing since his retirement fromFormula One at the end of the 2006 season.

Villeneuve accused Lewis of being too aggressive in his driving at the start of races, saying it was reminiscent of Michael Schumacher, who was attacked for 'dirty driving'. 'When will these chopping moves stop?' he asked. 'Lewis is not getting penalised and his behaviour off the start has started to look the way Michael used to.' The Canadian said he was surprised officials had not waved a black flag at Lewis, calling him into the pits for potential disqualification for dangerous driving. 'So far, he has been lucky, so we'll see if it carries on,' said Villeneuve – who won the title for Williams-Renault in 1997. 'He makes progressive moves that would have got some of the other drivers black-flagged.'

He also questioned whether Lewis was in the same league as Alonso, who had won in Montreal the previous year, and whether he would crack under pressure: 'Lewis is very fast, but he still has to step up to the plate and beat Alonso. And we still haven't seen how he reacts under pressure – that will be interesting to watch.'

Of course, Lewis would answer the barbs in the best style possible: by blasting Alonso out of the water come the race that Sunday, at the same time proving indisputably that he could handle the heaviest of pressure.

In the first practice session on the Friday he was two-tenths of a second slower than Alonso, but let's put that into perspective: this was the first time he had ever seen the Montreal track, let alone raced around it in a Formula One car. By the end of the second session in the afternoon some were questioning whether he was struggling in the heat and with the pressure growing on him by the day. He finished third behind Alonso and Massi, and made a few minor errors of judgment as he roared around the track.

So was he about to crack? No way! He seemed cool and collected as he talked about the day's work, explaining it had been as much about properly familiarising himself with the track as setting new records: 'Today was the first time I had the opportunity to drive here and I really enjoyed myself. We had done a lot of work back in the UK with our simulation programme and also I have watched a few of the past races here but you can't beat the real thing.

'We worked on set-up, tyre evaluation and also looking at the brakes as this circuit is notoriously hard on the brakes. There were no problems and it looks like we are in good shape.'

Indeed he was... By the end of Saturday's first qualifying session, Lewis was the fastest and that propelled him into the second session with a breezy confidence. In the morning, he finished four-tenths of a second ahead of Kimi

Raikkonen's Ferrari with Alonso third and Massa fourth. This set him up nicely for the final scramble for pole position in the afternoon's qualifying sessions and he did not disappoint, claiming the first pole of his F1 career with a fine display of driving. He set the fastest time of 1:15.707 and McLaren team-mate Alonso was unable to beat it with his final lap, finishing on 1:16.163, with Nick Heidfeld third in the BMW on 1:16.266. The Spaniard led earlier but lost six-tenths of a second in the final section.

Afterwards Lewis said: 'I feel fantastic; I have never felt so good. I had to wait for a few anxious seconds before discovering that Alonso had not beaten his time. It has been a fantastic day; it is already a fantastic weekend. It is not easy when you have a two-time World Champion hunting you down.

'I stayed strong and I did it. I owe it all to the team – we worked very hard to get it right. You come to that last corner at 200mph and on the final lap I went quicker than I have ever been; I almost touched the wall. For the final lap the car was sweet. I did not make a mistake and I got the time – I am thrilled.'

The result gave him the hope and confidence to believe he could now translate his brilliant form into a first grand prix victory the following day. 'It is going to be tough,' he said. 'I have not yet started from pole so that is another new experience for me. We have the car and strategy, and I just need to get a good start, get to that first corner first and stay consistent.'

Alonso, who started the race second on the grid, would

pay dearly for the mistake in final qualifying at the L'Epingle hairpin that cost him pole. He said: 'I was really going for it and was fastest for the first two sectors but went off the line and touched the gravel.' To give him his due, he did have some gracious words for his co-driver: 'I'm happy to be on the front row for tomorrow's race and for Lewis to be on pole next to me. The first row will be enough for today and tomorrow I will have another chance to try and win the race. I obviously want to win, but also I'm not going to win the Championship this weekend, so I will be sensible.'

Ron Dennis could not contain his excitement at Lewis' first pole: 'A fantastic qualifying result for the team for the second time in a row and for Lewis to achieve his first ever Formula One pole position. Fernando was unlucky on his second qualifying lap not to have improved following two great first sectors. We are confident that we will have a strong showing in tomorrow's race but certainly will not be complacent.'

And Mercedes boss Norbert Haug was equally effusive, saying: 'Lewis will start from his first Formula One pole position in only his sixth grand prix. Fernando was fastest in both the first and second sectors and until the final sector it looked like he would make it. Lewis and Fernando achieved the best possible qualifying result for the team for the second time within a fortnight.'

Not surprisingly, Ferrari team boss Jean Todt was in the doldrums, saying it had been the 'poorest [qualifying] of the season so far' and that he feared the worst in the race itself. Todt had always been a perceptive realist. He said: 'We were no match for our main rivals. Of course, the points only get given out in the race but the overall picture after today is not a favourable one and I hope that changes for the race.'

It wouldn't. Lewis gave a faultless show to take his first Formula One victory in only the sixth race of his career in a time of 1hr 44m 11.292s. He led throughout, maintaining his focus and concentration as the other big guns of McLaren and Ferrari seemed to lose theirs. He also survived four interventions by the safety car to earn an eight-point lead in the Championship over Alonso, who could only finish seventh. BMW's Heidfeld finished second, 4.343 seconds behind Lewis, with Alexander Wurz third in the Williams, their success finally breaking the McLaren-Ferrari stranglehold on the podium. Wurz's podium was Williams' first since Heidfeld finished second in a Williams-BMW at the Nürburgring in 2005.

Alonso set out like a man possessed, but overextended himself as if he were trying too hard, running wide at the first corner, and slipping down to third place behind Heidfeld. During a nervy ride, he overshot that corner another three times. The Spaniard also suffered when Adrian Sutil's Spyker was involved in a crash. Alonso was low on fuel and forced to make his first pit stop at the same time. Unfortunately for him that broke Formula One rules stating drivers cannot pit until the field has formed up behind the safety car – bringing him a 10-second stop-go penalty, and dropping him to thirteenth.

Fair credit to Fernando, he now set the fastest laps in his attempt to catch up, including the fastest of the day at 1m 16.367s on Lap 46, but he had too much ground to make up, despite the three further appearances by the safety car. The very fact that he finished meant McLaren maintained their record of completing every racing lap in 2007, with 768 so far.

There were other facts worth noting down in Montreal: Lewis became one of only nine drivers to win in his first year of competition. The others were Juan Pablo Montoya (2001), Jacques Villeneuve (1996), Clay Regazzoni and Emerson Fittipaldi (1970), Jackie Stewart (1965), Giancarlo Baghetti (1961) and Giuseppi Farina and Juan Manuel Fangio (1950). The win meant he had 11 races remaining to beat the record for the most grand prix victories in a debut season – the total of 4 set by Jacques Villeneuve in 1996. The Canadian Grand Prix was also the eighteenth occasion when a race featured a first-time winner and pole sitter, the last being Turkey in 2006 when Felipe Massa won from pole.

Lewis arrived back in the pits, fist aloft after his glory lap. Making his way up to the podium he came across the men at McLaren who had guided his career over the decade to this, the highest point: Ron Dennis, Martin Whitmarsh, and Norbert Haug. He headed straight for Big Ron and gave him a bear hug, before running up the steps and out on to the podium to celebrate his win. He said he was 'over the moon' as he savoured the sweet taste of victory: 'I've been ready for the win for quite some time. It was just a matter of when and where. I have to dedicate this win to my Dad because without him this would not have been possible.'

He then explained that holding off Alonso on that first corner had been key to his moment of glory. 'I didn't make a great getaway,' he admitted. 'Fernando got a better start and I had to make sure I didn't leave a gap for Nick behind me. Then I saw Fernando come flying down the outside and thought, oh no, I'm going to lose the lead, but he just went straight on at the corner. I continued on my line and got a fantastic exit, and then Fernando came cutting across in front of me. It was pretty exciting!'

He was talking ten to the dozen, like an excited schoolboy, and who could blame him? Now he had achieved the dream he had worked towards since he was first caught by the racing bug as a young boy of 6. All those years of hard work had paid off. He continued, 'I'm on another planet after this – I simply can't find the words to describe what it feels like to win my first Formula One race. The team has done a fantastic job and I'm so happy to be part of the Vodafone-McLaren Mercedes family. It seemed like every time I opened up a bit of a gap the safety car came out and I had to start all over again. It was only a few laps from the end [that] I realised that victory was within my grasp and I started noticing things like the fans cheering, and when I crossed the finishing line it was amazing. I now have to stay focused and keep up the good work.

'It's been an incredible start to my Formula One career so far, but I know there is a tough season ahead of us. Finally, thanks to the entire team at McLaren and Mercedes-Benz for all the hard work they have put into the car – it's an absolute pleasure to drive and be part of such a winning combination.'

Alonso's offered his congratulations, saying: 'I think this was a strange race with the safety car being deployed so many times, which worked to Lewis' advantage today – and my disadvantage. I came into the pits for the first time on Lap 24 as I had no more fuel so basically there was nothing I could do.

'It was a shame as this resulted in a 10-second penalty but I guess that unfortunately those are the rules but there was no alternative other than to stop on track with no fuel. After that I had to push as hard as possible because I was stuck in the middle of the field, and when you push to the maximum you sometimes go off track but at that stage there was nothing to lose. Whilst it was a difficult race for me, I'm pleased for the team and Lewis that we were able to secure some important points and Lewis winning his first race. I hope for a bit more luck for the US Grand Prix next week and at least I can leave Montreal with two points more than Massa.' And they say you have to be selfish if you want to be a champion...

Although Ron Dennis was beaming at the realisation that his boy had finally done it, once again, he was initially concentrating on the Spaniard's 10-second penalty and claiming he had been hard done by. He said, 'The whole team worked so hard to achieve the optimum result today. The frustration and disappointment of receiving a stop-and-go penalty, having been forced to stop in the pit lane when the pit lane was closed in the first safety car period, was obviously immense.

'However this in no way should detract from a mature and disciplined drive by Lewis to claim his first grand prix win. It's a very long time since the British national anthem was played for a race winner. His family should be justifiably proud of his achievement and whatever McLaren and Mercedes-Benz have contributed only compliments his talent and commitment. Lewis has done a great job, he deserved it and I am happy for him. Fernando was truly unlucky today but there is still a long way to go in the World Championship and we appear to be extremely competitive.'

Lewis was asked what could better this – was there an even more impossible dream to come true? He said: 'The next dream is obviously to win a Formula One World Championship but at the moment we have to be realistic again. It's always good to bear in mind that I'm still a rookie and this is my first season. There are going to be some hard times. I hope that there aren't, but it's just bound to happen – it's just the way it goes in this business and there'll be good days and bad days. But at the moment it's been consistent and that's down to the team and all the people around me. I've got a very well-grounded family and I think it works perfect.'

A lively question-and-answer session followed at the traditional post-grand prix press conference. One section of amusing answers from the Stevenage Rocket, involving also Heidfeld and Wurz, is worth recording here. It highlighted how the boy was developing, becoming much more assured, independently confident and able to handle being in the public arena.

Q: I read this week that you said pole position was better than sex, where do you rank this? (Laughter among the Press corps)

Above left: Lewis with his half-brother, Nicolas, who takes special pride in watching his older brother race. © *Getty Images*

Above right: With his father, and biggest supporter, Anthony after winning the Industrial Championship for Karting in Parma, Italy, October 1999. © *Rex Features*

Below left: Lewis aged 12, holding his trophy after winning the McLaren Mercedes Champions of the Future series. © *Rex Features*

Below right: Already proving to be great marketing material. Lewis jumps in the air at Earls Court in a shoot promoting Joe Bloggs clothing, September 1997. © *Rex Features*

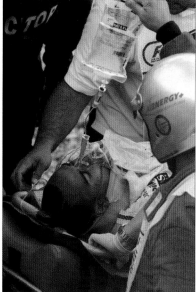

Above left: Focusing for the race at Silverstone. © *Rex Features*

Above right: Being transported on a stretcher after crashing into the tyre barriers during the European Grand Prix in July 2007. © *Press Association*

Below: A jubilant Lewis Hamilton celebrates with his family and friends after being crowned Formula One World Champion. © *Getty Images*

Above left: Lewis and then-girlfriend Nicole Scherzinger walk the red carpet in May 2014.
© *Getty Images*

Above right: Winning Sports Personality of the Year 2014.
© *David Davies/PA Wire*

Below: On the podium after winning the Abu Dhabi Formula One Grand Prix in November 2014.
© *Getty Images*

Above left: Lewis explores a somewhat slower mode of transport, the electric unicycle, as faithful bulldog Roscoe trots alongside in Miami. © *Getty Images*

Above right: Posing with the trophy after a US Grand Prix win in Austin secured the championship with three races left to run. © *Getty Images*

Below: Lewis Hamilton: Triple World Champion. © *Getty Images*

A: Heidfeld: He's too young still.

A: Hamilton: Yesterday it was a joke, it's a completely different feeling but... (More laughter)

A: Wurz: Did something change since yesterday? (More laughter)

A: Hamilton: It's definitely another level of feeling from yesterday, that's for definite.

Lewis was also asked what his father had said to him immediately after the race. His reply and gratitude to the man who had sacrificed almost everything to see him on that pedestal was certainly touching. 'I haven't seen him but obviously I could see him in the crowd while I was on the podium and it looked like he had a tear in his eye. So it's obvious that he was extremely proud and you wouldn't believe the amount of work he's put into my career. He had nothing when he was younger – just to see his family be successful is a real pleasure to him.'

Anthony was too choked with emotion to speak after Lewis' win, but a few minutes later he sufficiently composed himself and was told his son had dedicated the win to him. 'I hadn't heard that,' he said. 'But I'm glad I didn't hear it because who knows what would have happened? I was trying to hold it back as it was. This was the ordinary guy makes good. It's a special day for us but also for lots of other people, Formula One people and not Formula One people.'

He admitted the strain of the race had left him drained. 'Today has been hard work,' he said. 'I had to go through winning that race four times today. I did four grands prix today. Forget Lewis! He has just been laughing in his helmet and enjoying the race. That is what he does – nothing scares him.'

Would he and Lewis now be sitting down to make plans for a real assault on the world title crown? He smiled and shook his head: 'We never made plans to get to where we are; we just made plans to always do the best at what we were doing at that time. Getting to Formula One was just the next step that came along. We never, ever look ahead and say, "Right, we are going to do this, this, this and this".

'Wouldn't it be really painful if you start setting your heart on winning the Championship and it doesn't happen? We have plenty of time to win that championship, and if it happens this year, then that is a bonus.'

He conceded Lewis himself might be thinking about winning the crown now, but said he would be doing his utmost to keep him on the straight and narrow: 'What Lewis is going to think about is bringing the car home. Keep your mind straight, keep your feet on the ground and just bring the car home every time you take it out. And if we get a win along the line, that is brilliant, and if we win the Championship, that would be great.'

After his press conference, Lewis showed another side to his character by insisting he went to greet the fans from the UK, and indeed the rest of the world, who had waited patiently for him to emerge. They had cheered him to victory and now they wanted to congratulate them. He, in turn, wanted to meet them, thank them and celebrate a little with them even though, as the McLaren team was already reminding him, the next grand prix, in America, was only a week away.

Lewis insisted 'There's plenty of time to enjoy this win before going to Indy, and we'll obviously go there with great confidence. I've no doubt we can do well there as well. I just want to also thank the crowd; they were fantastic today.'

It was yet another illustration of how he differed from the stereotyped Formula One driver. He would never have dreamt of rushing off and locking himself away in his motorhome. Instead, he wanted to thank the people who paid his wages and whom, in the majority of cases, watched the races in what are often, let's be honest, uncomfortable surroundings – often fields with meagre facilities and zero comfort. Monza especially springs to mind...

By nightfall after his first Formula One Grand Prix win Lewis Hamilton was rapidly acquiring a new title: the People's Champion... It was party time for him in Montreal and the tributes and accolades poured in as the night progressed. Sir Stirling Moss led the way, saying of the young man who had become the 19th British driver to win a grand prix: 'He is a very impressive young man, the most impressive young driver I've seen in a long while. He has the car control and he has the calmness when he is driving, but he is also a fighter and has a great manner about him. He'll go a long way. I was impressed with him at the beginning of the season, but even more so now. It was obvious how good he was, but I never thought – and I don't think anybody thought – he would be leading the World Championship.

'For a guy who has just come into the sport, that is unbelievable, so I am terribly impressed and what has impressed me more than anything is that he is a racer.'

Another of racing's knights in shining armour, Sir Jackie Stewart, went even further, saying: 'He is probably the brightest star that has entered Formula One – ever!'

Damon Hill paid tribute to the way Lewis managed to maintain his cool in the heat of the battle: 'People should not underestimate what he has achieved in an incredibly short space of time. Yes, he's with a good team, and yes, he's got a good car, but to be winning grands prix, and be putting in performances like that race after race, takes something special. He may be young and in his first season, but this guy is the real deal. If you're good enough in this sport, you're old enough – and, boy, is Lewis good enough!

'He's leading the World Championship and winning races, so his confidence will be sky-high. And he's shown he can handle the pressure. We shouldn't get too carried away, but we could be looking at the next British World Champion.'

Another former World Champion, Niki Lauda, admitted he had the feeling that he was witnessing a new epoch in motor racing, thanks to Lewis' win – one that could take the sport to a new exciting level. He said, 'This was the best result ever, for him and for Formula One. I've never seen a guy driving such a perfect way. If he continues like this, he will be Champion. We all expected him, with no experience, to make mistakes under pressure, but he doesn't do any mistakes.'

Sir Frank Williams – who saw his own driver, Alex Wurz,

finish a distant third – said, 'He is absolutely a brilliant driver. You could almost describe him as a phenomenon, given that he is achieving so much with no Formula One experience. He is very, very remarkable.'

Simon Barnes, chief sportswriter of *The Times*, summed up best what the press back in the UK were thinking; his prose typically brilliantly flowing and rich: 'There was a sense of inevitability about it, almost a sense of serenity. Lewis Hamilton won his first grand prix in his sixth race and the dominating emotion was well, of course he bloody well did! What do you expect? The only mystery was why it took him so long– because Hamilton does not seem to be anything to do with precocious talent. By an extraordinary illusion, he looks exactly like the mature article, like the complete athlete: calm in himself, happy in his skin, as certain of his abilities as if they had been tried and tested a hundred times.

'No wonder his team-mate at McLaren, Fernando Alonso, has got the jumps. Being a World Champion is no defence against Hamilton's slightly spooky sense of self-certainty... Hamilton just drove. He drove with that sense of affinity for his conveyance that you occasionally see in very, very good horsemen – an almost passive sense of competitiveness, as if the driver or rider were merely a kind of vector for victory.'

Writing in *F1 Racing* magazine, Peter Windsor was also full of wonder at how easy Lewis had made such a difficult accomplishment appear: 'Lewis won this race because he won the pole; and then, from a slowish start, won it at the first corner – when Fernando blew it. He won it, in short, with a display of perfect braking, feel and balance on a torrid day. He won it with consistent precision at the big braking areas – at the hairpin and into Turn 1. He won it with a confidence level about which most drivers can only dream – with a quick trip to the circus on Saturday evening, followed by an early night, then a satisfying day at the races. It was simple. He made it look ridiculously simple. Such is his stature.'

The public was also eager to add their salute to the wonderboy, at the same time stressing how he had resurrected a sport many had turned their backs on. David, of London, said 'This guy Lewis Hamilton is really something else. His sudden appearance and success on the Formula One scene is reminiscent of Tiger Woods in golf. Both are mature, highly talented, no-nonsense professionals who have taken their respective sports by storm and just do the business. Formula One is worth watching again.'

And Derek, of Horsham, commented: 'Hamilton is showing great stability and consistency in every race. Alonso didn't become World Champion twice by being rubbish and this all makes for a very, very exciting season. Thank God the two are in the same car! No one can say that the other won because the car they were in was better... although Alonso is already trying to make his excuses.'

Catherine, from Powys, said, 'Lewis seems dedicated and modest. From the interviews I've seen with his father, he comes from a well-grounded background. I'm a 33-year-old woman and thanks to Lewis Hamilton, I've become interested in Formula One.'

There was even a surge of interest and admiration from overseas fans of Formula One. Pancho Villa jnr, from Mexico City, joked: 'Hopefully you Brits can be champions at one thing, since you all have not won a football championship since 1966 and we all know that it was rigged...LOL!' And Freddi, of São Paulo, conceded: 'Although I'm a Brazilian and a big fan of Massa's driving style, seeing Hamilton win yesterday was very nice and it perhaps gives us an idea of how the next few years of Formula One will be. I believe it will be exciting – with a nice competition among the new talents such as Massa, Hamilton, Kimi, Alonso and others. That's good news.'

It sure was. And while Lewis Hamilton was making fans as far away as South America, the good times were really about to roll in north America. Cue Indianapolis, one week on...

CHAPTER 12

AMERICAN IDOL

So, was it a one-off, or would Lewis Hamilton now take advantage of what had been a growing momentum? That was the question being floated wide and far as he arrived at the Brickyard for his Formula One US debut in the middle of June 2007. Obviously, the win in Montreal had filled him with confidence, but now he was in among the big boys. There could be no more hiding behind the 'rookie' tag; that was clearly a misnomer. No, as he revved up for the seventh Formula One race of his fledgling career, he had now become one of its hottest properties. The secret was out; the secret anyone connected with his career for the previous 10 years could well have guessed, that anyone who had watched his all-conquering season in GP2 the previous year would have acknowledged: Lewis was a natural and would take Formula One by storm.

He arrived in the States on the Thursday before the race to acclimatise himself after his Canadian triumph. In truth, this did not give him as much time as he would have liked, especially with this being another circuit he had never visited, let alone raced around. But needs must. After his win in Montreal he found himself much in demand. He explained his late arrival in this way: 'I was in New York for a couple of days – I had an appearance for Mercedes-Benz. Then I went to Washington yesterday for another appearance for Exxon-Mobil and getting back the flight was delayed from 4 o'clock to 8 o'clock, then eventually it was cancelled at 9. So we ended up staying in a hotel and luckily we flew out this morning.'

Not ideal for a man who, as already noted, is big on detail and likes to prepare himself fully, both mentally and physically at his own pace before a race. But he was also mature enough to accept that life would never be the same again after that thrilling triumph in Canada: 'I know that I had the front pages back in the UK after the race, which is awesome. I have had something like 200 text messages from friends and it's almost impossible to reply to them all, but I'm trying.

'It's a big stepping stone in my career and in my life. It was a great feeling to get the first win and definitely not expected going into my sixth grand prix, especially at Canada, which wasn't one of my strongest circuits. I think Fernando [Alonso] was probably quicker than me there but I did a solid job. It's obviously very positive for the team – we've extended our lead in the Constructors'

Championship... Great points for me... and coming here we've got to continue with that performance.'

His first impression of the Indianapolis Motor Speedway, also known as the Brickyard, was a good one. He admitted he felt a thrill of expectation shiver down his spine as he surveyed the track: a high-speed oval with tight twists and turns and a long straight made for putting your foot down. The home of American motor speedway and the world-famous Indy 500 shimmered in the sun as he put on his helmet for practice on the Friday prior to the big race. Even back then he admitted to a gut feeling: this was a race he could win; he could be the new King of America once the 73 laps had been completed on the Sunday, no doubt about it.

He also knew victory would put him in the history books, along with Graham Hill and Dan Wheldon, as British winners at the track. Hill, a legendary Formula One driver, had won the Indy 500 as a rookie in 1966 and Wheldon emulated his glory race in 2005; the first Brit to win at the Brickyard during those 39 years since Hill's romp. Lewis said, 'I am very excited about the race. It's an amazing opportunity for any driver to come here and compete. Watching the Indy 500 over the years, it's an awesome race and I've always wanted to go and watch and be a spectator. But to be here, racing on the circuit, is pretty cool. Just flying over, I could see what the track was like. It's quite a nice complex.'

But would the new level of expectation weigh heavily on him? Might it adversely affect his performance at the Brickyard? 'To be honest, I try not to focus on that,' he said, scratching his head. 'I came into the season with a very open mind and being realistic of the fact that I am a rookie and I've got a lot to learn, it is still a very steep learning curve. And yes, I have a great opportunity as I'm in the best team and have one of the best drivers to compare myself to.

'But I still feel there's going to be times during the season when there will be some lows, as well as the highs, and I think it's way too early to talk about the Championship. There are 11 races to go and I just have to approach every race exactly the same as I always have and try and do a solid job.

'Each time I go out in the car, I learn something new. I'm becoming more and more comfortable in the car, with the team, with the controls, and with the rules and the regulations and just the whole racing. I'm always learning bit by bit and I will continue throughout the season.'

It was that level-headedness that convinced many that he could push Alonso and Raikkonen down to the wire in the battle for the Driver's title. A cliché maybe, but for one so young, he had a wise old head.

The first day of practice at Indianapolis was spent studying the track, learning its bumps and curves; how to avoid its pitfalls. Fernando Alonso set the fastest lap in the first session with Lewis seven-tenths of a second behind him. The Spaniard was also top dog on the afternoon session, with a best lap of 1m 12.156s. But there were now ominous signs from Hamilton: as he got to grips with the circuit he was closing in on his team-mate. By the end of that day the gap was a little more than one-tenth of a second.

He knew he was once again on the brink of something big: 'As this was the first time I have ever driven here I spent some time just getting to know the circuit. The really tricky bit is the mid-section as it's very tight and twisty. We spent our time fine-tuning the set-up and evaluating the two different tyre options provided by Bridgestone this weekend.

'In the first part of the second session I ran a little wide and did some minor damage to the aerodynamic fences, which took a little time for the guys to repair. We have a pretty good idea of where we are going, and it looks like we should be competitive, but as always, Friday is only the start of the weekend – there is a long way to go.'

Alonso was fastest again on Saturday morning, with Lewis third, but by the end of the day the tables had turned dramatically. It was Lewis who grabbed his second consecutive pole after turning in a time of 1m 12.331s, 0.169 seconds ahead of Alonso. The Ferraris of Felipe Massa and Kimi Raikkonen would make up the second row. It was a terrific result for Lewis, who admitted he had not slept well the night before. Some pundits believed this could be down to hay fever, but he admitted: 'No, I wouldn't say I've got hay fever. I haven't been getting much sleep lately, probably just enjoying it too much! But yes, I didn't feel great.' Maybe not, but he couldn't conceal his delight at the outcome of qualifying: 'I'm quite surprised, to be honest. Going into qualifying we hadn't found the optimum set-up and I knew Fernando was quick here.

'To be on pole once again within a week is fantastic – I like north America! The fans here have been so enthusiastic and supportive for the team, and I hope they enjoyed today. I screamed into my helmet when I got the confirmation from the team of the pole position. It's a challenge to come to a track for the first time, and I have learnt new things every single corner and every single lap. I knew I had to push very hard in my second run in the final qualifying session. The car is working well, and the team has done a great job.'

Things got even better on race day as Lewis roared home first in 1hr 31m 09.965s to take his second victory in a row and forge 10 points clear of Alonso. It was also his seventh appearance on the podium in his seventh Formula One race. And he did it in style, completing a grid-to-flag victory and coolly dealing with Alonso's two attempts to pass him. Alonso, who would finish second, tried to get past Lewis as they pulled away from the grid, but it was the boy from Stevenage who won the tussle.

They clashed again after making their first pit stops 1 lap apart. The two cars went down the main straight side by side but again it was Lewis who emerged in front as they hit Turn One. After that, it was race off as he kept his position as leader until the chequered flag. The victory also meant Lewis entered the record books as only the fourth rookie, along with Jacques Villeneuve, Nino Farina and Juan Manuel Fangio, to win at least two races in their debut season.

Afterwards he was glad to be out of the searing heat of the day. He admitted he had been boosted by local fans backing him with noisy klaxons and the presence in his pit lane of American rapper Pharrell Williams as his VIP guest. Looking slightly dazed, Lewis admitted: 'It just keeps getting better and better – what an amazing week this has been! I can't believe that I have won. To come to two circuits [Montreal and Indianapolis] that I didn't know and to really come out with such pace and to see the team moving forward is great.

'The last 15 laps seemed a lifetime, but I was in the lead – I was able to do it and I'm very emotional now. Everything went right: start, pit stops, strategy... and I'm really happy. I was under pressure all the way from Fernando and we were both pushing as hard as possible. I made a good start to maintain the advantage but Fernando was right there. In the second stint Fernando managed to get really close when my tyres were graining, and he had a go at the end of the straight, but I was able to keep him behind. It's been a long and hot day, but I have really enjoyed myself and the support from the fans.'

Ron Dennis was at his most diplomatic, congratulating both drivers on their 1–2, but also pointing out that this time he had told them both to cut down their revs. Big Ron said, 'During the middle stint Fernando pushed hard and caught Lewis, and this created some positive but tense moments on the pitwall. We were obviously happy to let them race but had to be mindful of the fact that our competition was not threatening our 1–2 finish. Fifteen laps from the end both drivers reduced their revs to save the engines for the French Grand Prix but still continued to race. Their sporting behaviour, both on the track and especially during the podium celebrations, made the team proud to have two such great drivers.'

Lewis was told it was Father's Day and asked did he have a special message for Anthony? He said, 'I didn't even know it was Father's Day – I've just been so focused. I remember someone told me but I didn't know if it was Father's Day over here, or Father's Day back home. I'm never aware of those dates, but now it's even better.

'I dedicated the last win to him, but I don't really know what to do with this one. I think there's going to be – I hope – many, many more to come. I can't just keep on dedicating to a different... there are so many people in my family! As I said, I'm grateful to all of them. I hope he's happy, and I will say Happy Father's Day at the end.'

But he did not realise how big a star he had become until he arrived back in the UK. Now he was the talking point around the pubs and workplaces – he had become a national celebrity and a national treasure. The fans were desperate to send him their congratulations. Joe Neill of London said: 'Firstly well done Lewis! Your two wins in Canada and America are fantastic for Formula One. Also, full credit to McLaren for giving a British driver a chance – and for giving Alonso a run for his money! To me it looks like he is more than equal! It's great to see raw talent get a chance – let's hope he keeps it on the road all year – and that he goes on to win the title.'

Another racing enthusiast, Tim Leach of Burnley said it was time for Alonso to give a bit of credit where it was due: 'I have the greatest respect for anyone who drives a Formula One car, but after seven races Hamilton is 10 points ahead of Alonso. They are equal partners with the same backup and resources, which means that driving skills are the main criteria that separate the two team-mates.

'Alonso has to accept the fact that possession is nine-tenths of the law and barring a major disaster, he has his work cut out to catch Hamilton.'

Tom Bray of Dublin paid tribute to Lewis' cool style: 'It is really satisfying to have Lewis win these two north American races. His two wins from pole were solid – extremely high-quality calm execution with chaos often around him. I'm just glad to see that if he indeed does close up the Championship this year, it will include quality wins. I was worried for a while that we may have a non-race winning champion with this point system. But the cream does rise to the top. And has it ever!' Meanwhile Bill Lowe, of Banbury, was similarly effusive of Hamilton's driving skills: 'How much of the emerging gap between McLaren and Ferrari is based on Hamilton's skill as a driver? The Indy race, which I saw in person, was a masterful exhibition of driving ability.'

And tributes were also paid to Ron Dennis and McLaren for their gamble in bringing the youngster to world fame in such a short time. Alan Davies of Chester said: 'Win pole, protect your line, put your foot down, don't make any mistakes, bring it home! Five essential ingredients that make superb racing driver – yesterday at the Brickyard, Lewis was superb.

'Fernando will need to re-adjust his strategy and driving style in order to get back into the running. It's good to see that he opted to play it safe and bring home maximum points. However the star of this race is not just Lewis: it is also McLaren. The team has gone from being side-of-the-track scenery in the last few years to a dominant Ferrari-eating outfit. Five wins in seven races, three 1–2 finishes, and a bag full of podiums.

'They are clearly running away with the Constructor's title, leaving Jean Todt scratching his head and wishing for a Schumi resurrection. As far as the Driver's title is concerned, in 2008 McLaren might have *two World Champions* under one roof! What a combo that will be.'

And Jody Smith of Ipswich said that after his 2 wins in north America Lewis would surely now go on to pinch the title from Alonso: 'He has been consistent, got podiums, pole positions and two victories. Hamilton has shown his armchair critics that he is for real and is the new dominant force in Formula One today.

'Long-shot overtaking manoeuvers at the start of grand prix races are costing him dearly – Alonso had better learn to live with Hamilton's speed and consistency, and up his game, or the double World Champion will be left in his wake.

'Personally, I don't think Alonso can catch him now – Lewis is too consistent and will surely go on to capture the world title.'

Jonathan McEvoy of the *Daily Mail* also paid tribute to Lewis' showing in America – like others particularly admiring the way in which he dealt with all that came his way in such a mature, composed manner: 'Nothing seems to faze the new star. He arrived at a track he had never seen, following a nightmare journey... He charmed the crowd by waving, signing autographs and saying all the right things whenever a microphone was pushed under his nose. He is a natural.

'He was equally sure-footed in the cockpit. Yes, Alonso had the edge in practice and the first two sessions of qualifying, but when it counted in the shoot-out for pole, Hamilton banged in the fastest time on Saturday afternoon – all that in high temperatures and with hay fever. It was a masterclass in managing the weekend.'

Finally, the *Daily Telegraph* printed a note of congratulations that must have just about iced the cake for Lewis after his US win – it was from his cousin Michelle and read: 'Hi Lewis! This is your cousin, Michelle Hamilton, daughter of Randolph Hamilton, who is the son of your grandfather's (Uncle Davidson) brother (you know him as Uncle Fleet). Congratulations on your big win! We watched you all the way from the United States and we're so proud of you. Aunty Irva is here with us for the summer and she cheered you on the whole way.

'I hope the newspaper will forward this message to you. If not, we'll get in touch with your Aunt Vanessa. Again, congratulations and enjoy your big win!'

The ripple of applause continued all week, with tributes and accolades pouring in en masse. But Lewis knew he had to put it all to the back of his mind; it was not his scene to play the big 'I am'. No, he had another important date looming in his bid for world domination: it was less than two weeks until a 1 July showdown with Alonso & Co. in France.

The heat had been on in the US and now it was off as they

travelled back to a rain-swept Europe, but it would reach boiling point as the Formula One circus finally touched down at Magny-Cours for the eighth leg of an unrelenting pressure-cooker campaign. Alonso was agitated and fired up after losing out to his 'rookie' team-mate in north America and he was determined to avenge those defeats in Europe. Lewis knew he would have to pull out all the stops once again to keep at bay the man who was, after all, a double World Champion.

As events unfolded at Magny-Cours it became clear that Lewis now had to face up to a new problem as well as Alonso, and, like his team-mate, this one would not go away. It was the re-emergence of the prancing horse... as Ferrari finally put their early season problems behind them and put on a weekend's showcase of dazzling racing to take the limelight off Lewis and Fernando.

British fans hoping for a Lewis Hamilton hat trick of wins were disappointed when he struggled to live with the rejuvenated Ferraris. Kimi Raikkonen arrived at the French circuit clearly meaning business: he was fastest in the first practice session on the Friday and his dominance would continue right up to the end of the race on the Sunday afternoon. Even as he arrived in France, Lewis seemed a bit disorientated, claiming to 'quite like the track' and saying 'I've had some very interesting experiences here' before adding, 'I have always liked racing here, when you hear people talk about circuits that are technical, Magny-Cours is definitely one of them.

'It is important to have good speed in the slow corners, as

they tend to lead on to long straights. You have to have good mechanical set-up for the corners and the same with traction for the exits. My favourite sections of the track are the two high-speed chicanes at the back of the circuit. We go through them at speeds of up to 200kph, which is very fast for a chicane; very special to drive through and unique in Formula One.'

The bit about liking the track puzzled me, especially in light of his visits in Formula Three and GP2. Maybe it was just part of the ever-maturing Lewis Hamilton, putting on a diplomatic show for his French hosts? Certainly, his record at the circuit did not inspire his fans: he crashed there in F3 and had a similarly tough learning lesson there as he cruised to the GP2 title in the 2006–7 season.

He conceded: 'The French round of the GP2 Championship last season was not my best weekend as I had a coming together in the first race that led to me starting race two from nineteenth. I did make my way up through the field to fifth to score some points, so it is possible to overtake here. Although you always want to be on pole, you can pass at Magny-Cours, while there is a short pit lane that means there are more strategy options.'

The jinx seemed to have struck again on the first practice session – he was sixth fastest. Yet by Saturday night his fortunes appeared to have turned: he had done well enough to start from second on the grid. Lewis set a time of 1m 15.104s and missed his third pole position in a row by only seven-hundredths of a second, and he would have sneaked it, had he had not made a braking mistake in the final section of qualifying. He admitted: 'You can't be perfect all the time. On my final lap I braked a bit late into Turn 15 and ran wide. Without this mistake the pole position would have been possible for me today – I had it there.'

Was the pressure of leading the World Championship by 10 points and being hunted by Alonso, getting to him, maybe? Lewis said: 'I don't feel any more pressure, I just feel that I approach every weekend the same. It is great to be in the lead, but obviously there are 10 races left and it is way too early to consider winning the Championship.

'I am still in my first season. A lot of the other drivers obviously understand that I am still a rookie but as you go through the season they see that you are doing a good job or you have a close battle with them, and they can see you are fair or something like that and they build the respect that they have for you; it grows. But I still think they obviously know I am a rookie, they expect me to make a mistake at some point...'

Massa had won pole and Raikkonen would be No. 3 on the grid. Alonso suffered gearbox problems in the final section of qualifying, meaning he would start from a disastrous tenth position. As he wound down after qualifying he was in a grumpy mood, but managed a smile a little later saying he hoped the heavens would open in France overnight! Alonso said, 'I will pray for rain tonight. We know wet conditions are difficult and produce mixed results. But if you are quick in the dry, you can be two or three tenths of a second quicker than the guy in front. If you are quick in the wet, maybe it's two seconds so you can make up places much, much quicker. So I really hope it's wet tomorrow because it might lead to some uncertainties we might be able to benefit from.

'Starting tenth no doubt that makes it difficult for me to close the [points] gap to Lewis. I need points, but I also know that finishing higher than fifth might not be possible, but it is what I will try to do.'

He also smiled grimly when the word Ferrari was mentioned and said he himself had never written them off in the title race: 'After winning three races in Monaco, Canada and Indianapolis, people seemed to forget Ferrari, but not me. I know they are quick, that they can do a very good job and they are always strong. To beat Ferrari is always difficult, and it will be difficult until the last race.'

At least for once this enigmatic, often difficult man was spot-on. Ferrari would transform their season as Kimi Raikkonen and Felipe Massa finished first and second at Magny-Cours to end Lewis' run of victories. But the Stevengage Rocket was still in there battling, taking third place to extend his lead to 14 points at the top of the drivers' standings in what was his eighth consecutive podium finish.

Raikkonen took the lead on Lap 47 on his way to victory in a time of 1hr 30m 54.200s. He had overtaken Lewis by the first corner – the first time the Brit had been overtaken in Formula One – and powered on from there, finishing 2.414m ahead of Massa and another 32 seconds beyond Hamilton. Alonso put in a battling display to finish seventh, but out of the points.

Lewis tried to put a brave face on the weekend in France: 'I am sure we can bounce back at the next race, without a doubt. Going into my first British Grand Prix with the team I've always wanted to drive for, and leading the World Championship is one of the greatest feelings a driver can have.

'So long as we maintain reliability and consistency I don't see why we can't keep going for the win. At the start of the season such a thing was unimaginable, while I have said before that I never expected to finish on the podium in my first race, never mind to do so now for eight races. So I'm very, very happy with the job I've done, and the job the team has done. Even after the fact I was overtaken for the first time in a race, I am not disappointed. I don't like being overtaken, which is the same for everyone, yet it was inevitable it would happen at some point. But the fact is we have finished on the podium again. We are the most consistent team and I do think we are doing the better job. Obviously, you can't win every race, but I've extended my lead in the Championship so I couldn't be happier.'

McLaren team boss Ron Dennis admitted he had switched Lewis to a strategy to guarantee third place, recognising it would be impossible to overtake the Ferraris. He also tried to downplay the impact of the boys in red, saying: 'Obviously we are delighted that Kimi won over Massa (who would have been just 1 point behind Alonso had he won).

'We flattered them this weekend. They did a good job and probably improved the car a little, but we made them look a lot better than they were. Hopefully we will demonstrate that at Silverstone.'

Ah, Silverstone... There was just no let-up in what was becoming a punishing test of stamina. Lewis was certainly looking forward to the next stage of his examination: the journey home but even he was feeling the strain with the knowledge that the Prancing Horse was alive and kicking. Raikkonen and Massa had resolutely proved that to be the case with a dominant weekend for Ferrari in the wastelands of France.

Lewis was about to find out just how big a name worldwide he had become when he arrived back in England – and how he was being talked of as a pioneer for blacks who had never previously considered Formula One as a spectator, or indeed participant sport. Before we land back in England, let's now take a slight detour to examine the effect Lewis Hamilton was having on Formula One as its first black driver.

CHAPTER 13

RACE DRIVER

When Pharrell Williams joined Lewis Hamilton as his VIP guest at the US Grand Prix, the focus inevitably moved to the effect the young racing driver was having on the black community in terms of the sport. It seemed clear that as well as opening up Formula One to a younger, more vibrant audience, Lewis' achievement in becoming the first driver of black heritage to win a grand prix had encouraged other black people to follow the sport and, in some cases, to dream of breaking into it as he had done. As mentioned before, the natural role model comparison in the early days of his arrival on the scene was Tiger Woods. Just as Lewis was to storm to glory quickly, appearing nine consecutive times on the podium, so too had Tiger done in golf. Woods won his fifth Pro tournament and was World No. 1 just 42 weeks after he made his professional debut. It was also anticipated that, just as Tiger had opened up golf via his dominance over the years, so too would Lewis widen out motor racing.

But was that an altogether too simplistic view of affairs? Would the Lewis effect have black hopefuls queuing up to follow in his footsteps through Formula One's previously closed door? Of the Tiger Woods' comparison, Lewis himself would say: 'I'm not Tiger Woods, I'm Lewis Hamilton, but I think he's a sensational athlete. I hope I can do the same in Formula One.'

'The same in Formula One'... Yet even before his extraordinary wins in north America had been fully taken in, some pundits decried Lewis' achievements, arguing that even if he did turn out like Tiger that was nothing to shout about – after all, what had Tiger really done for the ethnic minorities in golf?

Matthew Syed led the doubters in *The Times*, arguing it must be said, with considerable aplomb and armed with convincing statistics to illustrate that Tiger had not changed golf one bit in terms of racial progress: 'The truth is that Woods has not had anything like the influence on global black consciousness that his cheerleaders suggest. Not one black player has joined the PGA tour since Woods turned professional in 1996 and there has not been a black player in the Ladies Professional Golf Association since 2000. There are today no home players from an ethnic-minority background playing on tour and of the 60 teenagers in the English Golf Union's elite programme only two come from minorities.'

Yes, that's quite an argument – well constructed and, on the surface at least, difficult to debate. I asked Ash Hussain for his views on Syed's contentions. Ash, 36, of east London, is an ideal man to talk about breaking down barriers. A national newspaper picture editor of Asian descent, he told me how he himself had to struggle to break through 'traditional barriers within the newspaper industry' to reach the top. He also admits he had to break through barriers within his own community: 'When I started out 15 years ago, the Asian community wanted doctors, engineers and lawyers, not photographers! But since then a few Asian youngsters have seen what I have achieved and have been inspired to pursue a career in media.'

He vehemently disagrees with Syed's view that Tiger has achieved nothing in breaking down those same barriers in golf, arguing that just because no one else has emerged at Tiger's level this does not mean he has failed as a role model for blacks. Ash said: 'I feel it is a bit too harsh because you get a lot of people who watch golf, especially in the ethnic groups, because of Tiger – he has actively encouraged people from ethnic minorities to follow the sport. I know of many who do so who did not previously and I also know many who have taken up golf because of Tiger Woods. OK, they are not champions like him but he opened the door for them; opened the door for a brand new audience and new participants. An audience who previously may have thought of golf as a rich man's domain, but who were enticed in by Tiger's success and personality.

'Tiger was the first black man in golf to win the Masters

at Augusta, the first to wear the green jacket. If that is not inspiring to youngsters, just what is? In the same way, Lewis has opened the floodgates for ethnic minorities in motor racing, which, like golf, was considered by many to be purely a rich man's sport.'

Ash believes the impact of Lewis Hamilton and the dynamic young Asian boxer, Amir Khan, is already opening up sport to minorities who might otherwise not be drawn in. He said, 'I think Amir Khan is another Lewis Hamilton in the sense that he is an absolute inspiration for the ethnic minorities. Amir is a new modern trailblazer for would-be black boxers in this country, having taken over the path already laid by Prince Naseem, and I strongly believe Lewis will similarly inspire kids from ethnic backgrounds into motor racing. In fact, I think what he has already achieved in the last few months has already inspired a whole generation of young ethnic drivers to compete in motor racing.'

In his forcefully-argued piece Syed also contends that Lewis will probably do nothing to help the lot of deprived black children. That he will, inevitably, become a 'yes-man' to the corporate giants who pay his wages rather than using his undoubtedly privileged position to try to improve the lot of ethnic minorities. Syed cites the example of Michael Jordan as a warning as to how Lewis could turn out; he argues the basketball star showed a 'shocking reluctance' to enter political debate in case it upset the sponsors who indirectly beefed up his massive salary. He claims Jordan could have used his position in his home state of North Carolina to unseat the Republican senator Jesse Helms in 1990. This would have been a noble cause as Helms once helped to create a campaign slogan that read: 'White people, wake up before it is too late. Do you want Negroes working beside you, your wife and your daughters in your mills and factories?'

Syed dismissed Jordan as being politically impotent, saying his response to the chance to get rid of Helms was to dismiss it out of hand: 'Republicans buy sneakers, too' – a reference to his shoe-manufacturing paymasters Nike. It leads *The Times'* journalist to conclude: 'Lewis Hamilton will soon become familiar with the rules of this depressing game. Even now the 22-year-old is being schooled in the art of saying nothing. His handlers recognise that by presenting their client as a blank canvas it will be easier to persuade multinationals to emblazon him with their logos. Like Jordan, he will soon become a walking billboard.'

Again, Ash Hussain has no time for those sentiments, arguing Jordan is given a particularly harsh assessment: 'I disagree with the idea that Jordan did no good – he did a lot for deprived ethnic minority children which has not been reported in the press. He also regularly helps out with children's charities and, of course, he did a film called *Space Jam*, which was aimed at the children's market – and many kids found its theme of achieving freedom inspiring. So just how is Jordan not an inspiration for coloured children? Much of what he does in his life is aimed exactly at helping and encouraging children.'

Syed also claims that, like Tiger, Lewis will be forced to pay lip service to his sponsors. He writes: 'It will be astonishing if Hamilton — a kid from Hertfordshire who has already signed lucrative deals with Vodafone and the watchmaker Tag Heuer — does not follow the example of the man destined to become the world's first billion-dollar sportsman. He will soon become accustomed to having a slick agent or two at his side during interviews, ready to deflect any question that might impact upon the sanitised image of his corporate clients.'

Ash Hussain believes Lewis Hamilton is no one's mouthpiece and that he is a young man of principle who will always say what he believes. He argues should he ever step out of line then his father Anthony will be there to help him: 'I think Lewis is a person who can speak for himself and always will – and the only person who will be at his side through thick and thin will be his dad, not some slick agent. His dad will keep him on the straight and narrow. He has steered him in the right direction so far, so why should things change now? He is a loving dad to him, not domineering, just loving and concerned his boy does not make mistakes.'

Amir Khan also believes Lewis is big enough, strong enough and wise enough to look after himself, and that he will not be taken for a ride by any 'slick-talking agents' or manipulative sponsors. The boxer, from Bolton in Lancashire, also believes that he and Lewis *are* opening doors for kids from ethnic minorities, and indeed all creeds. Amir, who has been car mad since he was a kid and even had motorsport ambitions of his own before he plumped for boxing, said: 'I truly believe Lewis and me are the future of

British sport. We are both pushing the boundaries and keeping alive the British sporting tradition.

'I want the pair of us to inspire young British kids to take part in more sport. And I'm not just talking about boxing and racing, because I think kids will look at us and take up all types of sports. We are natural winners and kids will look at us and say, "I can do that. I could be a winner like Amir and Lewis."'

Ash Hussain also had something to say to those who claimed Lewis was getting carried away by stardom and celebrity, that Pharrell Williams' appearance on the scene and the gradual emergence of other stars in Lewis' camp such as P. Diddy and Beyoncé was symptomatic of such a malaise. He said: 'People are questioning why Lewis is hanging around with people like that as if they are bad guys. But P. Diddy has got a school for deprived children in New York that he funds and Pharrell is a real nice guy. They are not as shallow as some would tell you; they have an altruistic side, and I know Lewis likes them for that as well as their company. I just can't be as cynical as some people seem to be towards Lewis and his friends. At the Goodwood Festival of Speed, Lewis came out and signed autographs in driving rain. He could have gone off home but he spent the whole day there. That is the sort of person he is – he is an ambassador for the sport; he's not just in it for the money or the fame – and he is also an ambassador, and an absolutely fantastic one, for the ethnic minorities.'

One celebrity 'knocked out' by the charms of Lewis Hamilton was renowned Buddhist Maxi Jazz, the singer in

Faithless and a motorsport fanatic. He admitted Lewis had become his hero, saying: 'As a 50-year-old man I never thought I'd have a 22-year-old hero. I met him last year and he shook my hand so hard he crushed it. He is manna from heaven. I want our children to be revering someone other than 50 Cent. To hear about Lewis and his dad's struggle to get somewhere, that's positive.

'The Government should be subsidising karting instead of going on about ASBOS. Kids won't have any energy for joyriding after they've been round the track. There are no affordable facilities for kids. Britain is the home of motor racing and yet we're not doing enough for the future of this sport.'

Writing in the *Observer* before the British Grand Prix at Silverstone in July 2007, Anna Kessel voiced the widely held opinion that Lewis' VIP guests and fans were merely a sign of the remarkable landscape change he was bringing about in Formula One. She said: 'Two weeks ago he appeared on cult urban music channel MTV Base and at Indianapolis hip hop mogul Pharrell Williams and singer Beyoncé hung out with Hamilton's family in the pits. In just four months Formula One has gone from hip – a fashionable playground for the super rich – to hip hop, and the predictions are that Hamilton's stock will yet grow.'

Two journalists from rival black-focus newspapers were quick to back up her belief that Lewis was the best thing in years to happen to Formula One. 'Lewis will be more popular than Tiger Woods,' said Michael Eboda, editor of the *NewNation*, a paper that serves the Afro-Caribbean community. 'He's turning the whole community on to the sport. People are glued to their screens when previously they would never have considered watching Formula One. One of my friends can't even drive and he's calling me up to talk about Lewis.' And Rodney Hinds, sports editor of the *Voice*, said: 'I get emails and phone calls after every race. There's a buzz about Lewis; people who don't know a goalpost from a lamppost are talking about him. He's uniting and exciting people. It's the relate-ability factor. I know Richard Williams [father of Venus and Serena] and he'll be over here around the same time as the British Grand Prix. I wouldn't be surprised if someone from their camp went to meet Lewis.'

The journalist revealed that the *Voice* had applied for Formula One media accreditation for the first time in its history following the news that Lewis would be racing. Yet Hinds admitted some of his friends were still wary of going to races live at the circuits: 'I had a phone call this week from two sisters who have followed Formula One for years. They've done the European circuit but they tell me there are no other black people there. We are the people watching sport via the remote control. We need to get a group down there to show solidarity. But there still remains that thought – how comfortable would we feel at these events? I would love to go to Silverstone and see large numbers of my community watching Lewis Hamilton.'

Three former England footballers – John Barnes, Luther Blissett and Les Ferdinand – were so inspired by Lewis that they set up a project to encourage young people from ethnic and disadvantaged backgrounds to get involved in motorsport. Luther told the *Observer*: 'Lewis is someone I can really identify with as a black man. In England we have a multicultural society, but that is lacking in motorsport, which is elitist and limited in its diversity. There is a lack of black faces, from drivers to mechanics. It was the same in football at one point until myself and Cyrille Regis made it common to see black faces.'

And Les Ferdinand said: 'Black kids are always looking for someone to aspire to and beyond football we have struggled to provide them with someone. Now kids will hear Lewis' story of how he got started, parents might start thinking they'll take their kids karting on the weekends.' Meanwhile, Michael Eboda came up with a vision that, if realised large-scale, could be even more far-reaching – and arguably the most remarkable of all the pluses from Lewis Hamilton's rise to the top: 'The most important thing to come out of this is Hamilton's relationship with his dad. Many of our young black kids don't have that and it may just make some fathers think again.'

Others within the black community were quick to praise Lewis and the way in which he had opened previously closed doors. Ron Shillingford of Operation Black Vote (OBV) said, after Lewis' first Formula One race in Australia: 'We hail the magnificent debut of grand prix sensation Lewis Hamilton who raced to glory on Sunday... For a black kid from humble beginnings just getting a coveted Driver's place was an amazing feat. It doesn't surprise me though because I first featured Lewis in the

Voice 14 years ago when he was embarrassing much older kids, thrashing them in karting races... I remember [his father] Anthony telling me when he was 8 that beaten adults were so astonished they thought Lewis was a midget! They just couldn't believe someone so tiny was so brilliant.' And OBV director Simon Woolley added: 'We're usually carrying negative stories about our community so it's refreshing for OBV to applaud in no uncertain terms the achievement of this talented black man. Lewis deserves nothing but praise.'

The *Voice* also lauded his achievements in a special comment before the British Grand Prix in July 2007, saying: 'The *Voice* celebrates 25 years this year and without question no sportsman or woman has so quickly captured the imagination as Lewis Carl Hamilton. Remember the name, as the rookie Formula One driver looks to replicate the achievements of some of the sport's true greats. Yes, his career is still fledgling and he has lots to learn – in and out of the car. But at a time when black youth grab headlines for negative reasons, here is a young man who quite simply is young, gifted and black... Congrats too should go to Lewis' family and father Anthony in particular, who has been the perfect role model for his own son.'

But the last word on the race issue must go to Lewis himself: 'It's going to be a pain, the whole fame thing, but I'm strong enough to handle it. When I'm at a race now I don't think, "Oh man, I'm the only black guy here!" I noticed it more in karting. On the day Senna died there was another black family at the track. But they weren't doing anything big because they didn't have the money. In karting, because some of the kids were immature, the odd racist thing would pop up. But I channelled my aggression; that's one of my great strengths. I was also taught that the best way to beat them is out on the track.'

Truly a great attitude from a great young man – and a real trailblazer and role model for coloured people in general as well, as those now taking an interest in Formula One. For bringing in newcomers from ethnic minorities who would not normally have taken an interest, as well as thousands of others who had deserted the sport because it had become dull and predictable, motor racing will always owe a mighty debt to Lewis Hamilton. Now let's return to his thrilling debut season and first appearance at Silverstone in front of 85,000 of his adoring home fans at the British Grand Prix...

CHAPTER 14

SILVER LINING

L ewis Hamilton would only realise the full impact of his extraordinary success on the world at large during a warm sunny afternoon in the Northamptonshire countryside at the start of July 2007. The heavens had been opening without relief for what had been a rain-soaked summer, but his return to Britain even brought an end to the mini-monsoon, or so it seemed. The sun shone brightly and everywhere you looked around Silverstone there were smiles.

And why not? The conquering hero was returning home after his exploits in north America. He had left as a minor name, but was returning world famous as the latest member of the celebrity club. It was amazing how a few heady weeks in Canada and the States had transformed his status. Lewis knew he had 'made it' when he appeared pitside after the race and was approached by the man whose crown as the world's most famous sportsman he was now confidently tipped to one day take. Even the king of bling, the comeback kid himself, appeared a mite nervous as he smiled and warmly shook Lewis' hand. David Beckham had certainly met and become friends with bigger worldwide names, but he had probably not come across one so ordinary, 'normal' and humble. His wife Victoria also seemed caught up in the magnetism of the day's star attraction, shaking Lewis' hand as if he were a long-lost friend.

After commiserating with him briefly on his third place finish in the race that day, the couple headed away into the late afternoon sun, but only after telling Lewis that he was always welcome to pop in, should he ever be 'passing through' Los Angeles. It did not go unnoticed that they had deliberately sought out the new star of motor racing, especially as they were actually at the circuit as guests of Honda and former British glory boy Jenson Button, not Lewis and McLaren! Still, even the high-flyers at Honda didn't seem to mind too much – it was, after all, Hamilton's big day. For it was Lewis that the record crowds of the weekend had come to see and he was bringing in the readies that ultimately, if indirectly, paid their wages.

David Beckham said that he thought Lewis was 'brilliant, a star and definite champion in the making' and admitted he had enjoyed the day: 'The atmosphere is breathtaking. It's different to a soccer stadium where fans sit in a very compact space.' And Posh gave her congratulations to Lewis on his win in America, saying he had 'helped prepare the ground' for their imminent move to LA, and admitted the whole day had been 'sexy': 'It was music to the ears and the eyes! To be on the grid just minutes before the race starts, to see those polished cars and the guys get ready – and then hear the noise as they start their engines...'

'Commiserations'... the Beckhams offered Lewis their sympathy – that was another puzzling, ethereal aspect to contemplate as the trucks were loaded and the Formula One circus moved out of Silverstone that Sunday afternoon. Just nine races into his top-level career, and nine podium finishes that had left him 12 points ahead of his nearest rival in the Drivers' Championship, a third place in a debut British Grand Prix was being viewed as failure. The BBC's Andrew Benson summed up the sighs of disappointment that could almost be heard throughout Britain after Lewis trailed in behind Raikkonen and Alonso: 'He denied it, but it looks as if the British Grand Prix opened up the first tiny cracks in the phenomenon that is Lewis Hamilton.'

The *Guardian*'s Alan Henry took a sympathetic line as he considered Lewis' admittedly rather lacklustre performance, proclaiming: 'The Silverstone race reminded the Formula One community of how relatively inexperienced Hamilton is. It was only his ninth grand prix and it was understandable if he were to make the wrong choice when it came to detailed car set-up.' *The Times*' Edward Gorman was much more severe: 'At Silverstone, it was more evident than hitherto the penalty that Hamilton can pay for his lack of experience,' and suggesting Lewis was suffering because of his activities away from the track:

'Hamilton has begun to look tired and perhaps McLaren should rethink his off-track schedule to give him every chance of producing the goods on the track.

'Promotional events for sponsors – sponsors whose logos already cover his driving suit and his car – seem hard to justify, given the historic nature of the prize at stake. Hamilton may also need to reconsider whether mingling with pop stars between races is the best way to preserve his energy for the battles ahead.'

The *Sun* also zoomed in on his off-track, albeit in a less censorious way, with a picture of a Page 3 girl to set off its back page story about Lewis and these nudge-nudge, wink-wink words: 'The reason behind Lewis Hamilton's pit-stop boobs at Silverstone may have been exposed last night – Nicole Baker's 32DD bumpers. Lewis, 22, blamed a couple of errors on his disappointing third place finish in the British Grand Prix. But we can reveal that Nicole's bodywork was the last thing the Formula One ace clapped eyes on before the race. The *Sun* Page Three Idol contestant was represent-ing Lewis as his pit girl when she caught his eye.'

The coverage in the press summed up the level of expectation that now travelled with Lewis Hamilton, the superstar. After Silverstone, he explained in a little more detail just how surprised, and caught unawares, he had been with the massive fan base he now had. He was becoming more in-demand off the track, being snapped out and about with singers and models. And on top of this, past and present drivers now queued up to praise him, as well as team bosses, with Sir Frank Williams describing him as 'superhuman'. This all led Lewis to say: 'It is still a very difficult experience to get used to – I don't believe I have got used to it. It's good that it's always fresh, always new and always exciting for me, and I hope that continues but it has been tough. As for the good things I hear from people like Sir Frank Williams, and all the people in the Formula One world, it's overwhelming.

'When I came into the sport, I came here to do a solid job. There's been a lot of pressure on from day one, but there's not been that many negative comments so I have been able to keep all this positive energy. It's definitely comforting to hear such nice things but having my world turned upside down... I'm very lucky I have good balance and a sense of awareness to get on with my life.'

Traditionally, Britain is a nation that loves to build up its heroes... then knock 'em down with equal fervour. Was that to be Lewis' fate? Some pundits now openly claimed this was the end of the road for the wonderboy's season, that it would all be downhill now. It seemed a harsh, destructive thought process, maybe even based on envy and jealousy. Let's rewind a few days and examine more closely how Lewis coped with his first British Grand Prix in Formula One...

In the build-up to the race it became clear that Lewis was carrying the hopes of a nation on his muscular shoulders. Day after day the newspapers were packed with stories about how he could win on his Formula One debut at Silverstone and items about how he was coping with the new pressures of stardom. Twenty-four hours before he was due to set up camp for the race weekend, he admitted his life had changed dramatically with his newfound fame: 'On Sunday night I was invited to the Princess Diana party (after the memorial concert at Wembley in her honour) but I didn't get back in time. Then I could have gone to the after-party but I was too tired, so I had dinner and went off to bed.

'Then on Monday I was playing golf in Woking and on the ninth tee I got a call saying P. Diddy has invited you to a special dinner. There was me, Pharrell [Williams] and Natasha [Bedingfield], we got in Pharrell's car and took that to an after-party thing. Pharrell got out first and I got out second and, just being a gentleman, seriously, I gave Natasha my hand and helped her out. Then somebody says something and next minute it's all over the place, and I don't even know the woman!'

He said he was coping well with the new stresses of fame and that he was relishing the idea of the race: 'Without a doubt, the British Grand Prix will be the biggest race of the year for me, as it's my debut home race. It is going to be another new experience, and I expect the atmosphere will be incredible. I cannot wait to race in front of my home fans.'

He asked his growing army of fans to be patient, but promised he would do his best to ensure a home victory. 'To win at this race would be immense, but we have to be realistic with our expectations,' he said. 'This is one race out of 17, and as with all the grands prix, I will do my best to win for the fans. But the most important thing for them is to enjoy the whole weekend, whatever the result will be.'

Lewis also went on to explain a little more about how he kept his feet on the ground; how he managed to keep things in perspective and how that ability to turn away from the track helped him when the time came for him to return to it. In a revealing interview with the talented freelance motoring journalist and author Rory Ross in the *Daily Telegraph* magazine, he would say: 'I think I am a fairly normal guy. I love very much being a family man, not just my immediate family, but aunties and uncles and cousins. Every year we meet up to have a big weekend together. I spend a lot of time with my brother, who is my best friend. I gain a lot of energy from my family and friends. I find it hard to trust people, and so I really feel trust needs to be earned. I can count my friends on one hand and I keep those closest to me.

Down to business, he was now camped out at Silverstone on the Thursday before the race; taking a look around the track and enjoying the pre-race laughter with family and the McLaren backroom boys before the serious business began with practice the next day. Jenson Button was asked about that Thursday's hype and what he thought about 'Lewis-mania'. He said, 'He deserves the amount of hype he's been getting. He's doing a great job, leading the Championship by 14 points in his first season. You can say that he's in the best car, which he has been for most of the year. But he's still beating his team-mate, so yeah, he has done a great job and he deserves the credit.'

As if Lewis did not have enough to cope with, there was also the small problem of the so-called 'spy scandal' that rocked the world of Formula One as he prepared to make his home debut. Motor racing's governing body, the FIA, announced they were to launch an investigation into the allegations that Ferrari engineer Nigel Stepney leaked design secrets to McLaren's chief designer Mike Coughlan. There were suggestions that Lewis could be one of the chief losers if the allegations proved true. Bernie Ecclestone was at pains to say he would be unaffected, although McLaren could be docked points: 'It is nothing to do with the driver. They [FIA] have got to prove that if any information was given by Ferrari, it was used. And if it was used, did it affect in any way the performance of the car, and if so where? In that case, they could take away Constructors' points from the team. But there is no way it would affect the driver.'

McLaren chief, Ron Dennis, was quick to defend his team's reputation. 'Personal integrity is important to me,' he said, 'and my company's integrity is more important. This matter does not involve our Company. I am absolutely confident, with the passing of time, that you will see how McLaren's position is one that is reflective of our statements.

'The team has never to my knowledge used other people's intellectual property. That is the key message. We are co-operating with the FIA and with Ferrari, and I have complete confidence in the outcome.'

Clearly he was affected by the revelations – he would even break down in tears as he defended himself and his team. But Lewis refused to allow the matter to affect him... on the surface, at least: 'I have managed to escape all that because of all the events I've been doing this week. I don't even know when it came out. I saw it on the Internet when I had half an hour at home, and I spoke to Ron [Dennis] about it.

'I'm not worried about it. Obviously it's not great, but McLaren have got a huge team so I don't think it's going to make a huge difference. And I don't think it has affected anyone in the team; they are still all completely focused. I think it was a small mistake that someone's made, and I don't really know them very well.

'I don't believe it will have an impact [on the Drivers' title points]. I don't think it will come to that. I've been so busy that I haven't had time to think about it, and it doesn't impact on my job. At the end of the day I have to come here and race the car, and try and win.'

It was a confident outward display, dismissing the issue as if irrelevant. But was there the possibility that it may have adversely affected Lewis during the race? That, as the talk continued about possible points deductions right up until the Sunday, it filtered through even subconsciously? One McLaren insider believes so, and told me: 'The boy had just too much going on by the Sunday; he would have had to be superhuman to have contended with it all and emerge unscathed. He was carrying the hopes of the nation, was expected to be the saviour of Silverstone's future, was expected to win, was expected to see off the challenge of a fired-up Raikkonen and Alonso... And then was also expected to put out of his mind 100 per cent any fears he had about the spy scandal. A scandal, I might add, that brought even the usually "nothing-will-ruffle-me" Ron [Dennis] to tears.

'Surely it had to have some effect on a young man like Lewis with everything else that was going on too? The fact he could suffer from no doings of his own?'

In the event, McLaren would be cleared at a hearing in Paris a month later, but Lewis would hardly have been human had he not been subconsciously affected by the threat of losing points or being banned in his debut season because of the scandal. The dirt would be dragged up again on 13 September, when McLaren were fined $100m and thrown out of the constructors' championship after being found guilty of being in possession of confidential Ferrari documents. No matter, on the Friday morning Lewis got down to the first serious business of his Silverstone weekend – the first practice session in windy conditions, and it appeared that he had somehow put all the pressures of the week out of his mind. He stormed around the circuit in 1:21.100, the leader of the pack, with Raikkonen just a tenth of a second behind.

After that disappointing second session, Lewis remained upbeat, saying: 'It is great to be here at my first home grand prix and to be driving a Vodafone McLaren Mercedes Formula One car in front of all the British supporters. Today has been really positive, and the work we have done seems to be taking us in the right direction. The car feels great to drive around this track, which is one of my favourites, and I am looking forward to the rest of the weekend, where I expect us to remain strong. We gathered a lot of useful data, which we will look at overnight and then continue our work tomorrow.'

He admitted it had been a thrill to roar around Silverstone for the first time in a Formula One car, that he was living the dream and that the reality had turned out to be just as good as he had hoped. Smiling, he almost purred: 'It is an awesome track – it really has always been one of my favourites. Turn one, the first sector, the high-speed corners, the history of the circuit and seeing how many people were there today, especially in the last sector. That's great to see and there are obviously a lot of British flags. So it's very exciting for me.

'I think it is a very physical circuit but extremely technical as well. Especially when it is so windy it makes it even harder to tune the set-up, even more so than on other circuits I have experienced. I go into qualifying with quite a bit of confidence in my car and I really do feel that at least on a single lap we will be quicker than the Ferraris.'

Saturday dawned and Lewis again appeared off the pace, finishing fourth behind Raikkonen, Alonso and Massa – but then the miracle. It seems to me that he works best when the chips are down, when he has something to prove and the pressure is at its most intense. Then, his natural instincts kick in – and so it was in qualifying at Silverstone, when he magically stole pole off Raikkonen, taking the top position on the very last lap of the day. His time of 1m 19.997s sent the crowd, and the nation, into raptures as he beat Raikkonen by 0.102 seconds, with Alonso, who was fastest in the earlier sessions, third on the grid. Massa was fourth.

Lewis knew he had put himself into prime position to

win the British Grand Prix at the first attempt. He said: 'That was an intense qualifying session. The Ferraris were extremely quick, as was Fernando. I lost a bit of time on my first flying lap, so I really just had to pull it all out and thankfully I did a sweet job on that last lap. I really couldn't have done it without the team, who changed the tyres so quickly and got me out in time. I just can't wait for tomorrow now, and I am going to do the best job that I can. It is great to see so many supporters; today has been fantastic. I nearly lost my voice – when I came across the line I was screaming just as loud as all the fans. They gave me a real confidence boost with their support; they were great.

'Usually there are pockets of supporters, but here it's the whole grandstand. I can't believe how many people are here today and it's been fantastic.'

Raikkonen could not hide his disappointment at his own showing, but still issued an ominous warning that it would be a different story on race day: 'I made a mistake at the exit of the final corner on my second run in the last session. I finished up slightly on the grass and lost traction, which cost me a lot, cost me too much time. But it's not worth spending too long thinking about it. What's done is done and it cannot be changed. But it's not over yet. We will do our best to bring home the best result possible.'

Alonso also said he was confident he could still win the race despite starting third on the grid. 'I am quite happy with the car,' said the World Champion. 'Obviously I would rather be on pole position but third is the best I could do today and hopefully tomorrow it will pay off and we can overtake people in the race.

'On Friday we tried to work a little bit with the set-up in terms of race pace to understand how the tyres perform in the long runs. I was not too happy with the car and our pace did not look too good. But overnight we did some changes and I found a completely different car. There's no reason why I now cannot be competitive.'

Both men were to finish ahead of Lewis as their predictions of dominance proved far from idle boasts. Raikkonen, in particular, appeared to be throwing down the gauntlet to Lewis with a drive that was not far off perfection. After winning the first race in Australia at the start of the season, and the one in France, a week before Silverstone, the super Finn became the first driver to notch three wins in the current season.

Lewis was unable to turn his pole position into a win, losing the lead at the first round of pit stops. But his one consolation was that Raikkonen's win meant Alonso ate less into his Drivers' Championship lead. He was now on 70 points: 12 points ahead of his team-mate and 18 in front of Kimi, with Massa fourth, a further point behind. At least he held off Raikkonen as they both hit the first corner, but he was destined to finish third after that disastrous pit stop on Lap 16.

Lewis tried to accelerate off before the crew had finished refuelling; he believed the lollipop was being lifted. It sort of summed up his day: after that he seemed resigned to *not* winning, almost embarking on a rather flat damage limitation exercise. Perhaps it had got to him – the full weight of the day and the expectation of the crowd and the nation for a new hero to cheer them. Then there was the almost-bullying driving of Raikkonen and Alonso in his slipstream prior to the pit stop and the clear fact that Kimi was in a faster car.

In the circumstances damage limitation would not be a bad option. He retained his lead in the fight for the title and finished just one place behind Alonso, who was closest to him. It also meant his podium record as a rookie continued: only Michael Schumacher and Alonso now had more consecutive podium finishes. Schumacher had 19 for Ferrari in 2001-2, while Alonso had 15 for Renault in 2005–6. Lewis joined several drivers on nine and was in position to move ahead of them at the next race: the European Grand Prix on 22 July 2007 at Nürburgring in Germany.

Luck was certainly on his side with Massa's misfortune. Starting from the pit lane after an engine problem, he managed a superb fifth place and, given the quickness of the Ferrari cars that weekend, would surely have beaten Lewis into fourth and ended his run of podium finishes had he had a clear run. Alonso would later make a point of saying that Lewis was 'a lucky boy', that Massa would *definitely* have beaten him into third. Yet that luck was also tempered by the skill of Hamilton in saving his day when he made the mistake in the pits. Although he tried to drive off while refuelling continued, at least he had the skill and guile to hit the brakes and avoid an even worse situation. Remember how his karting pal Nico Rosberg, son of former Formula

One champion Keke Rosberg, had suffered when he had accelerated off with the fuel hose still in the petrol tank on the fortieth lap at Indianapolis on 17 June 2007? Lewis said: 'I selected first gear ready to go and thought I saw the lollipop move a little, so I let the clutch out, trying to anticipate it and I was too early.'

Raikkonen was first home in a time of 1:21:43.074 for his twelfth Formula One win of his career, 2.459 seconds ahead of Alonso and 39.373 seconds in front of Lewis. Hamilton saw the race like this: 'I got a good start and tried to pull out a gap, but Kimi was extremely quick. Unfortunately I made a mistake in the pit stop, which obviously lost me a few seconds of valuable time. I tried to push, but continued to struggle with the balance. I tried to drive round the issues, and although I was a bit more consistent towards the end, the team chose to save the engine for the Nürburgring and backed off for a safe third.

'I think that the tyre choice played a big role in the race, and ultimately starting with the harder tyre was not the best way to go as the softer tyre was clearly faster. However, we have come away with more points. I have to say the fans have been tremendous this weekend and the race would have been harder without their support.

'Being on pole I felt quite strongly that we could have had a better result. However, to come to your first home grand prix and still get a podium after difficulties on your second and last stint... I have to look on the bright side, you know. We still have nine podiums in a row and I don't know if that has ever been done, but I'm very happy with that.'

He gave a touching answer when asked if he was using a particular role model to stay cool at the head of the Championship race: 'I don't particularly have a role model anymore because I'm 22 years old. But my brother inspires me because he has always got a smile on his face, no matter what – I think you can learn a lot from that. As I always say, whatever he does – he can't play football like the rest of us, he can't play any type of sport like the rest of us – he still gives it 110 per cent even though it is that tough. I think you can learn so much from that, so he inspires me.'

Ron Dennis confirmed Lewis had been told to save revs and offered praise for Alonso: 'Fernando did a tremendous job making every effort to turn our short fuel middle stint into a race win. Ultimately, both he and Lewis were asked to turn their engines down in order to ensure that we had the best ability to attack again in Germany. We didn't quite have the pace, but both drivers did a great job, and we still went away with valuable points.'

Alonso was sanguine about losing out to Raikkonen: 'Yes, I think second place was the maximum today. I don't know, we lacked two or three tenths [of a second] a lap to Ferrari in the same conditions with the same fuel loads. All weekend it has been like that so there were no surprises in the race. I am happy with the second place.' The Spaniard led the race's middle stages after using a short-fill at his first refuelling stop to race ahead of both Lewis and Kimi, but the ploy did not pay off as Kimi capitalised on a longer second stint to get back in front.

Alonso gave the impression that he could not resist

niggling Lewis for surrendering his pole advantage when, after the race, he was asked how McLaren could have held off the Ferrari. Fernando said: 'The only way to win that race was to go from pole – and put some distance between us and the Ferraris.' He added 'Sooner or later I will close up the gap on him [Lewis]. Since Canada I have been faster than him. At Indianapolis I couldn't overtake him, and at Magny-Cours I had that gearbox problem. Here, we had a normal race and I finished over 30 seconds in front of him.

'There are favourable races coming up now, like Germany and Hungary, and the target is to finish ahead of Hamilton and reduce the gap. I must be on the podium always one step higher than him. It's good that the Championship leader has more difficulties on track, and especially here in England and after starting from pole.'

To his credit, Lewis continued to rise above the jibes and the sniping from some press who believed he was 'now being found out'. He also refused to blame anyone but himself for his showing at Silverstone: 'I need to step up my game, which I intend to do. I'm still learning. I have to find time in myself through experience.' He then admitted he had got it wrong with his choice of chassis: 'Obviously we worked extremely hard this weekend. I think we made a wrong decision, or I made a wrong decision with the set-up. I chose a different rear end to Fernando and I think it really caused me problems during the race. Even in qualifying we didn't really have the pace that I should have had, but it was too late by then to change the car. It's a good lesson.' That attitude only served to endear him even more to the pit crew, especially after it was suggested that the man holding the lollipop may have been more to blame for the pit problem.

Alan Henry, writing in the *Guardian*, compared Lewis to Michael Schumacher in his refusal to blame his crew: 'The British Grand Prix was yet another indicator of Hamilton's remarkable maturity and composure. At his first refuelling stop, where he lost 2.5sec, it seemed to some observers that the McLaren mechanic holding the "lollipop" to signal when Lewis should rejoin the race was a little hesitant in warning him not to move prematurely. This may have been a trick of the light but Hamilton willingly took responsibility for the glitch.

'Similarly, when it came to assuming responsibility for the handling imbalance which slowed his car he took full responsibility for its set-up configuration, further strengthening his relationship with his mechanics who work around the clock fettling his machine.'

Alan Henry was spot-on. I spoke to one of the McLaren team and he told me that, yes, they felt a real allegiance to Lewis and that his willingness to take the flak only strengthened that bond: 'It's been one hell of a week, what with the Ferrari situation and Silverstone. If the same thing had happened to Fernando in the pit stop, he would be spitting fire, looking for someone to blame. Lewis took it on the chin as usual and accepted full responsibility. That makes the guys respect him all the more, if that's possible. He's the star of the show but he acts like he's just one of the team.'

Yes, Lewis may have suffered a setback at Silverstone but there was a silver lining... he had strengthened his bond with his crew and proved he could still get among the points even on a relatively bad day at the office. Two days later he proved he was back in business by blowing away the cobwebs of despondency at Spa in Belgium, ahead of Raikkonen and Massa.

The Lewis Hamilton debut season story in Formula One was far from over... on the contrary there were many twists and turns to come as the boy from nowhere battled to put his Silverstone disappointment behind him. Before we move on to the next stage of the season, with races in Germany and Hungary, let's examine another often-debated subject as we've been focusing on the British leg of his debut campaign... So how does Lewis rate among other British motor racing legends, and the man he himself maintains was the No. 1 driver of the modern era, the great Michael Schumacher?

CHAPTER 15

SCHUEY AND THE BRIT PARADE

The build-up to Silverstone led to many pundits being drawn into a debate about just how good a Formula One driver Lewis was, and how good he might become. Also, how, in the grand scheme of things, he compared with former British greats such as Jackie Stewart, Nigel Mansell, Mike Hawthorn, James Hunt, Jim Clark and Graham and Damon Hill. And just how did he measure up against his hero, the seven-times World Champion Michael Schumacher, who chalked up a string of wins at Silverstone during his remarkable career?

Even before his debut Formula One win in Canada Lewis had already made a case to be bracketed among the greats. After finishing second in Monaco, he notched up a total of 38 points in the Driver's Championship. At the same stage in his career, triple World Champion Jackie Stewart had amassed 19 points, Nigel Mansell had none, James Hunt eight, Graham Hill none, while his son Damon had 12, Jim Clark had eight and the first British World Champion, Mike Hawthorn, had 10.

In international terms, he also compared favourably: Michael Schumacher at that stage had four points, Ayrton Senna five, Niki Lauda zero, Alain Prost three, Jack Brabham zero, Alain Prost three and Juan Manuel Fangio had accrued 26. As for the British Grand Prix itself, Lewis would have to wait for that first Formula One win as he finished third on his debut at Silverstone. In comparison, Stirling Moss claimed his maiden victory in the British Grand Prix at Aintree in 1955, beating the great Argentine Fangio by two-tenths of a second. Jackie Stewart won at Silverstone in 1969 by more than a lap after a fascinating duel with Austrian Jochen Rindt and James Hunt triumphed at Brands Hatch in 1976, only to later be disqualified. A first-corner accident seriously damaged his car and, fearing a riot if the British hero was excluded from his home grand prix, he was allowed to participate with his illegally mended car. The race eventually went to Niki Lauda, who finished runner-up.

In 1987 Nigel Mansell was finally taken to the hearts of the British public when he won a mighty duel with team-mate Nelson Piquet. Mansell had been leading, but was forced to pit with 20 laps remaining because of a wheel vibration. When he rejoined the fray he was 20 seconds adrift of the Brazilian, but brilliantly closed the gap in 15 laps and won, after overtaking Piquet at 200mph on Hangar Straight. Seven years later, Damon Hill ended a family jinx by winning at Silverstone. His father Graham never won his home race, but Damon put that right in 1994.

In terms of achievement and winning their first ever grand prix the comparison between Lewis Hamilton and his British predecessors makes interesting reading. Mike Hawthorn won the hearts of the public by becoming the first Brit ever to reach the top of the sport. He started racing in 1950 and made his grand prix debut in 1952. While Lewis would win his first grand prix in his sixth race, Hawthorn would do it in nine while driving for Ferrari in France in 1953. He went on to win three races in 45 starts, earning four poles and six fastest laps along the way. In 1958 he won the world title in the Ferrari 246 Dino, but was tragically killed in a road accident near Guildford on 22 January 1959 just 3 days short of his 30th birthday.

Graham Hill won his first grand prix at the thirty-third attempt. A late starter, he competed in his first F3 race at Brands Hatch in 1953 at the age of 24, Nonetheless, he went on to win the world title in 1962 and 1968. In 176 grands prix he won five times at Monaco among a total of 14 triumphs. He earned 13 poles and 10 fastest laps. Hill was also the only man ever to have won the Triple Crown: the World Championship, the Indianapolis 500 and the Le Mans 24 Hour race. Tragically, he died on 29 November 1975, aged 45, in a plane crash in foggy conditions over Arkley Golf Course in north London. Five members of the Embassy Hill team, including up-and-coming driver Tony Brise, were also killed in the accident.

Jim Clark was another great British driver, winning two

world crowns and also triumphing at the Indy 500. The Scot spent most of his career driving for Lotus and lifted those world titles in 1963 and 1965. He was the best driver of his era with 25 grand prix wins and 33 poles from 72 races. Yet he too would not outpace Lewis in terms of that first grand prix win – it took him 17 races. Jim died at Hockenheim, aged 32, on 17 April 1968 when his Lotus left the track and hit a tree in a Formula Two race.

John Surtees won the Formula One world title in 1964 with Ferrari and he notched up his first grand prix win in his twenty-seventh race. Surtees also won seven World Championships on two wheels between 1956 and 1960, and he remains the only person ever to have won World Championships on both two and four wheels. In 1996, he was inducted into the International Motorsports Hall of Fame. The Federation of International Motorcycling (FIM) honoured him as a Grand Prix Legend in 2003 and he is still involved in single-seater racing cars as the chairman of A1 Team Great Britain. His son Henry competes in the Formula BMW UK series for Carlin Motorsport.

Jackie Stewart would push Lewis close for that quickest Formula One win, triumphing in his eighth grand prix. The triple World Champion (1969, 1971 and 1973) started racing in 1960 and would go on to win 27 of his 99 grands prix. Like Lewis, he had also previously won the F3 crown and raced in Formula Two. Stewart's Formula One record with Tyrrell also included 17 poles and 15 fastest laps. He retired in 1973, but returned with his own racing team, Stewart Grand Prix.

James Hunt won his first grand prix at the thirtieth attempt. He raced in 92 grands prix and won 10 of them, getting the pole in 13 and setting the fastest lap in eight. Initially he raced for Lord Hesketh's independent team, winning the 1975 Dutch Grand Prix at Zandvoort. He then joined McLaren in 1976 as Emerson Fittipaldi's successor, taking the world crown after Niki Lauda was sidelined following his horrific accident at the Nürburgring. Hunt retired and became a much-loved TV commentator, only to die prematurely from a heart attack at the age of 45 on 15 June 1993.

Nigel Mansell was to take an incredible 72 Formula One races in which to record his first win – at Brands Hatch. Yet in 187 starts he eventually claimed 31 wins, 32 poles and 30 fastest laps. Another late starter in the sport, it would also take time for the British public to take him to their hearts. Seemingly over-confident, he was really a rather introverted man. Mansell did not make his Formula One debut for Lotus until 1980, retiring in the Austrian and Dutch grands prix and failing to qualify for the Italian. Yet his 31 grands prix successes placed him behind only arch rivals Alain Prost and Ayrton Senna in the all-time rankings when he finally quit Formula One after winning the world title for Williams in 1992. Only Michael Schumacher has since eclipsed Mansell's number of grands prix wins.

The year after he turned his back on Formula One, Mansell went on to win the Indycar title and ended his racing career in 1998, finishing fourteenth and eleventh in the British Touring Car Championship at Silverstone.

Damon Hill followed his famous father Graham into Formula One, becoming the first son of a World Champion to win the title himself after his brilliant season with Williams in 1996. He won his first grand prix at the thirteenth attempt (in Hungary) and took part in 116 altogether. Out of these, he won 22, took pole in 20 and set 19 fastest laps. He joined Brabham in 1992 for his debut season in Formula One and then moved to Williams after Mansell fell out with Frank Williams at the end of 1992 over money and the prospect of Frenchman Alain Prost joining the Renault-powered team. Williams was reported to have neglected to tell Mansell that Prost had signed for 1993 at only the second race of the 1992 season, in Mexico. Mansell consequently left to join the Newman/Haas CART team in 1993.

Initially Hill played second fiddle to Alain Prost and then Senna. When Senna was killed at Imola, his chance had inadvertently come and he duly won the title. He then joined the Arrows team and finally moved to Jordan, bringing the latter their first grand prix win at Spa in Belgium in 1998. This was his last Formula One win and he retired a year later.

Recent Brits worthy of mention are David Coulthard, Johnny Herbert, Jenson Button and Eddie Irvine. Coulthard was the last Brit to win at Silverstone in 1999 and 2000, and won his first grand prix at the twenty-first attempt. Johnny Herbert – who won at Silverstone in 1995 – won his first grand prix at the seventy-first attempt, while Jenson Button achieved it at the one hundred and thirteenth attempt: in

Hungary in August 2006. Eddie Irvine succeeded at the eighty-second attempt.

Moving on to Lewis' living Formula One idol... Until Hamilton's arrival Michael Schumacher's first full season in Formula One had been deemed the best ever in the sport, with the young German garnering 53 points for Benetton in 1992. He also finished third in the Driver's Championship. 'Schuey' won his first grand prix at the eighteenth attempt; he also competed in part of the previous season. Similarly to Lewis, the young Schumacher grew up in karting, progressing through junior Formula races before making his name in Formula One.

I asked Formula One insider Darren Simpson to provide a rundown and full analysis on how Lewis is shaping up against his hero. His findings make intriguing reading: in some ways the two men have obvious similarities, in others there are striking differences linked to their personalities. Darren told me: 'Lewis Hamilton's performances in his first season are no fluke, and his honesty in the fight is already putting him apart from the greats that have gone before him ... especially Michael Schumacher. Comparisons between Hamilton's arrival and the early impact of Schumacher are now commonplace, but while he may match Schuey's skills, Lewis might have something the seven-times World Champion did not possess: an ability to fight in a less aggressive way and still win the day.

'Schumacher resorted to daring tactics that often led to collisions. His impregnable self-belief made it impossible for him to contemplate defeat, thus legitimising in his mind the use of any conceivable tactic. And by thus intimidating opponents he spread fear.

'Hopefully Hamilton can keep his enemies at bay without them going into the scenery. He has already displayed aggression. Whether Hamilton would buckle in the face of Schumacher's invincibility is, alas, unlikely to ever be put to the test in the cauldron of the Formula One Championship racing. But he would nonetheless relish the challenge.

'When asked which driver from the past he would most like to face, Hamilton replied: "The likes of Juan Manuel Fangio, Alain Prost, Ayrton Senna and Michael Schumacher because I have always wanted to race against him." He then joked, "The year I get here, he bales out – I don't know if I had something to do with that!"

'In the unpredictable world of Formula One, where hype can make or break a driver's career (just ask Jenson Button), is Lewis Hamilton the next truly great driver or a one-hit wonder? It is true that in Formula One, those who go on to achieve a higher level of success announce their arrival with verve rather than a slow build-up. Cast your mind back to Schumacher's first year, qualifying seventh on the grid in Spa on his debut, and generally showing his legendary team-mate Nelson Piquet that there was a new kid on the block and he was not willing to sit patiently and wait for his turn.

'The late, great Ayrton Senna and four-times World Champion Alain Prost also destroyed the competition in their first season before moving on to destroy each other. Hamilton has all the makings of a hero worthy of joining that elite group. He is calm, consistent and hardworking but also has an edge about him – for example, the way he chooses to drive so close to the wall, allowing him to maintain incredible speed coming out of corners. And the kind of tactics that he used in the US Grand Prix against his team-mate Alonso when he used a centre-to-right and then slight right-back to centre defensive overtaking manoeuvre that just about avoided punishment.

'Schumacher, however, was far more precise and rehearsed, using the stealth of a Ninja. His machine-like qualities were developed on the track over many years. Whereas Hamilton, although apparently bursting on the scene as a freshman, had been carefully crafted and tuned from an early age by one man – Ron Dennis – to be a monster the minute he hit the circuit in a tried-and-tested car.

'Comparing the two on their first season results is a bit of a non-starter because Schumacher started in the days when cars were much less computerised with no active suspension and no traction control by way of example, whereas Hamilton has started at a time when cars are almost radio-controlled. This, however, does not detract from his courage, or the natural aggression that all champions are made of.

'But there is an inescapable fact: Hamilton drives like a karter. He loves the edge of the track and takes a late turn in to the hairpin and clips a late apex. In fact, his driving does reflect that of Schuey's early in the German's career. Lots of sharp turn-ins, lots of brake lock-ups... Hamilton displays his lairy youth by pushing himself and his car to the very limit. Driving so close to the wall is a breathtaking tactic while it pays off, but will he, one day, end up in the wall like Senna? Of course, we pray not...

'Only once was the wall a problem for Schumacher, when he broke his leg in 1999 at Silverstone. The rest of the time Schumacher's ruthless "win at any cost" mentality, which on occasions resulted in Formula One driving becoming a contact sport, was the problem. Ask Damon Hill.

'One person I spoke to recently suggested that Lewis, because of his brilliance, is already in danger of becoming boring. He said: "The problem is he may be so successful with metronomic consistency that he may decide never to display the genius driving talents he may already have, or that he may develop in the future. If he wasn't English, we'd be saying he's boring like Sampras."

'Well, if metronomic wins races, then what's the problem? It is a very effective way of winning, especially if all around are being anything but metronomic and throwing their cars off the track. Comparisons to Schumacher are difficult – we really need to see how Lewis is doing in, say five seasons, and then look at them both again. Hamilton has got off to a flying start but he hasn't been a title contender in 12 out of 14 seasons and hasn't turned second-rate teams into World Champions.

'When you compare drivers, you have to take into account everything. How they drove/performed in different cars, different circuits, different situations, against different opponents... Hamilton may be awesome but we have only usually seen him sit coolly at the front of the field. Calm under pressure, yes, but would he be able to handle the rain like Schuey? Can he scythe through the field after a blundered pit stop or spin, or should he have to start from the back of the grid due to some technical issue or rule breach; would he still climb the podium at the end?

'Schuey proved he could do all of those things. We'll only be able to properly compare Hamilton to Schumacher in 10 years' time once all factors can be taken into consideration. The only way to settle the Formula One argument (don't even think about a true contest in the Race of the Champions) would be for them to go head to head in cloned cars on the same track – the young tiger versus the old lion. Sparks would fly and and set the entire Formula One paddock alight.' Indeed they would, but for now the idea of that happening remains a pipe dream, even though Schuey admitted during the 2007 season that he would love to take on the new young whippersnapper.

Let's now return to that thrilling debut season. Our next stop, ironically enough, is a wet weekend in Germany, where Lewis is tested to the extreme, with all the obstacles Darren Simpson has already suggested he might one day have to face and overcome, including a spin and having to start from the back of the grid...

CHAPTER 16

THE FEUD WITH ALONSO

Fernando Alonso would do well to heed that old show-biz maxim: never work with children or animals. Children, in particular... they would soon suss him out. One day I was talking with friends about the ever-developing feud between the Spaniard and his team-mate Lewis Hamilton when my 9-year-old son Frankie piped up: 'He's a bit like Dick Dastardly off *Wacky Races*, isn't he, Dad?'

Well, yes, I suppose he has similar intentions to win at all costs. Only while Dastardly manages to conceal his intent, at least until the end of each cartoon show, Alonso seems unable to do so. After Lewis' debut Formula One win in Montreal his face and body seemed awash with signs of discontent. Yet perhaps he could not see he was getting better treatment than his rookie co-driver, or so many of the British public thought, for although in public Big Ron

Dennis always appeared keen to talk about the parity meted out between his two drivers, that could have been merely to stop the British public getting restless.

If there was parity why did Dennis seem to tell Lewis to back off in Monaco? And why was he always so keen to talk up Alonso's performances? The fact of the matter was that for 25 years Ron had always run a team based on parity. Now he had signed up a double World Champion on break-the-bank wages. If you'd splashed out all that cash on the World Champion, wouldn't you be happy if he won again – and Lewis was runner-up? Wouldn't that be the ideal scenario?

Dennis' problem appeared to stem from an unusual flaw in assessing Lewis Hamilton. In my view, he knew better than anyone that the boy was a winner, but what he hadn't guessed was that he could have been a winner in his first season otherwise, why bring in Alonso to lift the title in the first place? Also, he hadn't counted on Lewis' determination to grab Alonso's crown; again he knew his personality better than most, but he had been left gasping at Hamilton's fierce desire to become World Champion rather than No. 2.

But could Alonso's problem have been altogether more serious: was Lewis Hamilton the better driver? Certainly the results suggested so as we headed towards the European Grand Prix in the Nürburgring on 22 July 2007. The public also seemed to agree and maybe it was that, more than anything, riling Alonso. Despite the outstanding achievement of being double World Champion, he was not receiving the public acclaim such an achievement would normally bring.

Before the Nürburgring, one British Formula One fan, Ade Johnson, succinctly summed it up: 'After heated outbursts from the two-times Formula One World Champion Fernando Alonso, McLaren have a choice to make. Do you keep him in the team, despite the fact that he may disrupt what is going on and the fact that he appears to be off the pace he was setting in 2005 and 2006, or do you sack one of the foremost drivers around? In my view, McLaren would probably be better off dropping Alonso from the team.'

If we study Alonso's behaviour more deeply, though, perhaps he deserves some sympathy for there he was, the outsider in a British team... a British team with a new boy who was not only British, but British and brilliant. Also, Alonso himself was racing under a dark cloud for much of the season and certainly from the French Grand Prix onwards. That weekend, returning from the Magny-Cours circuit to his hotel the night before the race, his preparation was unhinged when he was told that one of his closest friends, Emmanuel Longobardi, had been killed in a helicopter accident.

Naturally, an all-consuming melancholy appears to have swept over him. Certainly, from that weekend on, he seems to have lost a little of his love for the magic of Formula One. When told of the tragic news he admitted he had been left 'a little bit frozen'. Later, he would tell the Spanish newspaper *Diario As* – 'I was with him on Saturday afternoon. I have known him for years and we had a good friendship. He got on a helicopter to go to his hotel and we lost him. This sort of thing makes you think about what we do and what really matters. Really, the most important thing is to wake up every morning and be healthy.'

No doubt about it, Fernando Alonso Díaz is a complex character. Born on 29 July 1981 in Oviedo, north-east Spain, he has what many describe as a typical Latin temperament in that he is emotional and does not believe in keeping things in. Yet away from the circuit he also has a liking for the quiet life: he lives in England, in Oxford, and owns another house near the tranquil shores of Lake Geneva in Switzerland.

He won his first World Driver's Championship in September 2005, at the age of 24 years and 58 days, breaking Emerson Fittipaldi's record of being the youngest Formula One Champion and he is the youngest Double Champion. Yet he can also be a master of manipulation when it suits him. The previous season he played out a brilliant mind games campaign against his Renault backers before the penultimate race of the season in Japan. He spoke to the press about how he felt that Renault were not backing him well enough in his battle with Michael Schumacher for the title, which had the desired effect as the French team moved heaven and earth to help him in Suzuka in October 2006.

Alonso appears to have worked similarly against Lewis Hamilton as the season unfolded, with gentle trickles of complaints about favouritism from the British team for its British driver, building up to more specific allegations and an admission to the *Daily Telegraph* that he has 'never felt totally comfortable'. All this ended in anger by the time of the Hungarian Grand Prix on 5 August 2007 when his tactics saw him thrown five places down the grade from the pole position he had seemingly won.

His apparent discontent began in the build-up to the US Grand Prix. Clearly, he was rankled by Lewis' win in Montreal. McLaren's build-up was dominated by his public sniping on his favourite outlet, Spanish radio, about favouritism within the team. When it came to the crunch Ron Dennis brought both drivers home safely to preserve the points, but from Alonso's point of view the problem was that Hamilton had won again.

Lewis was asked if he was surprised by Alonso's jibes about favouritism. He said: 'I find it strange because I feel that ever since he joined the team, the team have been extremely motivated to push us both towards winning. Ron and the other guys on the team have been working very hard to make sure we have equal opportunity. It's probably always going to be difficult in a business, but obviously I've got a great relationship with all the guys in the team because I've been with them since I was 13. At the end of the day when Fernando came into the team, they were extremely excited and, I feel, built a very good relationship with him. So I don't see why he would say that. But I guess because he is Spanish and I am English, he might feel that way, but I don't agree with it personally.'

And did he think that Alonso had been taken by surprise at his results? 'I doubt very much that he was expecting me to do as well as I have,' Lewis admitted. 'But I don't know whether that's why he would be saying what he's saying. But definitely coming into the team he's the two-times World Champion and he's not really been challenged – well, I think he has [had] some challenges in the past, but not really had probably someone as close as me. So it's a very difficult situation.'

Alonso was also asked the same question. He admitted: 'Yes, and no. I think we knew from the winter tests that Lewis was very quick and was very close times comparing with Pedro [de la Rosa] and me. So no big difference between the three drivers of the team. So, you know, why not fighting for victories, podiums and Championship? But on the other hand, I think it has been a surprise for me, and a surprise for everybody, to see him doing so well and leading the Championship at this point.'

After Indianapolis even McLaren chief executive Martin Whitmarsh seemed to feel obliged to comment on the growing feud: 'Do I expect more speculation about our guys and their relationship? Yes. The reality is both our guys are winners, they want to win. If Fernando got out of the car and said he was delighted Lewis beat him today, I would be very worried. It can be a distraction, but at the moment it isn't. But when you have two competitive drivers they're always going to have a go at each other,' he added.

Lewis did not appear to be letting all these distractions – or the possibility that McLaren might found guilty at the spy scandal tribunal the following week – get to him as he hurtled around the German track for the first practice session on the Friday morning, 20 July. Indeed, although he admitted to suffering from a flu bug, he posted the fastest speed, 1:32:515. But that easy-going atmosphere all changed just 24 hours later as Hamilton crashed with only 5 minutes of qualifying left.

The accident happened just after Lewis set the fastest split time through the first of the track's three sectors. As he peeled into Turn 8 – a 160mph, left-right flick – his right front wheel buckled, and his McLaren MP4-22 darted over the gravel trap and into the tyre wall. For a dreaded moment, the whole of Formula One went quiet, memories of Senna's tragedy coming to mind. Then, as medical crews sped to the scene, Hamilton moved his legs in the cockpit and started to slowly pull himself from the car. He collapsed beside it and it was only when he finally gave a thumbs-up as he was carried away on a stretcher, drip in arm and wearing a neck brace, that everyone breathed a huge sigh of relief.

Later it was revealed that a faulty air gun was to blame for the crash. It failed to correctly locate a wheel nut when Lewis pitted for a fresh set of soft-compound Bridgestones. When he reached Turn 8, the tyre was cut, either by the rim – which could have been damaged through contact with the suspension – or else by a brake duct.

Ron Dennis explained: 'Our telemetry shows that the deflation was absolutely instantaneous. We are analysing the air gun to see which bit failed, but we know for sure that the problem was caused by mechanical rather than human error.' After the Brit's accident the session was stopped and Alonso returned to the pits, only to learn that he too had a loose right-front wheel nut, fitted by the same air gun.

Interviewed later, Lewis managed to put a brave face on it, but the damage was done. Although he would deny it, he must surely have suffered trauma and certainly he was badly shaken up. His crash meant that he was relegated to tenth for the start of the race on the following day. Optimistically, he said, 'I'm absolutely fine and we will see later if I am able to race tomorrow. Everybody has been looking after me really well. We know what caused the accident and I'm just pleased that everything is OK and I really hope I can race tomorrow.'

He would make the date on the Sunday at the Nürburgring after being cleared in a final check-up by FIA doctor Gary Hartstein on the morning of the race. Looking back, it might have been better if he had used the day to rest up and avoid a race it would have taken a miracle to win, or even finish on the podium.

Alonso went on to win an action-packed European Grand Prix, 8.1 seconds ahead of Massa in second, with Mark Webber 57.5 seconds further back in third. For Lewis, it was the end of his podium finishes run as he finished ninth and out of the points. Fernando was just two points behind in the race for the Drivers' title. In slapstick conditions, his third win of the season put him right back in contention to retain his title. Rain had been predicted early in the 60-lap race but it came on the first lap and left the track like a skating rink. Lewis suffered more than most; by the first corner he roared to sixth place and fourth by the second, but was then hit with his first crisis of the day: a puncture.

The monsoon meant race officials red-flagged the event until conditions improved and the drivers returned behind the safety car. Lewis then took a gamble, pulling into the pits to take on dry tyres on Lap 7. But the risk did not pay off, and he slid off the track.

The spin left him with a bank of other competitors on the dirt at the side of the track. To his credit, he was the only one of the beached drivers to keep his engine running. When a crane eventually appeared on the scene and lifted him back on to the track, he could legitimately continue in the race. He then proved just how good he was by trading fastest laps with Massa as he climbed up to eighth by the fifty-third lap. But as the rain returned he needed to go back into the pit for wet tyres, a move which dropped him back behind the Renaults and out of the points.

For Hamilton this had been an extraordinary weekend, one he would admit had been 'good for learning': 'Yes, this was a new experience for me – I made a good start and was sixth, then fourth when the two BMWs went off, then I picked up a puncture. The team took advantage of this and fitted rain tyres, but it just got too slippery and I went off. I managed to keep the engine running and a crane was able to get me free – thank you, Nürburgring marshals!

'After the restart I pushed as much as I could to catch up, but when you are almost a lap down you really have to rely on other people's misfortune. I was able to get ninth in the end, but no points.'

To give him his due, Alonso had driven brilliantly to take maximum points – his overtaking of Massa on Lap 54 was sheer genius and daring; the Spaniard keeping his nerve as his own and the Brazilian's cars touched. Alonso, who previously admitted he loved nothing more than racing in the rain, said: 'It was so exciting to drive, and also to watch, I hope. The first three laps were unbelievable. It was so wet, we were aquaplaning everywhere; it was impossible. Then in the dry the Ferrari was a little bit quicker than us. At one point when I was second I was saying to myself it is not the right time to rain. I was happy with second, Lewis was out of the points – 8 were enough for me. But I like rain – no doubt, I am always quite happy to go and have some fun in it.'

Big Ron was in a buoyant mood: 'This was motor racing at its best. Fernando did a fantastic job demonstrating why he is a double World Champion. First of all, he kept the car on the road during the first downpour. From that moment both him and the team made all the right decisions. However, his second stint following the switch to dry tyres was hampered by a wing adjustment tool failing and as a result he struggled with understeer, but fortunately in his third stop we were able to properly adjust the wing, and from there his pace was fantastic.'

With that, it was on to Hungary... but not without another of Fernando's 'distractions' along the way. This time he was asked to contribute to a magazine's bid to help a charity. *F1 Racing* asked all 22 current Formula One drivers to sketch a picture of their team-mate. Lewis' doodle was a nondescript, but pleasant image of Alonso, while Fernando's work was altogether more pointed. He drew

Lewis in his McLaren leathers and on the right-hand collar he had written the word 'McLaren' and on the left the word 'Boy'. The magazine's executives seemed surprised. In an accompanying caption, they wrote: 'Notice the word "Boy" scrawled by Alonso on Lewis' shoulder...'

The teams started to arrive in Hungary on the Wednesday before a meeting that would explode the notion that Lewis and Fernando were friends rather than mere co-drivers and that the rivalry was purely a figment of a feverish press pack's imagination. By the time the trucks were loaded up on the Sunday night, it was clear that all was far from well in the McLaren camp. Some pundits were even questioning whether Ron Dennis was to blame for the fallout. Shouldn't he have been harder on both drivers and have told them in no uncertain terms that they worked for McLaren, not the other way round?

Upbeat, Lewis arrived at the site of the hot and dusty Hungaroring – the eleventh race out of 17 in what was becoming a thrilling season, thanks in no large part to the warring. Traditionally, it had been a tough circuit for drivers and they would later complain that it was virtually impossible to overtake and that grabbing pole was key to the whole weekend. Given what would happen, those were prophetic words: grim for Alonso, but delightful for Lewis in the final analysis.

The week before the race Lewis and McLaren received a considerable boost when the team was cleared by the FIA, Formula One's governing body, in Paris of any wrongdoing in the espionage affair. An extraordinary hearing of the 25-

strong World Motor Sports Council (WMSC), the sport's highest body, ruled there was no evidence that the British team had benefited from the confidential Ferrari documents found in the possession of their chief designer, Mike Coughlan. On leaving the hearing at the FIA headquarters at the Place de la Concorde, a relieved Ron Dennis said: 'The punishment fits the crime.'

If they had been found guilty, it was feared Lewis faced having points deducted. There was an unpleasant rider on the verdict: the FIA warned that if McLaren was found to have used the information passed to their suspended designer by Ferrari's Nigel Stepney they could still be thrown out of the 2007 season and also banned from the following year's Championship.

For most Formula One observers this was all hard talk for the public domain. In reality they felt McLaren had merely been given a slap on the wrist and that was the end of the matter. Ferrrari, however, refused to see it that way. Fuming, they vowed to appeal and to continue their demand for their chief rivals to be docked points.

But Lewis and McLaren did not believe it would come to that. The spring was back in their collective step as they planned their latest assault on the World Championship at the Hungaroring. However, their problems would not come from outside the camp that weekend; instead they stemmed from tensions within that had been brewing for months and would now boil over with disastrous consequences.

As he met the press on the Thursday ahead of the weekend Lewis smiled. He said: 'I feel quite positive going into the race. I'm still leading the Championship, which I find quite amusing, considering Germany was such a bad weekend.'

The circuit was notoriously difficult to predict. McLaren had won six of the 21 Hungarian Grands Prix to be staged there since the event was added to the Formula One timetable in 1986. Kimi Raikkonen had been their last driver to win there, in 2005, but he was one of five different drivers to have triumphed at the circuit in as many years. Rubens Barrichello (Ferrari) won in 2002, Fernando Alonso (Renault) in 2003, Michael Schumacher (Ferrari) in 2004, Raikkonen in 2005 and Jenson Button (Honda) in 2006. It was into this cauldron of uncertainty that Lewis Hamilton made his Formula One debut on the track, a weekend he would never forget.

In the first practice sessions he was fifth, then started to come to terms with the nuances of the track, moving up to third fastest by Friday afternoon. Memories of the Nürburgring came flashing back as he ended the session by spinning off the track into the gravel. He said afterwards: 'Today went smoothly, apart from my spin towards the end of the second session, which meant that I missed out on my last run, so maybe I could have gone faster. The spin happened as I was catching [Sakon] Yamamoto on a flying lap and I was probably a little too fast going into the corner. Despite this we were able to make some positive steps and I am confident with our performance so far at this track.'

By the end of the third practice session on the Saturday morning Massa was fastest, with Alonso second and Lewis third. But it was to be the calm before a massive storm for

Vodafone McLaren Mercedes. The qualifying session that followed brought out the worst in Lewis and Alonso as both battled for the pole that would likely set either of them up for victory on the Sunday. And yes, in the interests of fair play, it must be said that Lewis was equally out of order on that extraordinary Saturday in Hungary.

At the end of the day, on paper at least, it appeared Alonso had edged out Lewis for pole position. But he had used dubious tactics to do so, remaining in the pits for too long as Lewis sat behind him. It meant he had enough time to complete his final lap, and claim pole, but thwarted his team-mate. Lewis arrived at the start line only to be greeted by the chequered flag. It was a mean trick, but it seemed to have paid off. He would most likely have outpaced Alonso on his final race around the track but it was Alonso who would now start in that all-important pole position. Or so it seemed...

Ron Dennis tried to defuse the tension by explaining that it had been Alonso's turn to benefit from 'the longer fuel burn' and saying Lewis should have slowed to allow him to pass him in the final qualifying session. Dennis said, 'He charged off. That was somewhat disappointing and caused some tensions on the pit wall.'

Certainly, Lewis' part in the events of the day was far from innocent; indeed he should have allowed Alonso past. Later he would admit this, saying: 'I made a mistake – I apologise, it won't happen again.' But equally Alonso should not have blocked him from his final attempt, and, turning to Ron Dennis: if he was quick enough to condemn his rookie driver for his wrong-doing, shouldn't he have been just as swift to deride his double World Champion who surely should have known better? Instead Dennis seemingly tried to defend the indefensible: 'He is under the control of that engineer; he determined when he goes. That's the sequence and if you think that was a deliberate thing, then you can think what you want.'

Yet Big Ron had not been slow in rushing to the engineer to give him a public blasting for not getting Alonso out on the track. Ron did admit, 'There are definite pressures in the team; we make no secret of that – they are very competitive. They both want to win and we are doing our very hardest to balance these pressures. We were part of a process that didn't work today.' Alonso himself claimed: 'The team held me back.'

The incident caused a temporary disagreement between Dennis and the young man he had trained for nine years to become a champion. In a heated post-qualifying exchange Dennis ended up throwing his headphones at the pitwall. Most pundits believed this was over his anger at Alonso impeding Lewis in the pit lane but subsequent analysis of the radio traffic between Dennis and his protégé came up with a different reason. Lewis, angered by the delay, had blamed it on Dennis, allegedly screaming over the team radio: 'Don't ever f****** do that to me again!' Dennis reportedly hit back, blasting: 'Don't ever f****** speak to me like that!' Lewis is said to have responded: 'Go f****** swivel!'

It was an undignified exchange that did neither any favours. Indeed, Dennis later denied it had taken place. But surely Dennis owed it to his team to come down heavily on Alonso for impeding his fellow driver? Instead, it was, rather unusually, left to the FIA to dispense justice. They ruled later on the Saturday, deciding Alonso should forfeit five places on the starting grid – he would start sixth with Lewis on pole. And for not bringing their own justice to the farce, McLaren would also be punished: they would not be allowed to score Constructors' points.

Alonso, Hamilton and Dennis were summoned to an FIA inquiry to explain why the Spaniard had stopped for such a long time. 'The commissioners decided that Alonso unnecessarily interfered with another competitor, Hamilton, and he has been penalised five places on the grid,' said an FIA statement. 'The attitude of the team at the end of qualification was considered prejudicial to the interests of competition and motor racing.'

But Lewis refused to criticise his opponent outright for his delaying tactics: 'There's not really much to say – you saw what happened.' When asked by how long he had missed out on what should have been his final lap, however, he said pointedly: 'About the same amount of time I was held up in the pit stop.'

The morning of the race McLaren released a statement that appeared to put the blame for the delay fairly onto Alonso's shoulders – a U-turn that again did not sit well with Ron Dennis' comments and attitude the previous afternoon. The statement said: 'The process of managing two such exceptional talents as Fernando and Lewis is made more challenging by having a race-winning car. We do not believe that the findings of the stewards and the severe penalty imposed on the team are appropriate. Every effort was made [in qualifying] by the team to maintain our policy of equality. However, in the heat of the battle there are occasions when the competitive nature of drivers sees them deviate from the agreed procedures.

'During this intense and frenetic period of qualifying, decisions are necessarily made in seconds to enable the drivers and the team to position their cars on the track at the optimal moment. We agree with the stewards that, when the team decided to hold Fernando for 20 seconds, there were four cars on the circuit. However, we do not understand the relevance of this observation as the team needed to estimate where all the remaining cars would be in the final minutes of the session.

'Similarly the team does not agree with the statement of the stewards that the 20-second hold caused Lewis to be impeded. Tensions were undeniably high and the problem at Fernando's first stop, the desire to enter a clear track and concerns expressed following the fitting of used tyres undoubtedly contributed to the delay in Fernando's ultimate departure.

'We do not believe that the findings of the stewards and the severe penalty imposed on the team are appropriate, and that our strenuous efforts to maintain the spirit of fair play and equality within the team have been misunderstood.'

Lewis meted out his own punishment to Alonso in the race: leading from start to finish and keeping the brilliant Kimi Raikkonen also at bay. The win meant that he increased his Championship lead over Alonso to seven points. So what looked like a nightmare scenario after final qualifying the previous day ended on a high note.

Lewis said, 'It's been an eventful weekend and quite emotional for all the team. With all the drama that has gone on over the weekend, it would have been easy to lose focus. It's been a bit of a downer for the team.

'It was one of the hardest races I've ever had. Just to get the points is so important for me and for the morale of the team. We've shown that we can beat anyone. We made a really good step forward with a great package but we still weren't sure whether we'd be ahead of the Ferraris. You could see in the race they had great pace. Kimi was on my tail for quite a long time – he drove a great race. But I know how to win races.'

But Alonso wasn't about to be silenced. He finished a credible fourth in the race. Asked if he would be at McLaren in three years' time, he said, enigmatically: 'I don't know.'

Kevin Garside of the *Daily Telegraph* summed up Alonso's comments in this way: 'Cleverly he has allowed questions about his future to hang in the air. If McLaren team principal Ron Dennis believes there is a real danger of the champion slipping through his fingers with two years of a contract still to run, might he not be minded to meet Alonso's demands from the team over the course of a tight run-in?'

When it was his turn to face the cameras, Dennis himself looked like an exhausted man. He seemed full of self-pity and could hardly drum up the enthusiasm to pay tribute to

Lewis for keeping his cool and winning the race. Without a hint of humour, he said: 'When you go through the period in your life from 30 to 60 you often get the expression "character building" but I can tell you at 60 years old I don't need my character building any more. This is extremely challenging for me, emotional and stressful. I'm not alone in having to carry that burden but nevertheless, we will continue to function as a grand prix team with specific values and if anybody does not want to be part of those values, irrespective of where they sit in the organisation, ultimately they all have a choice.'

Alonso did indeed have a choice, as did Lewis, as Ron wearily conceded: 'We have two drivers who are contracted for several years into the future. We will respect our part of that bargain and that part of the situation – we hope that the drivers respect theirs, because that's what a contract is about.'

However, Alonso swiftly responded with: 'What happened was something new for the team. Hamilton not listening, disobeying them, was something they hadn't experienced and I guess they wanted to make him see that. But anyway, in the next race I guess everything will be back to normal and we will both try to win the race.'

Remarkable comments. As much as the race wins it illustrated the power, belief and authority young Lewis Hamilton had brought to the sport. No doubt about it: his personality and success had opened Formula One up to the masses.

On the Monday after Hungary he revealed: 'He [Alonso]

doesn't seem to be speaking to me, so I don't know if he has a problem. If I walk in and I see him then I will speak to him, but I won't go looking for him and make him feel better.' Lewis added, 'I hope he still speaks to me. I'm easy to get on with, I don't hold grudges over anyone – but if he doesn't want to speak to me, then that's for him to decide. But I'm open.'

He also revealed that he and Big Ron were back in business: 'We sat down, we spoke about it and came to a mutual understanding and started with a clean slate. The relationship we have is very strong and something like this is not going to come between us, so we will move on to bigger and better things.'

As the summer break began, the surrogate father and his boy would live to fight another day, but how many more would Alonso survive? He himself could have done with a father figure such as Dennis to help him out. As Lewis took a deserved rest before the next race in Turkey, his double World Champion team-mate was looking more and more like the outsider.

CHAPTER 17

FROZEN OUT BY THE ICEMAN

As the final stages of one of the most significant, exciting and fascinating seasons of F1 ever loomed, one thing was clear above all else: that Lewis Hamilton – whether he won the title or not – had certainly come up with the greatest debut season ever in the championship's history, defying his critics and doubters. Everyone wanted a piece of the McLaren maestro: In September 2007, I was talking to an F1 insider who told me that it wasn't only Fernando Alonso who had been offered a way out of McLaren.

Every week during the summer a new angle on the Spaniard's future did the rounds: he might return to Renault, who were desperate to lure him back; he might take a year off; or he might see out his contract! But what of the future for Lewis? It is undeniable that both he and

Anthony had felt peeved at certain stages of the season by the controversy over Alonso – and what many viewed as the apparent lack of backing from Big Ron. But my trusty insider told me there had been another, behind-the-scenes development: that Ferrari had 'through sources' offered the Hamilton camp just over £20million to drive for them for three seasons if he tired of the rivalry which had been in the background – and increasingly in the foreground – since Melbourne in March. All he had to do was let them know...

Lewis at Ferrari: it was an unlikely scenario, but the very fact that it was even being discussed, albeit in whispers, would have done little to ease the pressure Ron Dennis might have felt as the season headed towards its climax. It had been arguably his greatest season for his protégé had come through as he had predicted; but the media's constant speculation over internal politics – and the effects of the dispute with Ferrari – had in some respects taken the shine off.

On the eve of the Turkish Grand Prix, Lewis added to the whispers about his future by admitting he was tempted to quit Britain and begin a new life in Switzerland. He said: 'Every time I go to London, cameras appear from God knows where. I'm definitely contemplating living outside the UK. I've always dreamt of living in London but it's becoming more and more difficult. My whole recent holiday [in the south of France] was in the papers. I was trying to relax, but I couldn't swim, because the cameras were waiting to get 10,000 for the pictures.

'If I can't live a normal life and enjoy my life without

being spread across the tabloids... we'll just have to wait and see. It's down to the media, really.'

In a way they weren't the wisest or best thought-out comments – and they brought the first real criticisms of the boy wonder from the press. The news boys saw it like this: OK, if you want to join Michael Schumacher and Kimi Raikkonen in Switzerland, go ahead and do it. But don't start moaning if you can't take the heat in the kitchen. Ever mindful of the public interest, the press always upbraid a 'star' for complaining of being photographed or asked questions, maintaining that press attention is part of the territory of being a public face.

On that holiday in the south of France, Lewis had been pictured in the sea with Sara Ojjeh, whose father is McLaren co-owner Mansour Ojjeh. Lewis denied that he was in a relationship with her, and it was this aspect of the press coverage that particularly infuriated him. He said 18-year-old Sara was engaged, eager to add: 'I'm not a playboy. I'm supposed to be dating one of the Ojjehs. I'm not. And the other day I went to the cinema with my best friend, his fiancee and my friend Mohammed. They said I was seeing this girl, meaning I'm cheating on someone else. I'm not. It's not me.'

But the talk of him and Sara did finally bring into the open what many had suspected for a while: that he had broken up with long-term girlfriend Jodia Ma. A spokesman for Lewis said: 'Yes, he has split with her, but they remain close.' My contacts in Hong Kong, however, said Jodia was devastated by the break-up. 'She was inconsolable – she really thought they had a future together,' my source said. The previous month, Lewis had been spotted with pop singer Natasha Bedingfield in the back of a taxi, and he was also linked with the glamour model and Celebrity Big Brother contestant Danielle Lloyd, though Lewis denied any romantic involvement with either.

It all seemed to be closing in on the boy who had taken motor racing by storm as he made his way to East Istanbul for the twelfth grand prix of the season. On the Thursday before the race, under a sweltering sun, Lewis took an early look at the 3.34-mile circuit designed by architect, Hermann Tilke – the man behind the new F1 tracks of Malaysia, Bahrain and China. He admitted he liked what he saw and felt he could increase his seven-point lead over Alonso in the title race. His optimism was founded upon his superb drive in GP2 in 2006. Back then, Lewis had sped through the field at the Istanbul Park circuit to take second spot with some daredevil manoeuvring through the field after he had spun off on the second lap.

Tellingly, at the press conference to mark the Turkish Grand Prix of 2007, Felipe Massa would also admit to a personal affection for the track. He said: 'It's a special circuit for me. I got my first pole position, my first victory here last year so it's very special. I like the place, the country, the city and especially the track. It's very challenging for the drivers, so hopefully I can have a great result here on Sunday.'

The brilliant young Brazilian had notched up his first ever GP win at the circuit 12 months earlier – and a similar result on the Sunday in 2007 would ensure him rocketing into contention for the drivers' championship. He was a dark horse who could yet upset the McLaren applecart of Hamilton and Alonso. A good friend of Lewis, probably his best on the F1 circuit, the Brazilian was in a similar boat: he too was seen as the number two to an established star (in his case Raikkonen), and he too was good enough to eclipse his more decorated senior co-driver, having possibly the best mentor in the business, Michael Schumacher. By the Sunday night in Istanbul, Lewis would know for certain that he had more to worry about than just Alonso as Massa once again lived up to expectations.

Talking of Alonso, Massa was asked at the same press conference if he thought the 'problems between the McLaren drivers' would ultimately prove beneficial to himself and Raikkonen at Ferrari. He said: 'I hope so. But I don't know. Actually we don't know exactly what's happened. We know that there's a big competition between the McLaren drivers but there's also a big competition between every driver.'

Certainly, prior to pitching up in Istanbul, McLaren had – at the insistence of Big Ron – held clear-the-air talks between Alonso and Lewis. Lewis explained: 'We're extremely competitive. We can't be best friends. I apologised, he apologised and we said, "Let's just get it over with and get on with the rest of the year." After the last race, everything looked as bad as it could be. But we were not in a war. We met up had a good conversation. Lewis said it was a really constructive meeting, with each driver saying they had no problems with each other.

When questioned about the meeting, Alonso simply said: 'I have a long-term contract with McLaren and at the moment I am not in any hurry to move.'

Ron did not attend the meeting, but said: 'We are leading both championships, and it's tough to have such a difficult situation – albeit such a positive one – but we just have to do our job. The important thing is everybody recognised what their contribution was to the difficult circumstances we had after Hungary and were committed not to allow those things to repeat themselves in the future races.'

The McLaren owner is the first to admit they are very competitive individuals, and their competitiveness will stay on the circuit. From the team perspective he was adamant they would rigidly stick to equality, crossing any further bridges as and when issues arose.

David Coulthard, who spent nine seasons at McLaren, said in public that he was convinced if anyone could keep the two at arm's length it was Ron Dennis, saying: 'Ron is as experienced as any team principal to deal with what happened. I remember watching Prost and Senna, and I am sure [feuds] happened with other McLaren drivers before them.'

Triple World Champion Niki Lauda criticised Alonso. Lauda told BBC Radio 5 Live that the Spaniard should 'stop complaining', adding: 'Alonso is using all kinds of excuses. Instead of complaining, moaning and bitching, Alonso needs to concentrate on driving quicker. My worry is if he continues to find the reasons somewhere else, and not in his right foot, he will lose out because Hamilton is doing a perfect job, simply concentrating on his driving and he's quick. It's what Alonso should do.'

In the first practice session in Istanbul a day later, Alonso seemed to have heeded those words. He finished third, a place ahead of Lewis, but behind Massa and the early pace setter Raikkonen. Lewis had brilliantly turned the tables in the steaming heat at the end of the second session that afternoon – finishing first ahead of Raikkonen, with Massa third fastest and Alonso down to sixth. Alonso said: 'Track conditions were a bit of a problem today. It was slippery this morning when we first went out, but we made some adjustments and that seemed to make a difference. Then this afternoon it was very windy, and we started to suffer a little from understeer, which we will work on overnight. We are definitely among the strongest here, but as expected it will be a tough fight with Kimi and Felipe.'

Lewis added: 'I am happy with the performance so far, especially as the conditions today were not ideal. It is a shame that both sessions were interrupted, however the work we did was productive and we made some good progress.'

The boy from Stevenage was still out in front at the end of practice on Saturday morning, with Massa, Raikkonen and Alonso behind him in that order. Lewis set the fastest time of 1:27.325, bettering Massa by 0.041 seconds and a tenth faster than Kimi Raikkonen, with Alonso four-tenths off the blistering pace.

By the end of qualifying that day, Massa, ominously, had pinched a possible pole off Lewis, clocking the best time of 1:27.329. Lewis would take second place on the grid after notching up a time of 1:27.373, with Raikkonen and Alonso behind him, respectively in third and fourth.

Significantly, during qualifying McLaren had given Lewis and Alonso each a separate pit area, with a separate pit crew, no doubt to avoid any repetition of the problems they had encountered in Hungary when Alonso's car had blocked Lewis in the pit lane. Lewis said: 'They decided it was easier to have two pit crews and it worked out quite well.' That was one of the benefits of racing at a modern circuit like Istanbul – the pit lane and garages are much larger than at older tracks, and thus able to accommodate two sets of mechanics per team if required.

After securing pole, Massa said: 'We have had many tight qualifying sessions this year. Pole position is always difficult. I was pretty competitive for the whole weekend. The balance was right and I just managed to put it together when it counted. It is very difficult to be concentrated and do everything right. We have a good race car but they [McLaren] are going to be very competitive as well.'

Lewis was also pleased with his own outcome: 'Going into qualifying I knew I had the pace. I was quite confident. It is also obviously a positive to finish ahead of Fernando. He has been improving all the way through.' Though he seemed to lack pace at the beginning, Lewis was very pleased that he was able to pull out the pace and get ahead of Alonso. His GP2 experience and knowing where and how to overtake definitely eased his mind. 'At some tracks you cannot get close enough, here is still tricky but it is possible. We have a good car, a good strategy and I am looking forward to having a good race with these guys.' As ever, Lewis credited his hardworking team, some of whom hadn't taken holidays in order to prepare the car for Turkey.

Alonso was also content despite ending up fourth on the grid. He said: 'I am happy with my qualifying today. I made the decision to go out on prime Bridgestone Potenzas for my final flying lap, but I do not think this was the wrong decision. That final lap was actually quite stressful as our planned timing was for me to run at the very end of the session with only a couple of seconds left to cross the line.'

He got stuck in traffic, so these factors probably played a role in not improving his lap time and coming fourth. No doubt he was also in a fairly good mood after receiving a special gift from Big Ron in recognition of the fact that the race in Istanbul represented his one hundredth grand prix. The Spaniard was given a huge metal scale-model of a 1954 Mercedes-Benz F1 car and smiled when Dennis quipped: 'It's something heavy for him to throw at us!'

The joking stopped the following morning. The tension was as high as the scorching trackside temperatures. By the end of a tough day for Lewis his lead in the drivers' championship over Alonso had been cut to five points. Lewis had driven well and was on course for a creditable third place finish before suffering a puncture on lap 43, with 15 remaining. It was a cruel blow, especially as Alonso soared past him as he led the McLaren back to the pits for remedial work on his right-front tyre. Credit where it's due: Lewis did well to get the car back to the pits as he still had a third of a lap to manoeuvre it around the circuit.

Unfortunately, there was also damage to the aerodynamics at the front of the McLaren. He finished fifth, with Alonso third and Nicklaus Heidfeld fourth.

Alonso trailed in 26.1 seconds behind race winner Massa, who led a Ferrari 1-2 ahead of Kimi Raikkonen – the Iceman finishing 2.2 seconds behind. It was the Brazilian's third win of the season and fifth overall of his career, and it moved him up to third in the standings, ahead of Raikkonen. The result also meant Ferrari had closed the McLaren lead in the constructors' championship to 11 points.

Lewis was defiant afterwards, saying: 'It was just a little bit of a problem. You always have setbacks. I'm still leading by five points. It is not over.' Of the tyre blow-out, he added: 'The team was fantastic all weekend. We had the pace of the Ferraris, but when you are behind you lose a little bit of downforce; we were just matching them for most of the race. I saw some bits fly off the tyre and then it just blew on braking into Turn Nine. It was lucky that I didn't put the car in the gravel and managed to control it back to the pits, as this meant that in the end I only lost two places.'

Norbert Haug, Mercedes Motorsport Director, made a telling point in his analysis of the race: 'It's a shame – the puncture on Lewis' car prevented him from finishing on the podium...however, Lewis saved four important points under very difficult conditions. These points could be decisive in the end.'

Alonso had got lucky – and he knew it. Until the tyre problem, Lewis had once again outdriven the double world champion. Alonso admitted: 'To be overtaken by two cars and find yourself sixth going into the first corner is not great. You just have to wait for the miracle and it only happened with Hamilton. If someone had told me on lap two that I would have been on the podium it would not have been easy to believe.'

It was later pointed out to Lewis that Nigel Mansell's world championship bid was wrecked by a blown tyre in Adelaide in 1986 – with his rival Alain Prost benefiting as Alonso had in Turkey. Did that send shivers down Lewis' spine? No, not at all...'I don't remember it; I was only one at the time!'

The boy who had taken F1 by storm in his debut season was made of sterner stuff. He still had much to do if he were to crown his remarkable feats by winning the championship, but he had changed dramatically as a person. He was tougher and stronger and now had begun to believe himself he could triumph – after months of playing down his hopes. He knew he had his work cut out after Alonso reduced his points deficit from five to three after the Spaniard finished first and Lewis second in Monza. And he admitted he was wary of the final three races in Japan, China and Brazil as he had never raced at any of those circuits, but still felt he could do it, saying: 'It is possible it could go to the final race in Brazil, but I hope not. I hope I get it earlier but at the end of the day it doesn't matter if I get the title earlier or the last race.'

Despite his apparent coolness, as Lewis Hamilton headed for Japan for the first of the three defining final races of his first season in F1, the pressure was on big-time. The race at the Fuji Speedway would take place on Sunday, 30 September and, tellingly, by that date it would have been almost two months since he last won a grand prix. On 5 August, Lewis had triumphed in Hungary after losing his way at the Nurburgring in the European GP a fortnight earlier, when he could only claim ninth position. After Hungary, he would finish fifth in Turkey, second in Monza and fourth in Belgium.

His back was certainly up against the wall as he arrived in Japan on the Thursday prior to the race. What had looked like – and should have been – a victory procession as the season moved towards its thrilling climax had become a fidgety, nervy run-in with our boy looking a different driver to the man who had made such an exhilarating start to his first season, achieving nine consecutive podium positions in his first nine races.

So what was going wrong – why did the odds-on favourite lose out in the final furlongs of the race?

And, to be honest, 'What went wrong?' is a fair question to ask of Lewis. Just what happened to that rampaging and conquering we saw earlier in the season? Why did he suddenly start to make mistakes and errors of judgment? It could have been a combination of inexperience, too much pressure finally getting too him, exhaustion from fighting on several other fronts during a busy season... and of course there was the Spygate scandal, which must have weighed heavy on his shoulders. Eventually it all got too much. He started making mistakes and taking chances he normally would not have done.

The Spygate scandal had refused to go away and was a major worry for Hamilton. Although in public he would dismiss the issue as irrelevant, I am told that in private he feared it might put an almighty spoke in his dream of winning the drivers' title: that he could actually end up being kicked out. Lewis would attend the extraordinary meeting of the World Motor Sport Council in Paris on 13 September.

He and Alonso would be spared the ultimate punishment, but the team was hit by a record fine, approaching £50million, and was also stripped of all its points from the season's Constructors' championship.

Dennis was so angry and upset he could hardly speak after the meeting, but, with tears in his eyes, he said: 'The most important thing is we go motor racing this weekend, the rest of the season and every season. However, I do not accept we deserve to be penalised or our reputation damaged in this way. Today's evidence given to the FIA by our drivers, engineers and staff clearly demonstrated we did not use any leaked information to gain a competitive advantage. We have never denied the information from Ferrari was in the personal possession of one of our employees. The issue is: Was this information used by McLaren? This is not the case and has not been proven today.'

Yet for all the end-of-term problems and letdowns, in Japan at least Lewis Hamilton would turn back the clock and somehow put everything else to one side and concentrate on his driving. As we have noted before in this book, in the face of real adversity, Lewis has few rivals. It would bring him his fourth and final victory of a sensational debut season and, at least on paper, make wrapping up the drivers' title in the final two races a mere formality.

Lewis had earned his fifth pole position of the year at Mount Fuji on the Saturday afternoon, with a time of 1:25.368. Alonso would line up behind him on the grid after posting a time of 1:25.438, Raikkonen was third in 1:25.516 and Massa fourth in 1:25.765. Yes, the big four were all present and correct as the clock ticked towards the final three races of the season – and at the Press conference after qualifying Lewis was, inevitably, in the chirpiest mood he had been in since Hungary. He said: 'That was a good session for us. The whole weekend has started off a little bit better than others, and we had a good car today. It was quite tricky conditions out there – we don't know the track in the wet, and we didn't get any practice this morning, and we're very fortunate that the team did a fantastic job getting the set-up right. When you're out there, you don't really know where you are – you really only have your pit board, you don't know how much time is left. They timed it to perfection, and I made best use of it.'

Lewis was asked if the pressure was now getting to him. He said: 'I'm quite relaxed to be honest. With the way this weekend has gone, hopefully I'll be more relaxed. I'm in the perfect position - obviously I have these two [Alonso and Raikkonen] breathing down my neck - but I'm not really too bothered. Again I just feel that the car's underneath me this weekend. Tomorrow's going to be a tough battle - we're all so close in time. The key is going to be to get down to the first corner, and leaving them.'

The key would also be the weather and how the teams dealt with the rain. Lewis would leave many old petrol heads amazed at how cool he could be under such immense pressure. It was also his first win in the wet and he certainly earned the congratulations and compliments after hardly making a mistake in two hours of tough driving conditions. Raikkonen and Massa were put at an immediate disadvantage after beginning the race on intermediate tyres rather than the 'extreme' wets ordered by race director Charlie Whiting. The Ferrari team was told to pit after just two laps and Raikkonen and Massa were always up against it from then onwards. Then Alonso crashed out on lap 41 after losing control in the rain and smashing into the wall as he approached Turn Six. He said: 'I aquaplaned and all of a sudden the car was in the wall.'

Heikki Kovalainen finished runner-up to Hamilton, trailing in 8.377 secs behind him with Raikkonen third. Both Lewis and Fernando could have learned something to their advantage if they had watched video of the race – and seen how Massa helped Raikkonen. While the McLaren team-mates had continued to fight for supremacy, with 10 laps to go Felipe had come into the pit lane to allow Kimi to take third place from him. When you consider the championship title would eventually be decided by just one point, that was certainly a decisive as well as a magnanimous gesture by the Brazilian.

Afterwards Lewis was delighted with his first win in almost two months. He admitted it had not been easy driving in the rain, saying: 'There were so many times I thought they should stop it. Sometimes it was very tricky, at others it was drying and therefore easier to drive. I was so eager to get going when we were running initially behind the safety car. After that I wasn't particularly feeling any pressure from Fernando, I was saving fuel and driving away. Then we made our stops, I came out, and heard that he'd been off and had got back on and was now several places behind.

'They were awful conditions and, in the end, I was fortunate I was able to finish the race after my collision [on lap 34] with Robert Kubica. When you're behind, and especially in those conditions, it is the responsibility of the car behind to be extra careful and I felt that it was a risk Robert needn't have taken. Still, I got through it and was able to see it home. It felt like the longest race of my life, what with the safety car coming on twice and the conditions being so difficult, but I'm ecstatic to get the victory.'

The result meant Hamilton led Alonso by 12 points and Raikkonen by 17 – with only 20 left on the board in the two remaining races in China and Brazil. It would take a sensational downturn for him to lose the title now. I would argue that his performance in Japan in the face of true adversity and pressure was on a par with his debut win in Montreal earlier in the season. Yet that moment of pure unadulterated brilliance would be matched at the other end of the scale by a display of wretched disappointment in the next race at China, one that would result in Lewis not finishing an F1 GP for the first time.

Lewis had arrived in Shanghai bubbling with confidence:

this was it, the moment when he would wrap up the world title. It was what he had worked for all those years; his moment of true destiny. He had the title in the bag, now he just needed to turn up, collect it and take it home.

All went to script on the Saturday: he duly notched up his sixth pole of the season with a time of 1:35.908. The order behind him was Raikkonen, Massa and Alonso, but it did not really seem to matter. Victory and the crown was his, as he said directly after qualifying that day: 'A very good qualifying for me and the team. I was pretty confident that we were fast enough to beat the Ferraris here; however, they looked very strong, particularly in the fast corners. I made my first run on the prime Bridgestone Potenza compound, which had been the more consistent tyre so far, however we opted to do the final run with the option tyres and luckily this worked perfectly for us. I still expect a very close fight for tomorrow's race but we have a strong strategy and I am optimistic.'

Yet, despite trailing by 17 points in the title shootout, Raikkonen also sounded surprisingly confident – although few picked up on that at the time, as most pundits believed he was well out of contention. Kimi said: 'Of course it would have been better to be on pole, but all things considered, second place is a good result, especially when you consider the uncertainty about how much fuel those in the top ten are running. I am very happy with the handling of the car this weekend: we have shown we are competitive in all conditions and I think that should be the same even if it rains, which seems likely. I am confident. We know the situation in the championship is pretty compromised but I will do my all to try and win.'

Indeed he would, and 24 hours later the Iceman had done just that, chalking up his fifth victory of the season and his 14th in total, at the same time also cutting Hamilton's advantage over him to just seven points after the British boy failed to finish after spinning off on lap 30. Alonso was second – and now just four points behind Lewis – with Massa third. It was a scenario few had expected. Lewis had dominated the opening wet stages of the race but stayed out too long and wore out his wet weather tyres. He also made the mistake of trying to race with Kimi Raikkonen when there was no need if he had looked at the race from a strategic point of view. That placed added pressure on tyres that were already struggling and on lap 30 he paid a heavy price. With his right rear tyre coming apart, he tried to make it into the pits but slid off the track into the gravel for his first retirement of the season; the marshals rendered helpless as they tried to push him back on to the circuit.

Afterwards McLaren boss Martin Whitmarsh tried to deflect any criticism away from Lewis, saying: 'In hindsight we left him out a lap too long. His tyres were very worn. It was our decision. We were getting weather information all the time. We didn't want to come in and get on the wrong tyre.'

Lewis tried to hide his disappointment by pointing out there was still one race left in which to complete the job. He also made it obvious that his team was not to blame for the setback: 'The tyres were finished. These sort of things happen. I'm sorry for the team, but I can still do it, don't worry. We were having a great race, and we didn't know whether it was going to rain again or not. The tyres were getting worse and worse and I came into the pits and it was like ice. I just lost the rear. I couldn't do anything about it. I couldn't see in my mirrors, they were completely dirty. I could just feel there was no grip. I was coming in that lap. It's unfortunate, but there is still one more race to go. When I got out of the car I was just gutted because I hadn't made a mistake all year, and to do it coming into the pits... Well, it's not something I normally do.'

Finally, there were some ominous words from Kimi Raikkonen before the teams decamped from China. He said: 'I am very happy! It is a really great result for me and the whole team, who did a truly excellent job. We needed this win and we got it. At the start of the race, I had a lot of understeer but then the situation improved. I was one of the last to switch to dry tyres but this was a help as after a little while the rain began to fall again. Even after the second stop I had a bit of understeer, but as before, the situation improved in the final stages. I knew Alonso was very quick but I was in full control of the situation. The car overall was working well both in the wet and in the dry. Last week in Fuji, we were unlucky but today things went right for us. We have had yet another example that in this sport anything can happen. The situation in the drivers' title is still difficult, but I will try everything to win in Brazil, even if the final outcome does not just depend on what we do. It should be a great battle, very hard to predict and interesting.'

It was all of those things and more, as what had been one of the greatest seasons ever in F1 finally reached its brilliant climax in Brazil on 21 October 2007. Lewis Hamilton had been the catalyst for the dramatic upturn in the sport's fortunes and he would be there for the final act in the drama. But, unfortunately and sadly, he would not have the final say: no, that would go to the man who had sneaked up and pinched the title at the last minute. Kimi Raikkonen, the self-effacing, witty, slightly off-the-wall master driver from Finland.

Lewis' arrival in Sao Paulo also marked an important chapter in his own life; it was almost as if he himself had come full circle. Here he was, in the hometown of the man whose legendary skills had so inspired Lewis. The man who had provided the blueprint for Lewis' own career – the late, great Ayrton Senna. Lewis had phoned ahead to ask Ayrton's sister Viviane if she would mind if he visited his hero's grave. She told him it was fine with her, but the visit would not go ahead. Lewis decided it would be inappropriate after his management warned him it would be a magnet for the paparazzi.

He told Viviane he would make the trip to the Morumbi cemetery another day, when the time was right. Viviane, 50, who had met Lewis, told the Sun: 'He called me to ask if it was OK for him to visit Ayrton's grave. We were flattered he is thinking of Ayrton during such a big event. I know Ayrton would approve of Lewis very much, both his character and driving. If he were here today, he would tell Lewis, "Be yourself because you are a champion – whether it is this time or the next time." Lewis reminds me of Ayrton in many ways. Ayrton never wanted to be a great man and he didn't care about money or fame. He just wanted to win and be the best, the same as Lewis. Lewis has a big, big talent and he is fighting to fulfil it. He is also a simple person like Ayrton was. He has great integrity and simplicity – I saw that in his eyes when I met him. It's difficult to compare them as drivers but I can see Lewis has an extraordinary talent.'

That talent would not be enough to lift the title at the Interlagos circuit that weekend. Lewis would fall short at the final hurdle. He had finished second in qualifying behind Massa on the Saturday, with Raikkonen third and Alonso fourth but could not replicate that result in the race itself. Asked how he was feeling the night before the biggest day of his life, Lewis said: 'I'm really buzzing. I'm really excited, I feel very relaxed, the car feels great underneath me, I love the circuit and the food here in Brazil is great and the fans are extremely enthusiastic. I've seen quite a few British flags out there, so I'm very very happy to see that we've got some support.'

Lewis would finish a disappointing seventh at Interlagos as Kimi Raikkonen, the rank outsider still at the start of the race, won an astonishing victory and with it his first F1 drivers' title. Massa was second with Alonso third. That result meant Kimi finished the campaign on 110 points… just one ahead of Lewis and Alonso (Lewis earning the runners-up spot by virtue of having secured more second places over the season than the Spaniard).

Lewis had struggled from the start of the race. He was

slow away on the grid with a belligerent Raikkonen easing past him before the first corner. A brilliant braking maneouvre by the Finn allowed Alonso through on the inside and it was now that Lewis' inexperience and judgment were called into question. He was fourth behind Massa, Raikkonen and Alonso but he appeared to have a rush of blood to the head as he tried to take on Alonso on the outside, only to end up going off the track. He rejoined in eighth place but hit more problems on lap eight when his car slowed with gearbox electronics problems. Lewis managed to rejoin the fray, but had lost 40 seconds and was 18th in the field. It was a disastrous setback – and one from which he could not recover although credit to him for weaving his way up to a final seventh.

Raikkonen took the lead of the race, and the championship, after Massa let him through during the second pit-stop period. Lewis Hamilton's wonderful, brave debut season adventure was coming to an unsatisfying end. But failure? Let's get real here... he had beaten his team-mate, the double world champion, to the title runners-up spot and was only a point away from the title itself in a fantastic debut season. And what a season it had been... largely because of the exploits of the boy from Stevenage. There was even a final dramatic twist when it emerged race officials were investigating the fuel used by Williams and BMW Sauber, whose cars filled fourth, fifth and sixth places. If they had been disqualified Lewis would have won the crown, but admitted he did not want to lift it by default. But the day belonged to Raikkonen, who said: 'We were not in the strongest position but we always believed that we could recover and do a better job. Even with the hard times everyone was sticking together and we did not give up. We worked hard and improved the situation.' He had won six races over the campaign and deserved his title. Even Alonso managed a little grace in defeat, admitting: 'You have ups and downs and you have better moments and worse moments. It is not a secret I had difficulties with the team. We tried to work together as well as we could and we finished third in the drivers' championship. I have great memories from this season.'

As did Lewis – he surely had the greatest memories of all. The boy who had seemingly come from nowhere to the very top had certainly provided us with the greatest memories. And he was dignified in the bitter disappointment, hurt and heartbreak he was feeling after Interlagos. Lewis said: 'Obviously I am pretty disappointed with the result today, having led for so much of the season and then not to win the championship. However I have to put the result into perspective, this is only my first year in Formula 1 and overall it has just been phenomenal. I am still very young and have plenty more years in me to achieve my dream of becoming world champion.'

'Phenomenal' – that just about summed up Lewis Hamilton's debut season. But what he would achieve in the next season would have both fans and critics struggling for superlatives.

CHAPTER 18

DOWN TO THE WIRE

They have a term for it in rock music: DSAS. Difficult Second Album Syndrome. In what would be a defining second season for Lewis Hamilton, it was clear that early on – as he struggled to match the brilliance of his debut campaign – he was suffering the motor racing equivalent of the rock musician's common dilemma.

While most everything he touched had seemed to turn to gold that first season, now it was an uphill struggle as he made surprising driver errors and the McLaren was found wanting.

Yet he would steady himself, the car would gradually but dramatically improve, and he would banish the cobwebs and emerge, at the tender age of 23, as the youngest ever champion in Formula One history. After the Brazilian GP at the start of November 2008, Lewis Hamilton would have answered all the questions asked of him and confounded the critics who claimed he was 'a bottler'. They had pointed to the previous season when he had allowed Kimi Raikkonen to overwhelm his massive points lead with just two races remaining. This time he would show a conviction, a resolute bravery and a coolness that mocked claims that he could not cope with pressure when it came down to it.

This time he would be so cool and calm, so convinced history was on his side and that he was the best, he would leave it right to the final corner before making the move that would bring the title he always believed was his birthright.

And he would book himself a place in the history books as one of the nation's greatest sporting heroes. A true legend: the boy who had proved dreams can come true if you truly believe.

But, yes, he would also put us all through the grinder as he left it late – so very, very, late – to claim the crown he deserved in that thrilling, nail-biting, last-gasp triumph over his only rival left standing, the brilliant Brazilian Felipe Massa.

So how did the boy who would be champion do the business? Let's remind ourselves with a look again at the season that Lewis Hamilton and his loyal followers will never forget.

It all got off to a blistering start in the heat and glitter of the opening race of the season in Melbourne on Sunday March 16. Lewis romped home and provided the perfect riposte to those who claimed he had 'lost it' after his anti-climatic showings at the back end of the last campaign.

He and the McLaren team pitched up on the Monday

before the race and he was beaming at the Press conference on Thursday. He was delighted the new season had finally arrived as it gave him a chance to blow away the cobwebs that had lingered since his disappointing finale at the end of the previous one.

He said: 'I think there is less pressure than last year. Last year there was a huge build-up and just a lot of weight hanging on my shoulders really because no one really knew if I was going to do well or what. And neither did I really.

'It is a slightly different feeling. I think I know even more now knowing what a season feels like. I am even hungrier and I feel even more determined and just more excited about racing. It has been too long a break.'

Now living in Switzerland, Lewis explained how he had unwound in that break between the old season and the new.

He said: 'I left Switzerland and stopped in Hong Kong for two days and just did a little bit of shopping just to break up the trip.

'Then I went to Brisbane for a day as my trainer is from there, so we spent a day with his family. We had a barbecue and just relaxed and then I went to the Gold Coast.'

By Saturday afternoon Lewis had claimed pole. He posted an impressive time of 1:26.714 with Robert Kubica behind him in the BMW-Sauber and his new team-mate Heikki Kovalainen third on the grid. Raikkonen would start 16th after failing to complete his qualifying session because of a fuel pump problem.

In the race itself on the Sunday Lewis kept his cool and emerged triumphant, dominating from start to finish to hold off the challenge of Nick Heidfeld's BMW Sauber and his old karting friend Nico Rosberg's Williams.

It was the fifth win of Lewis' meteoric career in a race that saw the safety car appear three times, the first on the opening lap.

Only seven cars finished with Raikkonen just getting in the points with his 8th place – even though he was forced out with engine trouble with five laps remaining. Massa also suffered from engine failure.

Lewis was delighted with the win and hugged Rosberg on the podium. He said, 'I feel fantastic. What a dream start to the season and my championship challenge.'

Next up was Sepang for the Malaysian GP, and disappointment for Lewis as Raikkonen kick-started his title defence. The Finn proved a worthy winner with Lewis finishing fifth after a slow pit stop and difficulties getting past the back markers.

Lewis said: 'I got a really good start and was pretty happy as we jumped four positions from ninth to fifth. We were in a good position for a shot at third place at least, but then I had the problem in my first pit stop which lost me a lot of time. So I did the best job I could.'

The heat was on and it was red hot when they arrived at Bahrain for the next race in the calendar. It would prove another frustrating weekend's work culminating in a 13th place finish on Sunday, April 6. After Raikkonen's triumph in Sepang, we would now witness the first stirrings of what would become a sustained and intense challenge from his Ferrari team-mate, Massa.

The little Brazilian repeated his feats in 2007 by winning the race once more... while poor Lewis would endure more agony.

In Friday's second practice session he suffered a crash into a wall that left us all praying for his safety. A tough little nut, he emerged unscathed and the following day, using a spare chassis, won third place on the grid behind Kubica, who had grabbed his first ever pole, and Massa.

In the race, Lewis got off to a terrible start as he struggled to fire up the McLaren, quickly dropping from third to 10th, and then gave himself no chance by hitting arch rival Alonso's Renault while trying to pass on the second lap. That bump knocked off Lewis' front wing and he had to head into the pits for repairs at the end of the lap.

His race became a battle to grab a single point and even that was out of reach. Massa won and Raikkonen was runner-up, a result that meant Lewis lost the championship lead. He was now five points behind the Finn.

Lewis was not his usual ebullient self as he and father Anthony made a hasty exit from the kingdom. He said: 'I am really disappointed and feel like I let the team down today. The whole weekend has not been ideal starting with the accident on Friday, but I will keep my chin up and bounce back at the next race.'

There now followed a three-week break as the campaign moved on from Australia, the Far East and the Middle East to Europe.

At the end of April, Lewis headed for the Spanish GP and Barcelona, one of his favourite stamping grounds. A year previous he had finished second to Massa in Catalonia and proclaimed 'I am living my dream' as he led the title race.

After the setback in Bahrain Lewis would go some way to silencing his doubters, but it was apparent to all that he was racing Raikkonen and Massa in a slower car.

And after finishing third in Barcelona to the now inevitable Ferrari one-two – with Raikkonen victorious – Lewis even publicly questioned the form of the McLaren car in contrast to the Ferrari.

He said: 'There are areas where we definitely need to improve. But it's comforting to know that we are relatively close to Ferrari.'

On May 5, Lewis did well to keep pace with Massa and the Ferrari in Turkey, his second place to the Brazilian leaving them tied at the top of the standings. It was Massa's third consecutive win in Istanbul while Raikonnen finished third. Lewis was pleased with the result and that the strategy of a three-stop race and starting on harder compound tyres had paid off. He said, 'I'm thrilled. We knew it would be very tough to challenge the Ferraris and that a finish in the top five would have been good. But the balance of car on those tyres was good and I was able to keep pushing and pushing.

'The three stop thing won't happen anywhere else. We knew that even if we had got the pole we weren't really going to be in line for the win, so for me this was probably the best race I've ever done. In the end you ask yourself and the team whether you could have done a better job and I strongly feel that I couldn't have. I feel we did a fantastic job as a team to bring it home second and to split the Ferraris.'

If that was 'fantastic' it was a struggle to find a suitable adjective to describe Lewis' showing in the next race on the calendar, in Monte Carlo. 'Supreme' perhaps? Maybe 'superlative' or 'stunning'? Yes, it was that good. As the rain poured down, our boy became the first Englishman to win the Monaco GP since 1969 and, more importantly, in his battle to win the world crown, he had ended Ferrari's four-race winning streak. Kubica was runner-up in the BMW and Massa was third while Raikkonen was out of the points after he endued a shocking day, failing to score after ploughing into the back of Adrian Sutil.

Early on Lewis had also suffered an accident as he ran into the barriers – but he came back superbly to become only the fifth Briton to win in Monaco. His sixth race win in 23 starts put him up on a pedestal with Stirling Moss, Graham Hill, Jackie Stewart and David Coulthard.

Afterwards he told his pit crew on the McLaren radio, 'I apologise for hitting the barrier, but we made up for it. Now let's go party!'

Later he elaborated upon his remarkable race, admitting, 'I am absolutely over the moon. To win here in Monaco is the highlight of my career. It was a very eventful race. I started well and immediately overtook Kimi, and also saw a chance to attack Felipe, but then the rain got heavier and visibility worsened.

'At the Tabac corner, there was a lot of water on the track, and suddenly I had oversteer and hit the barrier. It was just a slight touch, but the tyre was damaged and I had to pit. Fortunately, the first safety car period helped me to close the gap to the front. We changed our strategy, and I had to make only one more stop.'

But the brilliance of Monaco would not be recaptured in Montreal a fortnight later as Lewis messed up big-time in the Canadian GP, crashing into Raikkonen in the the pit lane and allowing Kubica to catch him in the standings. The BMW Sauber star registered his first F1 victory in style.

For Lewis, it was a race best forgotten. The smash wrecked his suspension, forcing him out of the contest, and also cost Kimi any hopes of glory, the back of the Ferrari being too damaged to continue. A perplexed looking Hamilton said, 'I don't know really what happened. I was comfortably in the lead. It was looking like it was going to be an easy win. We came in. It wasn't a great stop. I saw the guys in front of me, and all of sudden they'd stopped. I saw the red light but, by the time I saw it, it was too late to stop. I apologise to Kimi if I took him out, but that sort of thing happens sometimes.'

There would be no happy ending at the next race in France either as Lewis never recovered from a 10-position grid penalty, a hangover from that crash into the back of Kimi in Montreal. Lewis finished 10th after starting 13th on the grid and out of the points, at what was being billed as the last F1 race ever at Magny-Cours. His mood was hardly helped by the one-two finish of race winner Massa and runner-up Raikkonen, or indeed Kubica's fifth place. The Brazilian's third win of the season took him back to the top of the standings above Kubica and Kimi and left Lewis trailing in fourth place.

Lewis had also been hit with a drive-through penalty for

gaining an advantage over Sebastian Vettel on the opening lap, undoing all the good work that had seen him zoom up to ninth in 12 laps.

Lewis claimed he was hard done by, saying, 'I believe I was ahead on the outside. I couldn't turn in on the guy from the outside line, I lost the back-end on the marbles and went over the kerb. I continued and I don't believe I overtook by going over the kerb, I don't particularly see that as cheating, but rules are rules.'

He said he still felt confident he could win the world crown, 'I've been out of the points for three races now, but there are still ten to go. I'm ten points behind, but I'm determined to bounce back at Silverstone in front of my home crowd.'

And, in true Roy of the Rovers style, our boy would do just that, winning the British GP with a brilliant performance in another rain-lashed race, lapping all but two of the other finishers and regaining the joint lead in the drivers' championship with Massa and Raikkonen, after the Brazilian finished 13th and the Finn fourth.

Lewis drove brilliantly from start to finish. He made a great start when he beat Kimi Raikkonen and Mark Webber to the first corner and almost overtook his team-mate Heikki Kovalainen, who started from pole.

Hamilton eventually did go past the Finn and dominated in a style reminiscent of Michael Schumacher, as if on a one-man mission to entertain and conquer in front of an adoring home-crowd.

Aftewards he said: 'It is definitely by far the best victory

I've ever had. It was one of the toughest races I've ever done. As I was driving I was thinking, if I win this it will definitely be the best race I've ever won. That's not only because of its history, but also because I'm on home ground and I drove one of my best races ever.

'I was coming to the last lap and I could see the crowd beginning to stand up and I was just praying, praying and praying: keep it on the track, just finish and you could not imagine that we're going inside. I wanted to push. I just wanted to get it round.'

The win was all the more remarkable given the way Lewis stayed cool, calm and composed in dreadful wet conditions while those around him panicked. He added, 'It was so extreme out there, probably as extreme in some cases as Fuji last year. Obviously there wasn't as much rain. I was having big problems with my visor, I couldn't see a thing, especially the right side. I was having to lift my visor up and clean it every lap, especially when it was starting to rain.'

And the joy didn't end there: Lewis would travel to Hockenheim buoyed by his debut British win and notch up his first back-to-back victories of what was becoming a thrilling season as he, Massa, Raikkonen and Kubica battled for supremacy. The German GP triumph would consolidate his position at the top of the drivers' standings – opening up a four-point lead.

Lewis had dominated the field in qualifying and continued that fine form in the race itself and romped home ahead of runner-up Nelson Piquet Jnr, with Massa trailing in third and Raikkonen sixth.

Lewis admitted his win had been 'comfortable' and added, 'We had a good strategy and a good car. I made a great start. There was no real hassle from Felipe and I was able to focus on my job, being smooth and consistent.'

Hungary was up next and that would prove to be far from comfortable as Lewis – who had started from pole – limped home in fifth place after suffering a puncture. The puncture wrecked his hopes of a win on lap 41 of the 70, but at least he had the consolation of seeing main rival Massa's Ferrari engine blow up three laps from home when he had seemed a sure-fire winner.

His loss was Lewis' team-mate Heikki Kovalainen's gain, as the little Finn notched up his maiden F1 win and at the same time became the 100th winner of a F1 GP. And with Raikkonen only managing to finish third – Germany's Tino Glock was second – the weekend was not as bad as it had looked like being when Lewis had to contend with his puncture.

In fact, his fifth place finish meant he had actually increased his championship lead to five points over Raikkonen, with Massa dropping into third, a further three behind. Lewis knew fortune had shone on him. He said, 'The race could have been better for me, but at least I scored four points and maintained my lead in the championship, so this result is not too bad for me.'

McLaren boss Ron Dennis summed up the weekend at the Hungaroring when he smiled and admitted, 'From Lewis' perspective, as bad days go, it could have been a lot worse.' Indeed it could, and those four points and Massa's blow-up would prove to be crucial at the end of the season.

Lewis knew the Brazilian could not be written off. He sensed 'Little Phil' would be his chief rival; that Raikkonen did not seem as motivated now he had won the World Crown. That the No 1 role at Ferrari was now passing subtly but inexorably to Massa.

That theory would be backed up by this reality: of the remaining seven races, Massa and Hamilton would win two apiece; Kimi would not win any. In fact, he would only earn two wins in the *entire* season and, ominously for him, Fernando Alonso would join Lewis and Felipe in winning two of those final seven races, with Sebastian Vetell claiming the other. I was told by a Ferrari source that the Italian giants were assessing Raikkonen's showings against those of Alonso, who was in the slower Renault, and were seriously considering bringing in the Spaniard at the Finn's expense in 2010 when Kimi's contract runs out.

The threat of Massa to Lewis' title aspirations was apparent three weeks after the Hungarian GP when he beat him to the chequered flag in Valencia, winning a fairly drab European GP. At a circuit that makes overtaking virtually impossible, Massa dominated.

In a race notable for its absence of tactical manoevres on the track it was Massa and team-mate Raikkonen who managed to grab the headlines with two pit lane incidents. On lap 43 Kimi pitted and put his foot on the accelerator before the refuelling hose had been removed. One of the Ferrari mechanics was knocked over and suffered a fractured foot.

And after Massa's second pit stop he emerged into the

path of Adrian Sutil. He escaped with a 10,000 euro fine after the stewards decided his manoevre had been unsafe but that no sporting advantage had been gained.

This was the moment the whispers started up that Ferrari were being given special treatment: that if it had been Lewis he would have been punished much more severely; that the FIA wanted to see Ferrari win at Hamilton's expense. It would be a debate that raged until the end of the season, especially as in the next GP in Belgium Massa would benefit from what many pundits viewed as a harsh punishment of Lewis.

Massa's victory put him on 64 points, six behind Lewis in the drivers' standings.

Lewis, who had been suffering from flu and a sore neck before the race, said he was happy just to have got it out of the way and banked some points. He said, 'It's been a miserable weekend. I have had flu symptoms and a fever nearly every day. I had low energy and I had problems with spasms in my neck. I almost decided not to race, but I managed to get through it, even though it was tough.'

It would be just as tough at Spa on September 7, the 13th GP of a fascinating F1 season – but an unlucky 13th for Lewis Hamilton. The great Brit won the race fair and square, but was later demoted to third behind Massa and Nick Heidfeld for allegedly cutting a chicane. Now the conspiracy theorists were in full voice and, it must be said, not without reason. The decision was all the more galling for our man because, let's not forget, Massa got away with his unsafe pit lane release, when the expected 10sec punishment would have seen his victory wiped out. Now, he was benefiting unexpectedly from a 25sec penalty against Lewis. 'I would be surprised if there was a penalty,' Lewis had said before the stewards announced their decision. 'It was fair and square, it would be absolutely wrong if that happens, but we know what they're like.'

It was a fair point and, indeed, the controversial decision would outrage pundits and fans across the globe. On the face of it, Lewis had delivered a brilliant triumph as he soared past Raikkonen two laps from the end of the race as they battled for the lead on the Bus Stop chicane. He was forced on to the run-off area but still managed to rejoin the race in front of Kimi. He then allowed Raikkonen back into the lead, later admitting that he feared he would be punished if he had not done so. But, when they assessed the incident later, the stewards hit him with a penalty anyway, which cost him the victory. It was a cruel decision, all the more so as Raikkonen crashed out of the race soon after their altercation in the wet conditions.

'Kimi left me no room,' Lewis said, explaining his manoeuvre. 'I didn't want to crash and had no choice but to go over the kerbs. You aren't allowed to gain an advantage like that, obviously, so when I came out of the corner I let him through again.'

Lewis' lead had grown to eight points before he was brought into line, but after his penalty the deficit was cut to two over Massa and 19 ahead of Raikkonen. The FIA had effectively given Massa a championship lifeline.

Formula One chief Max Mosley tried to defuse the

situation by saying, 'Any suggestion there is a bias for or against any team or driver is completely untrue. Absolutely not. I'd love to see Lewis win the championship. It doesn't mean we are going to help him or hinder him. We are going to be completely neutral.' But the general feeling on the F1 circuit was that the boy had got a raw deal and that the FIA were not exactly unhappy about him falling back and could, therefore, maintain interest in the title race. After all, if Lewis was to pull clear of Massa, TV ratings might well suffer.

Certainly Massa himself had no sympathy for Lewis when asked about the verdict the day after the race. Massa said, 'I think he was maybe a bit too optimistic in thinking he could just hand back the position, albeit only partially to Kimi, and then immediately try to pass him again. Incidents like this have often been discussed in the official driver briefings, when it was made absolutely clear that anyone cutting a chicane has to fully restore the position and also any other eventual advantage gained.

'Maybe if Lewis had waited and tried to pass on the next straight, that would have been a different matter.'

So it was that all eyes were on Little Phil and Lewis as the F1 circus next descended upon Monza, Ferrari's Italian home and stronghold. Would the stewards, in front of the Tifosi, come to decisions that could result in assisting Felipe? No, the Brazilian had no need of a helping hand as he and Lewis finished down the field, with Massa sixth and the British ace seventh. Honours more or less even in a race that quickly became a lottery on a rain-lashed track, as exemplified by the fact that Sebastian Vettel took his and the Toro Rosso team's maiden win, at the same time becoming the youngest driver ever to win an F1 GP.

The German roared home in front of Kovalainen with Kubica third.

It had been a battle from the start for Lewis as he tried hard to salvage something after starting 15th on the grid, after putting the wrong tyres on his McLaren in a rain-soaked qualifying session. He roared through the field but had given himself too much to do to outrank Massa. Afterwards he admitted the race had really been an exercise in damage limitation and, although now the gap was down to a single point, that he was relieved to still lead the drivers' standings: 'I drove a really good race and was moving through the field very quickly when the circuit was at its wettest. If it had kept on raining, I'm confident I probably could have even won from 15th grid position. But as the circuit dried out, my tyres overcooked and I had to defend my position. Today was all about damage control: I came away with some points and kept my lead in the championship.'

It was certainly tough – and tight – at the top as Lewis and Massa continued their almighty struggle for supremacy.

Just four races now remained – and the first one of those would be a cracker, the first ever night race in F1, in Singapore. Lewis would finish third on the podium behind winner Alonso, and runner-up Nico Rosberg. It was a disappointment to be beaten by his arch rival, but the good news was that Massa finished outside the points, in 13th position.

The Brazilian was the engineer of his own demise. Like team-mate Raikkonen in Valencia, he pulled out of the pits before the refuelling had been completed and then – in a *Groundhog Day* moment – pulled out in front of Sutil, just as he had done in Valencia.

Lewis knew his main rival was out of the points and so drove a mature race, not going crazy to get past Rosberg as he might have done a year earlier, knowing that he would rack up six points while Massa would have none to add to his tally. Some called it karmic justice as Lewis had now been returned the six points the FIA had so cruelly taken off him after Spa.

Triple world champion Niki Lauda spoke for many when he said after the race, 'After the stewards' decision in Spa, I said that if there was a God he would find a way to give McLaren the points that were unfairly taken away and that's what happened today.'

And Lewis was just as philosophical, admitting he was happy enough just to finish third. He said, 'It's great to be on the podium. I'm delighted. I really can't complain. We got good points today. After I saw Ferrari weren't going to get any points I knew I didn't need to take any risks.'

But Japan a fortnight later would bring no such comfort, as he was controversially forced off the track when passing Massa and finishing 12th. The Brazilian would cross the line in 8th, but be bumped up a place, thus taking a point and cutting Lewis' title lead. Lewis went home empty-handed after clashing with both Ferraris and being hit with a drive through penalty.

Massa also received his own drive through penalty for hitting Hamilton, but unbelievably was promoted above Sebastien Bourdais after the Toro Rosso driver was penalised 25 seconds... when it was Massa who had driven into the side of his car!

Lewis' penalty came at the very beginning of the race. He set off sluggishly from pole and immediately found himself behind Raikkonen. With a rush of blood to the head, he tried to regain the lead and forced the Finn to take avoiding action.

Stewards investigated the incident and dished out a drive through for Lewis.

Massa's penalty came when he tried to get past Lewis at Turn Ten, but sped off the track on to the grass. He manoevred the Ferrari back on but hit Lewis in the McLaren, causing him to spin.

Massa claimed his manoevre had been fair but Lewis dismissed it as being 'as deliberate as it could be'. Massa left the Fuji Speedway with two points. He had reduced Lewis' lead to just five, with two races remaining.

To rub salt in the wound for Lewis, his old enemy Alonso was the man who stole the glory in Japan, winning his second successive GP.

No wonder the boy said he was happy he wouldn't have to wait long to put things right as the next race, in China, was just a week away, giving little time for much critical self-analysis in the McLaren camp.

And what did he do in China after his Japanese horror show? Of course, he went and won it! And he did it in real style by qualifying in pole, notching the fastest lap and ending first on the podium. A wonderful hat-trick of achievements.

Massa, defiant and stubborn to the end, finished 15 seconds behind him as runner-up to ensure the title fight would go right down to the wire in Brazil. Seven points separated the two gladiators as Lewis edged on to 94 after his comfortable triumph from pole to finish at the Shanghai circuit.

Raikkonen had allowed Massa to pass him after the final round of pit stops in what was the only real controversial move of the race. But nobody was quibbling. Lewis was on a high, knowing now that his lead meant he could finish fifth in Brazil and still lift the coveted trophy. He said, 'This is another step to winning the championship and achieving my dream. Our approach to this race was right, it was not to go out and win but look at both races and try and score as many points collectively. Going into Brazil will be different compared to last year. We know we have got to do a good job but it will be tough. I hope as a team we can pull through.'

So the stage was set for a final battle between the two men who had conspired to give us one of the most exciting F1 title fights since, well, the previous year...when Lewis had again been the key figure. How much F1 owed to the young man from Stevenage who had breathed new life into what for some had become an ailing, boring sport was now clear to see as for the second time in two years the British public waited with bated breath to see if their new hero could pull off the big one.

It looked simple enough on paper; it should have been an

easy task to finish fifth, to not have to take the necessary risks to actually win the race. But there were two main worries: as a driver of extraordinary skill, passion and competitiveness since he had first got in a kart, it didn't sit easy with Lewis Hamilton to sit back and cruise home. Could he tame his basic instincts?

There was also a suggestion that Massa might not be averse to some 'darker moments' if they were to bring him the title in his homeland. But that was never going to happen: the boy is a diamond – a genuinely nice, approachable guy who would never dream of cheating. A point he would make on the Wednesday before the race: 'Playing dirty has never been part of my game. I don't want anything to do with it. I will fight fair to try to win the title. The only thing on my mind is winning the race. I can't worry about what Lewis will do. I know it is going to be hard, but not impossible.'

Lewis was his usual calm and composed self as he approached the big day. He laughed off suggestions that he would 'bottle it' and that he did not have the maturity to just sit back and take fifth place. Renault boss Flavio Briatore had been the most skeptical of the many F1 personalities – including some drivers – who had questioned Lewis' mental make-up. He had dismissed the 23-year-old hero as 'no Muhammad Ali' and said history would repeat itself: that he would fall at the final hurdle as he had done the previous season.

Lewis merely shrugged his shoulders as if to say, 'Let them say what they want, it won't affect me'. A sign of his increased maturity and awareness came as he turned the tables on Massa, claiming the pressure was heavier on him…after all, he was racing in his homeland and was expected to win.

Lewis said, 'There's a lot of pressure on Felipe. When I was at Silverstone there was a lot of pressure. The whole country is relying on you, not having my whole country in my face will be easier. It really is who can stand the pressure more, I guess it will come down to who is the stronger. That is what makes the world champion.'

As a statement of intent – and indeed a summary of what was at stake and just how it could be achieved – Lewis' analysis was spot on.

Now it was time for the talking to stop… time to let the action do the talking.

You could have cut the tension with a knife as the drivers stepped into their cars at Interlagos. Even the skies were dramatic and the racing Gods themselves appeared to be looking down on Lewis and urging him on. Of course, his all-time hero Ayrton Senna had grown up here and it was as if he was there in spirit, cajoling and calming Lewis as the race was delayed by 10 minutes after the heavens opened.

Finally, they were off and an early indication of what was at stake – and how it could be lost in a moment – came when 37-year-old David Coulthard's illustrious 15-season, 246-race career ended abruptly when he crashed out on the first corner in the wet.

It soon became clear that Massa was on course to win the race – but could Lewis hold out to claim that fifth spot to keep the title out of Felipe's hands? He was yo-yoing between seventh and fifth but pitted for wet tyres five laps from home when the rain poured down again. That dropped him to fifth place behind Tino Glock, with Sebastian Vettel right behind him.

The whole of Britain appeared to be holding its breath as TV pictures relayed the drama. Could he hold off Vettel and win the title? No…with two laps to go Vettel stormed past him and a nation groaned.

On the final lap of a long, thrilling season, the nail-biting continued right to the very end. It looked as if he had failed, as if the dream was destined to end in tears again.

Live TV pictures flashed around the world of Massa's father Luiz Antonio celebrating his son's title win as Felipe took the chequered flag at Interlagos. Then, suddenly, something happened that would forever live in the hearts and minds of British motor racing fans.

The looks on the faces of Luiz Antonio and the Ferrari crew gave the first indication: from delirium, they were suddenly deflated and dejected. The tears of joy were turning to tears of incredulity.

Lewis Hamilton was passing Tino Glock on the final corner of a mammoth F1 season to move from sixth place to fifth to take an incredible world title against the odds. Glock's car was still on dry tyres as the rain lashed on to the track, and that had slowed him right down, allowing Hamilton to pass. 'It was just impossible on the last lap,' Glock would say. 'I was fighting as hard as I could but it was so difficult to just keep the car on the track, and I lost positions right at the end of the lap.'

It was the most incredible ending to any F1 season, and ironic that a German should be the man who would enable a Brit to scoop racing's biggest prize. Traditionally, it had been the Germans who had wrecked our nation's sporting dreams rather than made them come true.

Lewis had joined the greats at the tender age of 23 – he had won the crown by a solitary point.

Lewis jumped from the McLaren and saluted the crowd, then ran to hug his mechanics and finally ended up in the arms of his girlfriend Nicole Scherzinger, the singer in The Pussycat Dolls, and his beloved brother Nic.

For the record, Alonso was second in the race ahead of Raikkonen and Lewis finished the season with 98 points while Ferrari had the consolation of winning a record 16th constructors' title. Not that that meant anything to the disconsolate figure of Massa, his father and his crew. He was a victim of that cruel thin line that separates glory and failure.

Lewis had become the first British world champ since Damon Hill in 1996 and the first McLaren driver to win the title since Mika Hakkinen in 1999.

'I am speechless,' Lewis said. 'I'm very emotional, I've cried. I don't think it has hit home yet that I am the world champion. I can only thank God I managed to get past Glock and it was just amazing. I have just had the most intense race of my life, my heart is still racing.

'I am going to celebrate with my family. We will party together as a team, that's for sure. I had a problem with my tyres, they were beginning to grain. There was nothing I could do. I was just trying to keep the car on the track. My heart was in my mouth when I was trying to get back in front of Sebastian Vettel but fortunately there was an opportunity to get past Glock.

'It's been a long journey in which I had the support of many people. My team did a fantastic job during the entire year and we sacrificed ourselves a lot. I am happy for having achieved this for all of us. Massa did a fantastic job today, congratulations to him for his win and for challenging me all year. But it's great to finish on top.'

Indeed it was. Mission accomplished… but it would not be game over for Lewis Hamilton. Now he wanted to retain his crown and go on to win it again and again. And who would bet against him doing just that? The era of Lewis Hamilton in Formula One was truly upon us.

CHAPTER 19

A LOAD
OF BULL

After he had roared to his debut title win in the Brazilian GP at the back end of 2008, the general consensus in F1 was that Lewis Hamilton would now go on to dominate the sport for many years to come. The twenty-three-year-old had faced head-on the challenges of old pros such as his McLaren teammate Fernando Alonso and younger tyros including the ever-improving German duo Sebastian Vettel and Nico Rosberg. Lewis's clear dominance of the field appeared to indicate that he would indeed go on to establish his own dynasty of F1 triumphs, that no one was good enough to beat him and that, anyway, he had the best car: the fastest car in F1.

But all the speculation of a Hamilton-dominated era proved to be misplaced. From being the undisputed world No 1 in 2008, Lewis would now suffer four years of relative failure; four years in the wilderness trying to work out where it had all gone wrong. How and why a young man who, quite literally, had the whole world in his hands would become an also-ran was a mystery. The truth of it was that from 2009 to 2013 McLaren lost its edge and Lewis's decision to sever his working relationship with his father backfired.

From having the fastest car on the grid in 2008, McLaren would now struggle to keep pace with the emerging power of the Red Bull racing team. And Lewis would break away from his father, Anthony, who had been the biggest calming and supportive influence on his racing career. Lewis sacked Anthony at the start of 2010 and he would struggle to reach the previous high of 2008 without him. Some pundits questioned the wisdom of it at the time, warning that Lewis appeared to be on a path to continued failure as he struggled to become his own man. Others voiced the fear that Lewis was becoming too big for his boots and that he was living the life of a celebrity without Anthony's calm, guiding hand.

There was an element of truth in the accusations. I would agree that Lewis was indeed trying to follow his own individual path and he also had money to burn. But he was no playboy. He continued his strong, loving relationship with Nicole Scherzinger, the pop star whom he had dated since 2007, and was far from the spendthrift type some pundits claimed him to be. Of course, he bought himself nice cars, a fine house and smart clothes, but so do many successful sportsmen at a young age. He never bragged or boasted about his privileged existence – certainly, he was no spoilt brat like some twenty-three-year-old unsavoury Premier League footballers I could name.

But, yes, he did seem to miss his dad's support and wisdom.

Lewis would also find it more difficult at McLaren when his long-time mentor quit the racing team in April 2009. Ron Dennis had been arguably the most influential figure in Lewis's rise to the top, after securing his signature with the team from an early age. When Dennis departed to concentrate on McLaren's new sports car project, Lewis lost his closest confidant in the pit lane.

With the personal and professional changes in his life and the challenges of Red Bull with their faster car, it was perhaps inevitable that Lewis Hamilton would encounter this period of relative disappointment and frustration. It was still a surprise: few people expected him to become an also-ran in the following four seasons. And few had anticipated his relative fall from grace. From 2009 to 2013, he was F1's 'King without a crown': the man-boy we had believed would go from strength to strength found his route to glory thwarted by Vettel, the new kid on the grid.

After he won the crown in 2008, Lewis's results over the next four years would read like this: fifth in 2009, fourth in 2010, fifth in 2011 and fourth in 2012. It was some comedown after 2008 and the facts did not lie: they showed a driver struggling in a team that was struggling. OK, I know in 2013 Lewis would finish fourth again in his first season at Mercedes. But at least he had grasped hold of the branch that shouted 'Hope' once again: at least he knew good times were around the corner, given the investment and developmental skills of the German racing team.

At McLaren from 2009 to 2013, there was a sense of deflation. That was echoed in the results of Lewis's teammates in those years. They suffered in terms of glory for the majority of the time: only Jenson Button would break the hoodoo with some fantastic drives in 2011. Otherwise, the results of the co-drivers were even worse than Lewis's figures in 2009. Heikki Kovalainen notched just 22 points to Lewis's 49, in 2010 Button accrued 214 to Lewis's 240 and in 2012 Button achieved 188 points to Lewis's 190. Only in 2011 did a co-driver beat Lewis over the season – Button taking 270 to Hamilton's 227.

Even that total was not enough to bring the title back to McLaren, Button finishing runner-up to the now dominant Vettel in his Red Bull.

After Lewis took the drivers' title in 2008, Button would win it a year later with some fabulous results in his Brawn-Mercedes. Then, as Lewis continued to languish down the field, Vettel would steal the limelight and the championship – staking a claim for immortality by winning it on four consecutive occasions in 2010, 2011, 2012 and 2013 (the latter when Lewis was still getting to grips with a new car and a new team at Mercedes).

It must have been difficult for such a fierce competitor – and natural-born winner – like Lewis to stomach those four wins from the young German superstar. Especially as Vettel also snatched Lewis's record of being the youngest champion in the sport's history in 2010. He was six months younger than Lewis had been when he claimed his first title two years earlier. The Lewis Hamilton era that we had anticipated was upon us when he won that thrilling debut title in 2008 was suddenly snatched away – with Vettel stepping confidently into the void as *the* man of the moment. The young German superstar would lift four titles on the trot as Lewis struggled for consistency and speed in a car that was clearly not in the same league as the newly dominant Red Bull mean machines in which Vettel and co-driver Mark Webber were racing.

The 2009 season got underway at Melbourne at the end of January and provided key clues and insight as to how we might expect things to pan out over the next ten months and, more pertinently, given how Lewis would a year later hand over the baton of wunderkind, to the ever-emerging threat of Vettel. There would be no second successive title for Lewis as Jenson Button snatched it from his grasp with a brilliant campaign in the Brawn GP car. Button's brain and Brawn's, well, brawn combined to give the Somerset racer the crown he had so craved and had now so supremely earned.

Button even triumphed with a race to go, such was his dominance, as he and Brawn GP won the drivers' and constructors' titles in Brazil. It was Jenson's first title and the tenth occasion that a British driver had won it. The history books also record the fact that it was the first time the drivers' crown had been lifted by English racers in consecutive campaigns.

It was telling that the runner-up to Button was Vettel, who had taken the seat vacated by David Coulthard at Red Bull that season. For Lewis, it would be a sobering season as his McLaren struggled to keep pace with the Red Bulls and Brawn GP cars. Changes to the car – with the intention of making the sport more attractive by encouraging more overtaking manoeuvres – played an important role in the supremacy Red Bull and Brawn would enjoy. The official F1 website best sums up the rather complex technical developments that would lead to Lewis's demise. The website explained in commendably simple terms the changes: 'Slick tyres were back. Kinetic Energy Recovery Systems (KERS) were optional and promised ... a potential gain of 0.6 secs in lap time. And aerodynamic changes aimed at improving overtaking meant less bodywork "furniture".

'It was the aero side, allied to the new rule banning testing during the season, which were to create the main talking points ... because Brawn, Toyota and Williams all hit on the idea of running a double diffuser.'

The official F1 website then made the point that the testing ban made it hard for those teams without the double diffuser to keep pace – although they did after 'four or five races'. But by then Button had built up a commanding lead in the drivers' championship. Indeed, the great Brit won six of the first seven races, only losing out to Vettel in China.

It was fortunate for Jenson that he had got off to such a fantastic start, as Vettel would be the man in form for the second half of the 2009 season, winning three GPs including the final one of the season in Abu Dhabi as Button was unable to triumph in any. Button's early season victory parade earned him the title but Vettel was clearly going to take some stopping the following season if he started as he had ended.

To give Lewis credit, he won two GPs in the second half of the season in his McLaren – claiming victory in Hungary and Singapore. It illustrated how brilliant a driver he remained, but his car was simply not good enough, as exemplified by the fact that Brawn took the constructors' crown with 172 points as opposed to McLaren's 71 points. There was a vast 101 points difference – a gap that highlights the problems Lewis had faced and, indeed, would face in 2010.

He finished fifth at the end of the 2009 season and retired after twenty laps in Abu Dhabi – just when it seemed the car was coming good and after he had posted the fastest lap in qualifying to earn a pole position. Towards the end of the season, Lewis outlined his views on his 2009 campaign in a post-Brazilian GP press conference. He told reporters, 'It's been a fantastic year for me. It's been very tough and demanding at times, but I think I'm actually a very different person now than I was a year ago – and some of that comes directly and indirectly from being world champion. I think this year has helped me to understand and appreciate more the challenge and thrill of Formula One. I'd like to think I'm a more rounded individual as a result of my season, and I definitely think I'm a better driver.

'In many ways, though, I'm still the same. I'm still a fighter, and I still want to make sure that I keep my family, and my friends and my team close to me. I'll be bringing the fight to the first race of next year – I'm already looking forward to it. It can't come soon enough. I'm encouraged by our progress because I know that it's all feeding in to our development for 2010.'

They were optimistic words from a man who had just handed over the crown he had craved for so long to fellow Brit Button. It would also prove to be rather ironic that he spoke of keeping his 'family and friends … close', given that he would split from his dad Anthony – dismissing him as his manager – early in the 2010 season. Lewis dropped the bombshell news on the eve of the Bahrain GP – the season opener at the start of March 2010.

Lewis explained the move at the post-race press conference, telling reporters, 'Dad will miss being here but it was me who initiated the break. He's got other things to focus on, but I don't want my dad to be my manager any more. I will at some stage have a new manager, but I am in no rush. He's still taking care of a lot of stuff, but he's slowly backing out. He tried to take it as a dad. We had sat down with several different managers over the past three years, yet never felt quite comfortable with them. But at some stage I felt that I would be able to start taking on quite a few of my own things.

'Dad has started to take on quite a lot of his own things and he wants to be a success in a different way in his own life. He is very determined.'

Lewis was asked if Anthony would have approved of his trip to Los Angeles for a romantic weekend with girlfriend Nicole, close to the opening race of the campaign. He said, 'A lot of times in your career you are so strict with yourself that you do things that are maybe better for your physical condition but not, perhaps, for your mental approach. I took the view that I would be better prepared all round if I went out to LA. So I did.

'It was brilliant and I had a really nice weekend. We went out, ate good food and just relaxed. I think that's the key. Sometimes you need that. I had two hectic weeks of testing and media. The story broke about me and my dad. So much had gone on. It was good to switch off, turn my phone off. It was like a different life for a couple of days and coming here I feel better than ever.'

Of course, it was understandable that a man of twenty-five wanted to take control of his own life but it also seemed a terribly sad moment. Anthony had done everything he could to help his son reach the pinnacle in motorsport; he had made sacrifices and dedicated his life to that end. Now he was not to continue as manager as his son moved on with his career.

Some commentators contended that Lewis had become too big for his boots and that he had fallen under the spell of his pop-star girlfriend. But Anthony would later confirm that had not been the case. In 2011, he told the *Daily Mirror*, 'I don't believe for one minute she would ever say to Lewis "fire your father, make your own decisions". I'm sure she would actually encourage him to contact me, not the other way about. She is a loving, respectful, very family-orientated individual. We know each other extremely well. She's stayed here several times and had dinner with us. She's got strong bonds with her family and is part of this family.'

However, he admitted that the split was painful, adding, 'Lewis was right to go his own way. Was it right the way it happened? Probably not. If I'd had my way it would have been done differently. But it is what it is...

'And I can honestly say we have both become better people for it. It had to happen at some stage. One would have had to say to the other, "I'm leaving you". And it wasn't going to be me. I was so focused. I couldn't think about anything – except Lewis's career.'

Without Anthony by his side, Lewis would suffer a frustrating few years – but that could as easily be put down to Red Bull pulling ahead of McLaren with their cars as to a lack of parental guidance. Having said that, Lewis won three races in the 2010 calendar, just one less than the eventual title winner, Vettel. It remained clear that Lewis was the *best* driver on the circuit, but he just did not happen to have the best car. He would be joined in the McLaren team by reigning champion Button who, inexplicably, was not retained when Mercedes bought out Brawn. It meant McLaren had both the current champion and his predecessor champion in their ranks.

Lewis's first win in 2010 came in Turkey at the end of May and he swiftly followed that up with victory in Canada a fortnight later. He then triumphed at Spa in Belgium at the end of August and was in the running for the title right up until the last race of the campaign in Abu Dhabi in mid-November. Ultimately, Vettel would emerge triumphant and seal his first drivers' crown but Lewis's resilience in fighting right until the end in a car that couldn't match Vettel's Red Bull showed his brilliance as an F1 driver and his right to be called one of the greats of any motorsport era. Lewis finished second to Vettel in Abu Dhabi with McLaren teammate Button completing the line-up on the podium.

Four drivers had arrived in Abu Dhabi with a mathematical chance of winning the title: Vettel, Lewis, Webber and Ferrari's Fernando Alonso. Lewis set the fastest lap on Lap 47 but was unable to beat Vettel to the big crown. Alonso finished runner-up in the drivers' standings, courtesy of his seventh-place finish in Abu Dhabi, and Webber beat Lewis to third place after finishing eighth in the final race of the season.

Given that he didn't have the fastest car on the grid throughout the campaign, Lewis's achievement was not to be sniffed at. His disappointment was apparent at the post-race press conference when he summed up the season from his point of view. He said, 'It has not been the most spectacular season for us. But huge congratulations to Red Bull and to Sebastian. They really did a fantastic job throughout the year, so fair dos to him. I think for us it was a great end-of-season result, for me and Jenson. I think we pushed very hard throughout the year, so a big thanks to all the guys back home at the factory for not giving up. Next year will be a better year.'

Did he really believe that – or was it just hype? It was hard to see how Lewis would hunt down the Red Bulls after losing to them in 2010. Their cars were becoming more competitive each season – so surely 2011 would see both Vettel and

Webber pull even further away from Lewis and their other closest rivals? There was no doubt that they had riled Lewis. The expectancy that he would embark upon a period of dominance after his 2008 triumph had been extinguished by Button's win in the Brawn in 2009 and now the era of Vettel appeared to be imminent in the Red Bull.

Lewis tried to put a brave face on it, dismissing Red Bull as 'just a drinks company' before the 2011 campaign got underway in Melbourne. He said he was confident McLaren had the initiative to make up ground and overtake the Red Bull upstarts, telling reporters in a pre-Melbourne press conference, 'They [Red Bull] have not been there as long as our teams. Our teams have got status they would like to keep. For many, many years it has been McLaren and Ferrari at the front and now we have got a new team that has come and knocked us off the top. But I am really certain that either team will do absolutely everything in their power to make sure they can remain at the top.

'Red Bull are not a manufacturer, they are a drinks company. It's a drinks company versus McLaren/Ferrari history. I don't know what their plan is. Our team is building to become a bigger manufacturer, like Ferrari, and I can only see our team being there for a ridiculous amount of time. It is a pure-bred racing team.'

They were strong sentiments, but would those words withstand the gauntlet Red Bull threw down from that opening race in Australia? Or would they prove to be a red rag to a bull – giving the team the necessary incentive to ram the words back down Lewis's throat? We were about to find out.

CHAPTER 20

DARK BEFORE THE NEW DAWN

L ewis had indicated that he believed Red Bull's 2010 triumph in the drivers' and constructors' titles had been merely a flash in the pan. That Vettel's title win was more down to luck than skill and that he would now win back the title from the young German. Lewis's attitude to the Red Bull stable had best been summed up at the end of the 2010 campaign, when he had come up with that derogatory phrase that they were 'just a drinks company'.

Unfortunately, he had miscalculated – and in a big way. That throwaway barb probably served as an incentive for Red Bull to show him who was boss, and Vettel was both ambitious and tough. No way was he going to lie down and let the 'Lewis Show' steal his limelight: his aim was to consolidate his position as the new No 1 and he would do just that in a season that left Lewis once again in his slipstream as his McLaren failed to keep pace with the powerful Red Bulls.

Vettel stormed to his second world championship in two years – becoming the youngest driver, at twenty-four years and ninety-eight days, to do so. He had eclipsed the brilliant Fernando Alonso to earn the right to be known as the youngest double world champ in F1 history. And to rub salt into Lewis's and McLaren's wounds, Red Bull also won the constructors' championship for the second year running. The 'drinks company' was clearly more than just that: Red Bull had now established itself as a major player in F1, and Vettel was going to be a major rival for Lewis for years to come, given his age.

The season was a big disappointment for Lewis. He won only two GPs and finished fifth in the final standings behind Vettel, Button, Webber and Alonso. It was especially galling that he ended up below Button, his teammate and supposed No 2 at McLaren. The gap between the top five drivers told the story of the season: Vettel was so dominant in the Red Bull that he finished 122 points ahead of runner-up Button and a quite staggering 165 clear of Lewis.

The stats also summed up just why Lewis had failed to keep pace with Vettel and the other three drivers who finished above him, as he won just three out of nineteen GPs compared to Vettel's eleven. It was a comprehensive drubbing for Lewis by the German driver.

Yet Lewis would get off to a bright enough start in 2011's first GP in Melbourne, Australia, as he finished runner-up to Vettel and ahead of Webber, Alonso and Button. OK, Vettel had continued where he left off, taking first place on the podium, but there had been enough in Lewis's performance to suggest he might actually make a fist of it and push Vettel for that coveted No 1 spot over the season.

But when Vettel then won the following GP – the Malaysian in Sepang – it looked as if Lewis might be in for another season of trying but failing to keep up with the championship leader. Lewis trailed home in eighth spot – a result that was confirmed after he and long-time rival Alonso clashed on the track as they battled for third place. In the event, Lewis would be the bigger loser as he was dropped down to eighth while Alonso finished sixth.

Lewis was, inevitably, downcast at the post-race press conference. He said, 'This is racing, I guess. I started second and did everything I could to keep up and I don't really have much to say. Through the race my tyres went off and I just have to take it on the chin and see how it goes.'

But the smile of hope would return by the end of the next race as he won the Chinese GP in Shanghai in mid-April 2011. Lewis had started third on the grid after Vettel had taken pole. Vettel finished runner-up with his Red Bull teammate Webber coming home third. The win cut the German's championship lead to twenty-one points and gave Lewis and McLaren renewed hope that he could compete. Lewis had overtaken Vettel four laps from home in the fifty-six-lap race and was delighted to have chalked up his first victory of the season. China had become one of his favourite races; it was something of a good-luck charm, as he had also won there in 2008 and this win meant he had become the first driver to win the event twice.

Lewis was also mightily relieved as his post-race comments illustrated. 'It's been a long, long time,' he said. 'I can't remember the last time I won a race. I feel absolutely overwhelmed. It was a worry before the race, when the car wouldn't start. But I tried not to show I was concerned. I think today the strategy that we came up with definitely helped. My new-option tyres seemed to last longer. The pit stops were fantastic. The car felt great and I was trying to nurse my tyres while picking up pace. It was one of the best races I've experienced. It feels amazing to be able to bring home a victory for the guys in the factory. No one made it easy today, which makes the win all the more pleasing.'

It looked as if Lewis might be turning the corner with his first win of the campaign but, in the event, it actually turned out to be little more than a false dawn. His next win would not come until the F1 circus pulled into Germany's Nurburgring at the end of July. In between, he would encounter controversy in what was proving a difficult season. At Monaco at the end of May, he criticised the race stewards after twice being penalised as he finished sixth. He got a drive-through penalty for a clash with Ferrari's Felipe Massa and was also hit with a twenty-second penalty for a subsequent clash with Williams driver Pastor Maldonado. Lewis told BBC Sport that he felt victimised when, in actual fact, he believed he was the victim. He said, 'People want to see racing. But you get done trying to put on a show, trying to make a move. Fair play, if I feel I've gone too late I'd hold my hand up to admit I've caused an incident. But it's not the case.

'I'll just try and keep my mouth shut and try to enjoy the rest of the season. It's not too late to win the title but it's not looking great. I gave my all today and the team did a great job. It's character-testing, whether it's right or wrong. I'm going to go chill, do some jet-skiing, and try to stay out of trouble.'

But while everything seemed to be going wrong during spring and early summer, it all went according to plan at the Nurburgring. Webber had started on pole but Lewis beat him to first place, much to his apparent joy. The win put him third in the title race, although he still had a mountain to climb if he were to overhaul Vettel, who was still eighty-two points ahead of the British ace.

'We never expected to come here and be so fast,' Lewis told a news conference. 'It's one of the best races I think I have done. It was really fantastic for me to make that step forward. The race was about real perfection and about not making mistakes. All the emotion, effort and energy the team put into the car, when we don't see results like this, it [the pressure] slowly builds up, so, when you finally hit the sweet spot, it just couldn't feel any better.

'Bit by bit, I've learned more about how the car is behaving, with driving style I've learned to look after the tyres a little bit more. There were just certain areas I was losing out. I was really surprised my tyres lasted so long later on in the race – so I guess there are still areas we need to improve, particularly on heavy fuel at the start of the race, but it is a massive step forward.'

There were nine races left in the season and, if Lewis was going to make a serious challenge to Vettel, he would need to keep winning. But Vettel would prove too strong in the Red Bull and it would be the German racer who dominated the latter end of the campaign, winning five of those nine GPs. No one could deny him the drivers' crown for a second successive season and no one could deny that he had earned it with eleven wins out of nineteen races.

Lewis would triumph in one of those final nine meetings – at Abu Dhabi, the penultimate GP of the year – but the season would be remembered more for his run-ins with other drivers than for winning races. It was a campaign that he would probably rather forget, as Vettel compounded Lewis's misery with his mastery.

At least there was that win in Abu Dhabi and, as it was at the end of the season, it gave Lewis hope that he could look forward to the following one with some optimism. Lewis started second on the grid but roared home, much to the delight of the McLaren garage. Vettel had won the race the previous two seasons it was held but this time he was forced to retire after the first lap with a puncture. Lewis took the lead from then and never relinquished it, with Alonso coming home second.

'I'm ecstatic,' Lewis said in the press conference following his win. 'With the pressure I've been under and the doubt that has surrounded me, I feel massively proud. I think it was one of my best races. I don't feel I've made a single mistake. I think it's very rare for us and for me to get the opportunity to be able to maintain a gap, to be able to control the race but today I had the pace. My fans have been incredibly supportive and so have my family, particularly in recent weeks and that's made a big difference. To be able to walk away with a smile feels just fantastic. Victory is good for the soul.'

That last sentence showed how wrong some pundits were to portray Lewis as a one-dimensional, chav-like figure whose head had been turned by riches and bling. 'Victory is good for the soul.' How many F1 drivers would say that? It proved to me that Lewis Hamilton has much more depth to his character – certainly much more than some pundits would have you think. He was a young man who had grown up as a star but who remained committed to family, his girlfriend Nicole and his F1 career.

In the final race of 2011 in Brazil, he even found time to make up with Massa, who had been something of a nemesis because of their constant run-ins during the campaign. Lewis retired from the race and afterwards sought out Massa and gave him a hug in public. Afterwards, Lewis said, 'It was good to have a nice chat with Felipe. I have great respect for him and I'm looking forward to racing him again next year.' And Massa said, 'It was a very nice gesture on his part.'

That was another soulful act on the part of Lewis and ended any misunderstandings with his fellow driver.

And his father was of the opinion that we would see a more mature Lewis in the following season. Anthony said, 'He's turned a corner in everything he's done, his lifestyle and his love of motorsport. You've not seen Lewis Hamilton yet, you've seen a young Lewis Hamilton. Now a new Lewis Hamilton is coming.'

Lewis definitely was maturing as a person and a driver. Of course, he remained the bravest, most daring racer on the F1 circuit but he now tried to avoid confrontations and run-ins with his fellow drivers – although that wasn't always easy to achieve given the nature of the sport. It would take him seven GPs before he won a race and he would end the 2012 campaign in fourth place. He seemed to be stuck in this fourth/fifth-place rut but would work hard to become No 1 in the world again. The truth of it was, of course, that he wasn't lifting the title because his car wasn't as good as the Red Bull. It was never the case that he was being outpaced by Vettel because the German was the better driver. No, Vettel was in the faster car and, as long as that remained the case, Lewis could not reclaim his crown. In 2012, Vettel would claim his third consecutive drivers' title: he was on a marvellous run and it was difficult to see how Lewis would overhaul him, as the German had the better car.

Given that Vettel had a natural advantage, Lewis did well to win four races in 2012. He was first home in Canada, Hungary, Italy and the United States. That was just one less than Vettel – and in a slower car. That fact highlighted how competitive Lewis remained: he may not have been the champ but he still drove like one in a less competitive car.

Lewis's first win of the season came at Montreal in the Canadian GP. Vettel started on pole but finished fourth as a determined Lewis romped home. Vettel and Alonso suffered as their tyres degraded at the back end of the race, but Lewis had pitted for new tyres – a decision that led to his well-earned victory. It was a victory that took Lewis to the top of the drivers' championship by two points from Alonso. Lewis was, of course, bubbling after the win and immediately thanked his thousands of fans who had stood by him over the past three years when he had struggled to keep pace with Vettel.

He said, 'I want to dedicate this one to all the fans out there who have always supported me, no matter what. Thank you.'

For their part, the fans were under no illusions that Lewis was working miracles to stay ahead of the Red Bulls. One fan, calling himself 'icemangrins', said, 'I'm so glad and thrilled for Lewis. This is perhaps his best win in the past three years ... kind of equalling his win at the 2011 Chinese GP in terms of pure race craft. In all fairness, the Spanish GP is the only event where he made a judgement error ... 5 technical issues in 7 races is mind-blowing.'

The win was Lewis's way of letting Vettel know he could not expect to walk the title even if he did have the best car. No, Lewis would push him all the way. But the Red Bull's superiority would eventually tell as the German won four races on the trot at a key stage of the season. Towards the end of September, he triumphed in Singapore and he then won the next race in Japan, the one after that in Korea and the Indian GP at the end of October.

After coming home first in India, Vettel led the drivers' standings by thirteen points and, with just three races left, had set himself up for a remarkable third consecutive title. Kimi Raikkonen won in Abu Dhabi, Lewis then triumphed in the penultimate race in America, and Button was first home in the final race in Brazil. A fourth-place overall finish in the standings was nothing to be scoffed at, but by the autumn of 2012 Lewis had had enough of being an also-ran. He believed – and quite rightly, too – that he was a better driver than Vettel but that the only way to overhaul him was to race in a car that was faster and more consistently reliable.

Could the McLaren team give him that promise of competitive reliability? He doubted it. At the same time, though, could he bring himself to leave the racing team that had nurtured and developed him; that had spent a massive chunk of his life and their resources on making him a world champion in the first place? He had his doubts and, although it would certainly be a wrench to walk away from McLaren, Lewis was strong enough to do it if he believed it would mean he could prosper once again as a racing driver.

And in September 2012, he did just that, announcing that he would leave McLaren at the end of the season and join the Mercedes racing team. It was a deal that would leave him super wealthy – estimated at £60 million over three years. A cliché maybe, but Lewis stressed that it wasn't just about the money. He had stayed loyal to McLaren from 2008 to 2012 but had gone backwards in terms of results on the circuit. Now he felt the power and riches of Mercedes would take him back to where he belonged – at the very top of the tree: world champion. He knew it might take a year or two; that he would need to settle in and establish the crucial relationship between team and driver and that the car would probably need time to be fine-tuned. But he was convinced Mercedes had the clout to do what McLaren had been unable to do for the last four years: provide him with a car that would give him a realistic chance of regaining the drivers' title from Vettel.

Lewis told a news conference just why he had decided to quit McLaren for Mercedes. He said, 'It is now time for me to take on a fresh challenge and I am very excited to begin a new chapter. Mercedes-Benz has such an incredible heritage in motorsport, along with a passion for winning, which I share. Together, we can grow and rise to this new challenge. I believe that I can help steer the Silver Arrows to the top and achieve our joint ambitions of winning the world championships.'

There had been rumours that Lewis and McLaren had grown tired of each other – but now was no time for unsavoury comments. Both paid tribute to the other. Lewis thanked McLaren for everything they had done for him since the age of twelve, while they thanked him for his lifetime's work.

McLaren team principal Martin Whitmarsh said, 'It's entirely appropriate that I should take this opportunity to pass on our thanks to Lewis. He wrote a huge chapter of his life and career with us, and was, and always will be, a fine member of an exclusive club: the McLaren world champions' club.'

And that, as they say, was that. After the final race of 2012 in Brazil, he was gone. But would Mercedes now give him the backing and the car that would enable him to depose Vettel, who had clinched his third consecutive crown? That was the big question and Lewis was convinced he knew the answer: an emphatic yes.

CHAPTER 21

MAKE MINE
A DOUBLE

I t is fair to say that Lewis's initial impact at Mercedes was rocky and testing. He had, of course, arrived at the team with much hullabaloo after spending so many years in the cocoon of McLaren: he had grown up within McLaren and his life was structured and he had become comfortable with the team and his yearly routine once he embarked upon his F1 career. But now everything was new and he would surely need time to settle into Mercedes; to get properly acquainted with the car, the bosses, the mechanics and his new teammate, his long-time friend from way back in their karting days as youngsters, Nico Rosberg.

Alarm bells should probably have started ringing when Mercedes made it clear that there would be no No 1 driver – that Lewis and Rosberg were on an equal footing. They could compete against each other for the world drivers' championship and could expect equal billing and equal financial, crew and car commitment from the company. Team principal Ross Brawn had emphasised Lewis and Rosberg were equals pretty much as soon as the British ace joined Mercedes. Brawn told Sky Sports' *F1 Show* that all Lewis asked for during contract negotiations was equal billing with his German co-driver. He continued, 'Of course Lewis wants to race – in the contractual negotiations we had with him, never was the issue of who was No 1 or No 2 ever mentioned from his side. All he wants is parity – he wants the same opportunity and that is great that he has that confidence and that approach and that he doesn't want favouritism – he just wants parity.'

I have no doubt that Brawn – who would leave the team after the 2013 season – was outlining the true nature of the situation. That Lewis wanted Nico to be given equal billing and an equal chance. But even he must have been surprised at just how determined Nico would become as the season wore on. In Lewis's first two campaigns at his new team, Rosberg would not only be a competitive teammate, but would also become his number-one rival. And their long-time friendship would undergo immense strain and be put to the test at every GP as both men battled to become the undoubted king of the sport.

Each of them seemed hellbent on beating the other and both refused to be the one who had to give way to the other on the track – even when the team ordered them to do so.

Lewis got off to a bad start at Mercedes when he crashed the car during his first testing session in February 2013. That session ended prematurely after fifteen laps when he lost control as the brakes went haywire at Jerez in southern Spain. The only consolation for Lewis was that Rosberg also failed to complete his session: he was brought to a standstill after an electrical fault on Lap 11. Lewis, still settling in at the team, declared himself 'quite happy' with the car, despite the testing fiasco. He told BBC Sport, 'I'm just glad that firstly I'm safe and that it's happened now, not when we're in the season. This is what testing is about. It's about getting through those development phases, errors or whatever they may be, and working on them and that's what the guys are doing.'

A month later, Lewis showed what he was made of as he brought the Mercedes home in fifth place at the first GP of the 2013 campaign in Melbourne. OK, he hadn't ended on the podium and at face value the result was eerily similar to those he had been chalking up in his last couple of seasons at McLaren: neither glory nor misery but more towards competent and sound. But he had finished the race in a new car and had notched ten championship points on his debut, while Rosberg had earned none at all as he retired from the race after twenty-six laps.

Just a week later, Lewis did make the podium for the first time in the Mercedes by finishing third in the Malaysian GP. But the first inklings of what was to come appeared as the German was told not to overtake Lewis by Brawn. The team principal told Rosberg on the radio that Lewis had also been warned to go steady as the car had fuel consumption issues. Brawn felt it was only fair that both men should cruise home, given Lewis's fuel problems.

Before the following race in Shanghai, China, Rosberg told reporters at a press conference that he was confident there was no No 1 driver at the team. He said he had been assured both men had equal billing and added, 'I am very confident that there is no Number One and Number Two. But you can also see if that is the case yourselves in a few weeks' or a few months' time.' He put down the friction at Sepang to poor communication. Rosberg added, 'The difficulty was that we hadn't really discussed it beforehand. That was the mistake we made. It's important going forward that everything is discussed and then whichever way it goes, if I'm in front and Lewis is behind or vice versa, we will respect it. As long as one is prepared for it, it's discussed and it's understood, that's the important thing. That's the main mistake we made as a team [in Sepang].'

Lewis earned his first podium finish for Mercedes in Shanghai by finishing third in the race itself. But it brought only anguish for Rosberg as he was forced out after just four laps with a suspension problem. While Nico struggled for consistency with his troublesome car, Lewis appeared to be settling in nicely at his new team. After Shanghai, he was fourth in the drivers' table and seemed to be happy with how things were panning out. He himself was realistic enough to accept that he was hardly likely to win the title in his debut season with a new team, but he did believe that this first season could provide him with a springboard to do just that in the following year.

But after the optimism came a strong dose of realism as Lewis struggled to maintain his good start at Mercedes. By the time the Monaco GP came around at the end of May, he had been outqualified by Rosberg for the third consecutive time. That statistic was enough for Lewis to come out and admit that he had had difficulties with the car – difficulties that had still not been resolved. He told reporters, 'I've been struggling all year. Considering it is a new car, I've done pretty well, but I definitely seem to have been struggling as we've got into the season. Winter testing wasn't too bad and when we changed something in China it felt good and I got pole, so the confidence came. But that is the only race I've had that confidence, I don't know why. It is really just the uncertainty of what the brakes are going to do. I think I solved it later in qualifying so let's hope for a good race tomorrow.'

Taking into account his worries, Lewis was relatively pleased to finish fourth in the race in Monte Carlo. But that result was tempered by the fact that teammate Rosberg won the race. Nico would also add insult to injury by roaring home in first place in Lewis's home GP at Silverstone, Lewis once again finishing fourth.

It had been a sobering couple of months for Lewis as he continued in his teammate's slipstream, but the one characteristic Lewis has above all others – his determination to be a winner – would finally turn his season around. At the end of July, he won his first race in the Mercedes, in Hungary, finishing a full ten seconds ahead of runner-up Kimi Raikkonen. And teammate Rosberg's race ended in misery as he suffered engine problems just six laps from home. Lewis was smiling like the proverbial cat that had got the cream as he went on a lap of honour, fist pumping triumphantly in the air. The win meant he had equalled Michael Schumacher's record of four triumphs in Budapest, and Lewis told reporters, 'This is probably one of the most important Grand Prix wins of my career, having moved to a new team. I could not be happier. I hope there is plenty more to come. It's an incredible feeling and I'd like to thank all the fans. My team did an incredible job, we studied a lot last night and were hoping the tyres would last. We had no idea it would go that well.'

Lewis was on a high but would soon realise how difficult winning the title would be as Vettel now won the remaining *nine* races of the season! At the end of the 2013 season, Vettel had easily retained his drivers' championship title, while Lewis finished fourth and Rosberg was sixth. How could Lewis possibly turn around an almost 200-point final deficit (Vettel had 397 to Lewis's 189) to snatch the crown off Vettel? It seemed like mission impossible – but then Lewis Hamilton had always been someone who willingly attempted to triumph over adversity.

And with a full season behind him at Mercedes and an improved car ... well, who was to say he couldn't pull off his second F1 title win?

The 2014 season got underway with Lewis driving with number 44 on his car. F1 chiefs had decided that drivers could choose a number that would follow them to the end of their career and Lewis went for 44, which had been a lucky number for him during his karting days. Drivers were now able to choose any number between 2 and 99, although the reigning champion would still have to have number 1 on his car. So, if Lewis did win the 2014 crown, he would get number 1 back on the Mercedes – but for now he was happy to drive with 44.

But he was less happy when he was forced to retire with spark-plug problems in the traditional season opener in Melbourne. Lewis had been aiming to get off to a flier but here he was, still bedevilled by problems with the car and, to make matters worse, his new arch rival and competitive teammate, Nico Rosberg, won the race and the first twenty-five points of the campaign. It was a sickener for Lewis: it couldn't really have been a worse start to the season – especially one in which he had been convinced he could finally have a proper pop at the title after years of finishing behind Vettel in the McLaren.

However, some pundits made the perceptive point that the loss in Melbourne may have actually been just what Lewis needed to inspire him. As we have noted throughout this biography, he often seems to perform best when he is up against it – and now he was really up against it. He had got off to the worst start possible and needed a strong statement of intent to show that he was not only as good as his co-driver Rosberg, but that he was, in fact, better. As the sport's very own website, *formulaone.com*, so succinctly put it, 'Perhaps we should be thankful for the spark-plug insulation problem that brought Lewis Hamilton to a halt in the opening race of the season in Melbourne. The Mercedes racer wouldn't see it that way, but that trivial little failure had a massive effect as it put Hamilton on his back foot right from the start and forced him to attack. As he retired, teammate Nico Rosberg won and opened a 25-point lead. With only a seven-point difference between first and second place (apart from in the double-point finale in Abu Dhabi), that meant Hamilton had his work cut out clawing back that gap.'

Indeed he did. It went right down to the wire, the end of the final race of the season, before Lewis knew for sure that he had finally won back the title after so many wilderness years. The battle between himself and Rosberg was tense and competitiveness between the pair simmered over the season as each man tried to pull clear of the other, but failed time and again. Both had strong cars, both had a winning temperament and each wanted to outwit the other and claim that elusive drivers' championship title.

Lewis had lost that first race of the 2014 season to Rosberg in Australia but then made a real statement of intent with four consecutive wins. The super Brit triumphed in Malaysia, Bahrain, China and Spain. Rosberg was second in Malaysia, giving Mercedes their first 1-2 finish in an F1 GP since 1955. The win in China earned Lewis his first consecutive hat-trick of victories and certainly put the pressure on Rosberg to come up with a result in Spain.

The German was unable to halt the Hamilton juggernaut there, but finally did so in Monaco, with Lewis finishing runner-up. Now it was Rosberg's turn to take the spotlight – after Lewis's run of four wins on the trot, Nico now won three of the following five races. Lewis was happy enough to split those wins up with a wonderful victory on home turf at Silverstone, but he was now more than ever aware of the threat that Rosberg posed to his ambition of reclaiming the title. Rosberg, clearly, was not going to give up, or even give an inch if he could help it, as the duo continued their battle for hegemony in F1.

The fact that their Mercedes bosses refused to stop them racing made the season a much more exciting than usual visual feast, although it left both their drivers on a continual nervous edge. They both grumbled about the other's antics at the end of July in Hungary. Lewis had to start the race from the pit lane after a worrying engine fire in qualifying, and he showed just how talented a driver he was by finishing the race in third place, ahead of Rosberg. He also showed how defiant and mono-dimensional his pursuit of glory was by refusing to let Rosberg past.

It was the first time he had allowed his growing resentment towards the German to leak out into the public domain and it only served to worsen their already deteriorating relationship. Both drivers were called in for a team talk with their Mercedes overlords and afterwards Lewis said the matter had been sorted and was now in the past. But Rosberg refused to discuss it, which suggested he was not of the same opinion. Lewis told a post-race press conference in Belgium, 'I am hired to race and as far as I am aware the team has never said you have to slow down. Maybe not get in the way or not make it difficult sometimes for strategic reasons, that's clear. But he was never up my tail or going up the inside.

'It was an awkward position, not a very clear situation

with the team orders and I'd like to think I handled it quite well.'

However, Nico would only say, 'It's best I don't add too much.'

The pair were now at the point of no return – or so it seemed. The press pack, always hungry for a feud tale, made much of the incident. It would only be when all was lost and won at the end of the season that Lewis and Nico would hug and say the niggling episodes were something that they regretted and that they hoped could be left behind in the 2014 season, and not taken forward to 2015, when both men were likely to be competing seriously against each other again.

Having said that, at the time it hardly helped to cool their competitiveness when Nico and Lewis collided in the race at Spa, in Belgium, after that press conference – causing Lewis to retire on Lap 2 with a punctured tyre. Rosberg then ended well up in the points as he finished second, behind surprise winner Daniel Ricciardo, who had taken Webber's seat at Red Bull.

But – as had been the case throughout this thrilling season – Lewis came back against Rosberg once again, winning the Italian and Singapore GPs to thrust himself back into the lead in the race for the drivers' championship crown. Lewis was now on brilliant top form and he made it *five* wins in a row with victories in Japan, Russia and the United States. His form was wonderful, but so was his composure and refusal to be rankled by Rosberg. The last of those five wins – in America – meant he had won five on the trot for the first time in his career and that he had notched his thirty-second win in F1, the most *ever* by a British driver. He now led the drivers' championship and was still in the lead after the penultimate race in Brazil, in which he finished runner-up to Rosberg.

Yet, still, Lewis could not take it for granted that the title was tied up. There remained one race and it could well have been a 'winner takes all' if Lewis had been forced to retire with engine trouble or had finished so far down the field that a win for Rosberg would have given the German the drivers' crown they had both fought so hard for over the past eight months. That was down to the fact that the final race offered *double* points to give it more of an exciting edge.

The tension was high and the nerves almost overpowering as the pair lined up side by side for the final race in Abu Dhabi at the end of November. Rosberg was on pole but the pressure was on them both to win as Lewis led the title race by just 17 points – he had 334 to Rosberg's 317. But it was a cool, calm and collected Lewis who would win the race and the title as Nico struggled with mechanical problems. After Abu Dhabi, the final standings table showed Lewis had 384 points to Nico's 317. Lewis had triumphed by sixty-seven points, much to his delight. He rushed into the arms of his dad and brother and embraced girlfriend Nicole as the win finally sank in.

Lewis declared the triumph as 'the greatest day of my life' as he spoke to his joyous fans from the podium, saying, '2008 [when he won his first drivers' championship title] was a great year in my life. The feeling I have now is way, way past that. The greatest feeling ever.'

'It is very hard to soak all this up,' he then told BBC Sport. 'I didn't sleep. I went to bed at 12, woke up 5am, went for a run and thought for sure I would be tired when I got to the race but I felt composed. My family came and surprised me at breakfast. I had wanted them to be here but I didn't know if I would be able to give them time. I didn't want to get to the end and say, "I wish I had done this or that".

'It's really going to take some time to sink in.'

As far as the stats go, it was his eleventh GP victory of the season and he finished sixty-seven points clear of title runner-up Rosberg. In contrast to Lewis's eleven wins, Rosberg triumphed in just five GPs. To be fair, the German was magnanimous as the season wrapped up, admitting that, overall, Lewis deserved to be champion and congratulating him on his magnificent triumph. Rosberg told reporters after the race, 'I'm very disappointed but all in all Lewis deserved to win the championship. That's clear. All in all he just did a better job than me.'

But there would be one more victory to round off an incredible 2014 for the best driver in the world. In December, he attended the BBC's prestigious Sports Personality of the Year award event in London. Lewis had twice come second in this – in 2007 and 2008 – and he did not expect to beat nearest rival Rory McIlroy to the title this time round. The win was a definite shock, as the book-makers had installed the golfer as clear odds-on favourite. There was a feeling among some critics that Rory would win easily as he was 'more likeable' than Lewis: that he connected with the people, while Lewis was more distant and was not so personable.

But all those theories went out of the window as Lewis romped to yet another victory. He got 209,920 votes from the public, while Rory polled 123,745. A clearly surprised, and emotional, Lewis thanked the public after picking up the SPOTY award. He said, 'I am so proud of being British. I am proud and honoured to be among such talent. A huge thank you to all the people who called in. It's been such an incredible year. I couldn't have done it without my team and my family. My father did four jobs to make this possible. Being here is a reminder of how many great sportsmen we have, and I never thought I would be up here with the greats. This is a dream.'

It was truly the icing on the cake for a wonderful 2014. Lewis Hamilton was the man who had it all – two world titles, millions in the bank, a gorgeous pop-star girlfriend and a loyal, loving family. What more could he achieve? 'Another world title or two,' he answered, laughing when the question had been put to him at the post-race press conference in Abu Dhabi. And that just about sums up the boy from Britain who had achieved fame and fortune against the odds. He would never stop dreaming and never give in.

CHAPTER 22

NICO'S NOT MY FRIEND

As 2015 dawned, Lewis Hamilton was in high spirits. He had enjoyed a very merry Christmas with family and friends, although there had been nervous smiles when his bosses at Mercedes learned that a large part of it had been taken up skiing and snowboarding! They would have preferred him to limit any risks to the racing track rather than the snow, but Lewis had made it clear after winning his second world crown that he intended to 'have a bit more fun' in his life.

Sure, he would always maintain the ultra-professional attitude he had towards winning on the F1 circuit, but he had lived in the racing bubble all his adult life and now wanted to let his hair down away from the circuit. This meant he would attend more parties, drink more booze, be seen out on the town with big-name celebrities – and not be afraid to ski and snowboard when the opportunities presented themselves during Christmas 2014.

The week before Christmas, he went skiing in the Alps with his brother Nic and five pals. Lewis also took his bulldog Roscoe along and posted a pic of the group boarding a private jet. Lewis said the trip was to celebrate winning the Sports Personality of the Year award after twice missing out in 2007 and 2008. Girlfriend Nicole Scherzinger could not make the trip as she was stuck in London performing on the West End stage in the Andrew Lloyd Webber musical *Cats*. It was maybe a sign of things to come – apart pre-Christmas on this ski trip, Lewis and Nicole would split for good by the end of February 2015. They had parted ways a couple of times previously, but the 2015 split would be final as both moved on with their lives in separate directions.

Lewis posted an Instagram picture of himself with Nic on the slopes, along with the caption: 'My brother @nicolashamilton and I hitting the slopes last week! Great fun! #latergram #Godisthegreatest #HamiltonBros.'

On Boxing Day 2014, Lewis told his Instagram followers how he had enjoyed a white Christmas with another pal, American racing driver Ken Block, in Canada. The duo went snowboarding and Lewis once again posted Instagram pics and messages to his followers. He said: 'Had a blast out in BC with my good friend Ken Block and some friends boarding. Thanks for having us bro. God Bless!'

New Year's Eve would be a quieter affair, as Lewis saw in

2015 with Nicole after a romantic dinner in New York City. The couple raised a glass to the future and later shared a pic with Lewis's 2.3 million followers on Instagram. He accompanied it with the message: '#latergram Merry New Year!!! @nicolescherzy & I are wishing you all success & happiness in 2015 #NYC #blessings #GodBless.'

He would continue to take time out to enjoy himself even as he prepared for the new season. In February 2015, he attended the Elle Style awards in London and told how he was really getting into his music, posting a picture of himself in a studio with the caption: 'Other than being in a car, this is my favourite place to be. My fortress of solitude. #Music #TeamLH.'

The previous week, Lewis had been taken ill while testing the Mercedes. He completed just eleven laps at Barcelona before having to quit with 'a high fever'. Mercedes tweeted: 'An unplanned stoppage keeping us off track at the moment. @LewisHamilton is unwell and not able to continue driving today...'

Inevitably, there were suggestions in the press and among fans that Lewis was not focused on the new season, that he was not putting in the hard hours on the track and in the car and yet frequently featured in the gossip pages, pictured leaving nightclubs and celebrity events. One fan, who wished to stay anonymous, said: 'Lewis I am one of your biggest fans but you are starting to try my patience. Not that you obviously care. You were ill last week. You couldn't commit to testing & yet you show up at this cr#p that has nothing to do with your day job that starts again on Thursday? Give me strength bro. You'd better do the biz this weekend [when testing resumed].'

While another, Dave, complained: 'F1 racing is a very short career, much like a footballer. Unlike a footballer he has to fit into a very tiny cockpit. He has to be able to withstand massive G force, much like a Red Arrow Pilot. This guy is one amazing athlete & he is now putting everything he & his family have put into getting where he is now at risk. Come back down to earth Lewis or go & be rock star.'

However, although he was being seen out on the town more, Lewis was not in fact putting his career second. No, it was just that he had been seen *so little* previously that was emphasising the difference. Now, he was becoming a more relaxed, assured person and felt more confident in social circles – he was not in any way gambling with his fitness or No. 1 position in the Mercedes team. He was one of the fittest guys on the F1 circuit and never neglected maintaining that level; Lewis worked out hard and he simply wouldn't have been able to drive the car with such remarkable control if he wasn't still at the peak of fitness.

One fan, Steve, in Arlington, America, best summed up the Lewis Hamilton of February 2015, saying: 'Lewis Hamilton is a great athlete and person. The reason people try to be mean is because they can't dispute the fact that he is a two-time champion. So they have to find something to criticise, and all they are left with is his clothes and hair to talk about. Lewis is not an alcoholic or drug addict. He is very popular and has boosted the F1 fan base worldwide. So

Lewis, continue to do you and be you. Wear your bling earrings, your hats, your sneakers and your RUN DMC chain. Make your music, party like a rock star and at the end of the day (and the season) you will still be the CHAMP!!!!'

Spot on, and prophetic too. Lewis would up his efforts as the new season loomed, and he was at peak fitness when the traditional curtain-raiser in Melbourne finally arrived in March 2015. When he told the press just what his privileged position as a top F1 driver meant to him, Lewis stressed that in no way was he gambling with his career by partying to excess: 'Winning the World Championship is the goal. I would give up everything else for the World Championship. I am the strongest and the happiest I've ever been in my life. I love my job – it is the greatest job in the world.'

As we have touched on, he even lost the 'love of his life' Nicole when they split up in February 2015, just a month before the start of the new campaign. But he refused to let even the trauma of their latest split come between him and the dream of that third world title. A few days before heading to Melbourne, Lewis said: 'Of course, in previous years it has been the case where it's affected my life in general. Last year, I adopted, maybe the word is a mental attitude that was impenetrable. But I feel that I still carry that kind of mentality from last year and whilst it's not been easy, I feel stronger than ever. Having been in this position before, I don't feel that it's going to be a problem. Apart from having the flu, I generally feel good and excited.'

By the time the race got underway in Melbourne it was

clear that Lewis meant what he was saying as he brushed aside any lingering effects of the flu bug and the break-up with Nicole to storm to victory in the first race of the season. Mercedes teammate and pal-turned-rival Nico Rosberg finished runner-up as the team made a statement of intent in the Constructors' Championship. The rivalry between Lewis and Nico that had tarnished their one-time close friendship the previous season would intensify in the 2015 campaign, and ultimately lead to a situation that meant they could hardly bear to be in the same room as one another. It would also culminate, at the end of the season, with team boss Toto Wolff warning that the feud could mean Mercedes dropping one of them because it was not good for the morale of the duo or the team as a whole.

In December 2015, Wolff would warn at a press conference: 'We are having huge unity within the team, but the difficult relationship of the drivers is one of our weaknesses. And that is not good. If I were to analyse what are the biggest strengths and the biggest weakness of the team, I would say the biggest strength is the quality and the characters of the personalities within the team. The biggest weakness is the dynamic of the relationship between the drivers – and sometimes between the drivers and the team.'

The clearly worried chief added: 'We took the decision of having two evenly matched drivers in order to make the team progress faster and better. It was a very conscious decision three years ago. Going forward, we will consider if it is the best set-up for the team. Personality and character within the team is a crucial ingredient for the team success.

If we feel that it is not aligned with the general consensus, spirit and philosophy within the team, we might consider that when we take a decision, in terms of the driver line-up going forward. I think it is important to have talented and fast drivers in the car. But we want to work with nice guys.'

However, in Melbourne, there were no signs of the rift that would rock the team. It was as if the warring duo had been told to keep a lid on it after their run-ins the previous season. Lewis and Nico were all smiles as they celebrated their one-two on the podium – it had been the perfect start for the champion as he began the defence of his title and his attempt to win it again in consecutive seasons. Even the post-race press quotes suggested peace had broken out as Nico actually praised Lewis! 'It is a nice feeling to be second today because it is an awesome start to the season for the team,' Nico said. 'They have given us a stunning car. Lewis has done a fantastic job this weekend. I could not quite beat him but I was trying all the way to the maximum. I will give him a big run for his money and hopefully beat him.'

While Lewis said: 'The team did an amazing job today and it is incredible to continue on from last year. I am very honoured to be a peer among these great drivers.'

It was a key win for the Brit. It showed just how revved up and determined he was to retain his title and also sent out a message to Nico and his other main rival, Sebastian Vettel. Nico had won the Australian opener in 2014 but Lewis had now taken the honours and would clearly take some stopping this season. He had also shown his strength of mind before the race by refusing the chance to take the

No. 1 on his car for the season. Instead, he decided he would continue to race with No. 44 on the Mercedes. Lewis had told the BBC: 'I'll always be No. 44. I'll keep number 44 on the car. That's my number since I started, so I want to keep that.'

It meant that for the first time since 1994 – when reigning champion Alain Prost retired – there would be no No. 1 car on the F1 race circuit. The opportunity for the champ to use the number on his car had been introduced in 1975. Vettel, who had used the number in 2013 after his title win, would also be denied the chance to keep it on his car – he would now become No. 5 for the 2015 season.

The same trio of drivers – Lewis, Nico and Vettel – would occupy the same top three spots when the F1 season moved on to Sepang in Malaysia. But they would not finish in the same order. This time Lewis would have to settle for the runner-up spot as Vettel won in his Ferrari and Nico finished third. Vettel's win was a surprise as he had only joined the Italian giants at the start of the campaign, replacing the outgoing Fernando Alonso. With the victory, he showed that he would be Lewis's most formidable opponent when the car was 100 per cent firing. Yes, certainly more of a threat than Nico – Vettel was, after all, already a four-time champion at the age of twenty-six after his period of domination at Red Bull from 2010 to 2013.

Sepang was also notable as being the first occasion that saw the simmering rivalry between Lewis and Nico boil over. Nico had appeared to block Lewis in final qualifying, although the latter still started on pole thanks to an earlier qualifying time. It would be the fortieth time Lewis had won pole, and he was fairly relaxed when the inevitable questions about whether Nico had set out to deliberately obstruct his progress came his way.

Lewis simply smiled and replied: 'No'. He added: 'I just bailed out.'

Nico appeared less keen to draw a line under the incident, saying: 'How do we make that a fact, that he bailed out before he came across me? That is the interesting one, because me just saying it isn't going to bear much weight. So, we need to think of one, which I don't have an answer for to make that a fact for you. I will have to think about something later on. Or you can ask Toto [Wolff] who is coming. That is maybe a good one. That will give some more weight to it.'

The German was clearly riled by the incident and the view in the press box and the paddocks that he *had* tried to block Lewis. It was only a minor blow-up in the scheme of things, but it also marked the first time Wolff had to have words with them since he had hauled the duo into his office at the end of the last season.

In mid-April, on the third leg of the so-called 'long-haul' section of the F1 calendar, the Mercedes pair had reverted to the old one-two as Lewis triumphed in Shanghai, with Nico second – and Vettel, inevitably, third. But the victory would once again be tarnished by inflammatory comments from Rosberg who was finding it hard to come to terms with the fact that Lewis continually appeared to have the upper hand. An oft-mooted criticism of F1 is that the cars win the races, not the drivers. That if you put any driver into the best, fastest car, he would win the title hands down. But here, that theory was clearly being proved wrong. For Lewis and Nico both had the same car, the same quality of back-up and the same chance of winning. Yet Lewis was time and again beating Nico. It was possibly this realisation that most irked Nico – there was nowhere to hide. Lewis was a faster, better racing driver and he could not blame the car for his own failings. Also, ever honest, Lewis would not try to make out all was well in his relationship with Nico. He admitted they 'were not close friends' off the circuit and made it clear he would do his damnedest to beat the German on the circuit, even if it caused ripples within the Mercedes team.

After the Chinese Grand Prix, Rosberg now moaned that Lewis had driven slowly at certain stages to try to 'back him up' into Vettel, who was on his tail. Rosberg told the press: 'It compromised my race massively at the time because the best possible race for Lewis was to back me off into Vettel so Vettel would try to undercut me and I would have to respond. It was very frustrating, Lewis was taking it as easy on his tyres. Interestingly, he said he was just thinking about himself and that says it all. What upset me is we went through exactly that before the race.'

Once again, Lewis diplomatically played down the incident. He told reporters: 'That's absolutely not the case. I wasn't trying to back him up into Sebastian, because ultimately we do need a one-two and that is a priority to the team. If he wanted to get close to overtake, he could have done. I'm not really quite sure what his problem is. We came here to get one-two and we did. There shouldn't be too much aggro really.'

He was quite right – and it made me think that if Toto Wolff was to replace one of them some day, it would surely be Nico. It was the German who continued to ruffle feathers and who continued to struggle against Lewis's superior driving skills. Wolff seemed to be edging towards Lewis even after the Chinese GP when he tried to defuse the row in Shanghai by backing the British ace. Wolff said: 'There wasn't any animosity. There wasn't any intention from Lewis to slow Nico down in order to make him finish third or worse. He didn't know the gaps behind Nico. What he knew was that he had to take that tyre longer than we had ever run it the whole weekend. This is why he decided to slow down in the way he did.'

And so it was on to the final race on the 'long-haul' trail – the Bahrain GP in Sakhir. Once again, Lewis would emerge triumphant, with Rosberg trailing in third and Kimi Räikkönen a surprise runner-up in the Ferrari. The night race in the desert provided Lewis with a comfortable win: he led from the start to notch his third victory in four races. It also extended his lead over Rosberg to twenty-seven points. This time the German blamed the car for his defeat – saying there was a problem with his brakes. At least Lewis didn't have to fend off yet another icy blast from his temperamental teammate! Lewis said of his win: 'It's great to be having a fight with the Ferraris. They gave us a really good run for our money and we'll need to keep pushing as a team. We're trying to win both championships [drivers and constructors] so we aren't 100 per cent happy as we wanted to finish 1–2.'

Was that a coded message to Rosberg? That he needed to raise his own game so Mercedes would romp to the constructors' title? I wouldn't have blamed Lewis if he had been out to rile his teammate after Rosberg's continued taunts and complaints as the 2015 season took shape. But, no, I believe it was simply the Hamilton desire for perfection and his innate ambition to win, whether it be as an individual or a team. As the F1 circus packed its bags and exited from the Bahrain desert, Lewis had completed stage one of his dream to become a triple world champion – and the first Briton to win the crown three times since Sir Jackie Stewart.

He was top dog after the 'long-haul' GPs and could now take a breather, a holiday and a period of well-earned relaxation before the start of the European leg of the season. It would be three weeks before he competed in the Mercedes once again – and he was supremely confident his rich vein of form would continue in Barcelona in the middle of May. The triple-crown dream was on.

CHAPTER 23

THE TRIPLE WORLD CHAMPION

Barcelona in the spring, May 2015. Sunshine, sangria and high spirits. Well, not so much of the sangria, but Lewis was certainly in the mood to tango as he arrived in Catalonia in the hope of not only consolidating his lead in the World Championship, but opening up an even bigger advantage over Rosberg and Vettel. He had told reporters he planned to 'go easy' in the break between the 'long-haul' GPs and the return to Europe. But it hadn't worked out quite like that. Typical of Lewis, he busied himself away from the circuit when bored with downtime.

The British ace even flew from his home in Monaco to Rome for a cameo role – as himself – in the new *Zoolander* movie! He also did some promotional work for the Mercedes team and then linked up with fashion mogul Sir

Philip Green for a trip to Las Vegas to see Floyd Mayweather beat Manny Pacquiao. The duo then hotfooted it to New York for a charity ball. And in between, Lewis still managed to fit in a Los Angeles holiday with brother Nic!

No doubt that would not have been the schedule the more sedate Sir Jackie Stewart – the British great whose triple world-champ record he was hoping to match – would have followed in his heyday. But times change and Lewis was a fashion icon and a celebrity as well as the F1 reigning world champion, and he seemed much at home handling all that was thrown at him away from the circuit as well as on it. He is very much the modern sporting legend – akin to football's fashion and celebrity icon, David Beckham.

And Lewis was absolutely focused on winning when practice and qualifying got underway at Barcelona. He had won here the previous year and hoped to build on that and his improving relationship with the Spanish F1 fans, who had applauded him when he crossed the finishing line. That was quite a change from the times when they booed him when he was teammate – and rival – to local hero, Fernando Alonso, in their McLaren days.

Well, he may have become more popular in Catalonia, but Lewis was in for a shock – or two, actually – as arch-rival Rosberg beat him to victory in Barcelona *and* the next race in Monaco. Lewis finished runner-up in Barça, but could only manage third place in Monte Carlo. The latter was down to the team, who pulled Lewis into the pits after the safety car emerged following a crash. He had been in the lead but then lost his position as Rosberg and Vettel took advantage by staying out on the circuit and passing Lewis before he rejoined.

To his credit, Lewis, although clearly upset, congratulated Rosberg who had cut his lead in the title race to just ten points. And to their credit, Mercedes publicly apologised to Lewis for their blunder in bringing him in and handing the points to Rosberg and Vettel. Toto Wolff said: 'We got the maths wrong. That one goes on the team and I apologise to Lewis. He is a great driver and I am sure he'll understand we sometimes make errors.'

But Mercedes non-executive chairman Niki Lauda was less diplomatic in his views than Wolff, saying: 'A top team should not make mistakes like this. I am really upset because it was not necessary. It was the wrong decision to bring him in. It was very obvious. There was no risk to keep him out. It was heartbreaking for Lewis, for me, and everybody in the team. Lewis did say he was not happy with the tyres, but then we overreacted by bringing him in. It was completely unnecessary, a huge mistake because this is Monaco where you cannot pass. I apologised to him and his team because we ended up destroying his race.'

After Monaco, the season took its traditional twist to the European stage of the season…by heading to Montreal! Yes, the Canadian GP is always a tangent on the circuit, but Lewis would be the last to complain given his success rates there. In 2015, he had little trouble notching his FOURTH win at the Circuit Gilles Villeneuve, leading from start to finish, with Rosberg runner-up. It increased Lewis's title lead to seventeen points and ended any hopes Rosberg had of overwhelming the Brit after the German's spirited showings in Spain and Monte Carlo.

Lewis said: 'I love Montreal. I love this track. I love this city. Really, just a fantastic weekend, great to get back on the top step. I didn't feel I had the most comfortable balance – I had a bit too much understeer. Nico was quick but I didn't feel under too much pressure. I felt I could pull it out when I needed to. Did I need this win? I think so.'

A fortnight later, 21 June, the racers returned to Europe after the mini hiatus in Canada, with Lewis keen to widen the gap at the top between himself and his teammate. Lewis felt victory, and a compelling display in the Mercedes would also set him up nicely for what he termed 'the big one' – the following race in his homeland at Silverstone. Unfortunately, Lewis could not pull off the confidence-seeking win at the Spielberg circuit after a poor start allowed Rosberg to get past him and stay ahead for the rest of the race. Lewis claimed a fault with the car sabotaged his race when he let Rosberg speed past him on the first bend after he had started on pole. He said his clutch had not responded right and that was why he could not keep the German at bay.

Lewis said: 'I had a bad start because of the clutch and it's not the first time this has happened. I had a problem with the wait revs. I took my foot off the gas and it was still on and then I dumped the clutch and just had lots of wheelspin. Nico was having bad starts and they changed everything and now he is having good starts and I am having bad starts. It's the way it goes, but it's disappointing when the car just doesn't get off the line fast enough.

'There is nothing you can do about it on a track like this where you just can't overtake unless you're much faster.'

So it was a case of lick the old wounds, and home, James. Yes, Lewis headed back to Blighty and his annual reunion with Silverstone, bruised, but still determined to prove he was the world's No. 1 racer. And where better to do just that than at the home of motor sport? He would be aiming for his third British GP win and he had always admitted that winning on home territory meant more to him than any other victory on the F1 global circuit.

The omens were good. He did well in practice and won pole in qualifying to set him up for the Sunday showdown with Rosberg. After Nico's win in Austria, it was essential that Lewis get back on track and show him who was boss. It would be good to reopen the lead at the top of the racers' board and to show his appreciation of his British fans, who he referred to as 'fantastic, wonderful and the people I try to win more titles for'.

On race day, it rained as the race moved to a thrilling climax, but that was nothing to worry about – Lewis was renowned as F1's top man when the heavens opened. But he didn't get off to the best of starts; indeed, he slipped from pole to third before getting his act together. When the rain fell in the latter stages, Lewis showed his talent for getting the big decisions right by switching swiftly to intermediate tyres just as it started. The move helped him take control and emerge triumphant, with Rosberg second and Vettel third.

Lewis's win also earned him a new entry in the record books as he became only the third British driver to secure a hat-trick of wins on home territory. He joined Jim Clark, who won five, and Nigel Mansell, who had four British GP victories to his name. Afterwards, a joyous Lewis told his adoring mass of fans who crowded into the paddock: 'I am so happy with that win. Thank you to all the fans who came. That was for you. It's a very special weekend for me. I started to tear up on that last lap. I was gunning the whole way and I really just wanted to do it for you guys. I'm going to keep pushing for this championship.

'The race was very tough. It was a very bad start for both of us, but if I'm honest it made it more exciting. For the first time in my career I made the perfectly right choice on the rain and coming in [to change tyres]. I could see the rain coming more and I've never had that before, so I feel extremely happy about that. After that, as I was going around Turn Seven and the last corner, I could see the crowd just cheering me on every time I came by and just spurring me along. I didn't want to drop it for them. I'm really honoured just to be here representing the Brits, to have the British flag up there.'

Great stuff. The plan was clear now: keep up the adrenalin and momentum in Hungary, three weeks later. He managed to do just that, but hardly in the circumstances he would have envisaged. Lady Luck was definitely on his side as he finished sixth after an error-strewn performance. It came after he dominated in practice and qualified, yet again, on pole at the Hungaroring. But in the race itself he started badly, allowing Rosberg and Vettel to sweep past him, and then ran into the gravel at Turn Six, leaving himself plenty to do to even get among the points as he languished in tenth spot.

However, the safety car was employed on the twenty-sixth lap and that enabled him to close the gap. Yet he still managed to make life difficult for himself, damaging his front wing after clashing with Daniel Ricciardo, which meant he had to pit to get it fixed. When Lewis rejoined the fray, he was in twelfth position and looked likely to have let Rosberg cut back his title lead once again, especially as he'd suffered a drive-through penalty because of the run-in with Ricciardo. The German was now second and pushing for the win, but now he too hit trouble – and once again it was with the hapless Ricciardo. Their clash left Rosberg with a puncture, which meant he too had to pit – and when he rejoined he would finish eighth, two spots behind Lewis.

The enormous piece of luck meant Lewis had actually increased his title lead, but he knew he had had a bad day at the office and could easily have conceded vital ground to Rosberg. Lewis told BBC Sport: 'I was all over the place. I don't really have any words to describe what happened. There were mistakes all over the place. I don't know if it was a lack of concentration or what. I pushed, and I kept trying right until the finish line, but there were so many obstacles along the way.

'It's like there was the choice to take two different directions and each time I chose, it was the wrong one. I can take a lot from today, learn a lot, and take it on the chin.'

He then told the press pack: 'Do I deserve any points? I think that I drove as hard as I could and I had good pace, but through all that went on, I think by the grace of God I have some points. I've got to come away from this, take a breather and come back strong next race.'

Lewis was ahead of the pack and on target still to win that coveted third drivers' title. And now, he also had time to unwind, relax and have a bit of fun as the annual almost-month-long summer break began for the F1 teams. And boy, did he unwind! Taking in quad biking in Colorado, festival fun in Barbados with singer Rihanna, and dancing in New York with movie star Jamie Foxx and pals, Lewis made sure he had a good rest from the circuit. He also kept fit in the gym and by walking with his bulldogs Roscoe and Coco so that when racing began again at the end of August he was ready and raring to go.

When he arrived at Spa for the Belgium GP you could sense and see the change in him. Gone was the carefree guy who had even posted a reel of his holiday exploits on YouTube; in his place was a dedicated sportsman with a mono-dimensional mission – to get his hands on that third crown. OK, the pre-summer break had ended poorly as he struggled in Hungary, but the fact of the matter was he was still twenty-one points ahead of Rosberg and on target to achieve his dream.

And to prove exactly how focused he was, Lewis not only triumphed in Spa, but also in the following race in Monza, which meant he collected the full fifty points for two wins. Meanwhile, Rosberg struggled to a total of eighteen points as he finished runner-up in Spa but retired on lap fifty in Italy with engine problems. Vettel was Lewis's nearest rival, but even he finished a full twenty-five seconds behind as the great Brit romped home in style. The only downside to a great day was that Lewis had to wait more than two hours for his victory to be confirmed after controversy over his and Rosberg's tyre pressures – although they were eventually cleared of running them too low. Having said that, Lewis's team had taken no chances when warned there would be an inquiry, telling him to push hard for the finish line in case he did suffer a time penalty over the tyres.

Afterwards Lewis told the press: 'I thought, "Why am I pushing? I'm twenty seconds ahead, so I don't have to push." So I didn't understand. I was thinking all the different scenarios of what the problem could be. As they said it, my tyres took a drop in degradation. So I'm starting to slide. And I'm thinking did I speed in the pitlane? I'm pretty sure they didn't, or they would have pulled me in for a penalty. I was thinking all these things, though I thought I'm going to do what they asked me to do. I couldn't think what could be the reason. So the last few laps were a bit off-putting.'

No matter, he kept his cool and notched his seventh win of the season and his fortieth in F1, and the general feeling in the paddock was that he was now cruising to that third crown as he opened up a fifty-three-point lead over Rosberg.

Lewis knew that he was also now just one victory short of his hero, Ayrton Senna: this was turning out to be a truly memorable, landmark season for the boy from Stevenage who had become the world's No. 1 racing driver. It was a watershed win: Lewis now seemed sure he was going to win the title as he described the display as 'the best I've ever driven' and said that it was 'the best weekend ever'.

Inevitably, maybe, given the euphoria, he would now come down to earth with a mighty bump as he failed to finish in Singapore a fortnight later – and Rosberg collected twelve points with a fourth-place finish. Lewis had suffered a power-unit failure on lap thirty-two. Some news organisations around the world claimed Lewis had been angry with the team for the loss and that he had lost confidence in them. He was quick to rebuff those claims and say he had been misquoted when he turned up in Suzuka for the Japanese GP just one week later. Lewis told SkySports News: 'I have full confidence in my team. There have been a lot of stories misquoting me but I have never had a loss of trust in them. And why would I? We've had unbelievable success.'

Indeed, they had... and it was about to reach unprecedented highs as Lewis and the team now stormed ahead to glory. Wins in Suzuka and then Russia meant he was on the very brink of that triple crown. The Russian victory was memorable for him sharing the podium with President Vladimir Putin – and Putin's mighty swift exit from proceedings when Lewis uncorked and started to spray the champagne around! Earlier, the two men had embraced, with Lewis resplendent in a Cossack hat. Of more significance was Rosberg's early retirement from the race in Sochi with throttle trouble – that, allied with the Hamilton victory, meant Lewis needed only finish two points ahead of Nico and nine ahead of Vettel in the next race and he would be champion again.

On 25 October 2015, our boy delivered the goods and that third crown in some style in Austin, Texas. His American GP win meant he finished seven points ahead of runner-up Rosberg, and ten points ahead of third-placed Vettel. He had won the title with something to spare – and with three races to go, too. It was a remarkable achievement as he now matched Sir Jackie Stewart in becoming only the second British driver to notch those three titles. The stats tell the story that he would then finish runner-up to Rosberg in those three remaining races in Mexico, Brazil and Abu Dhabi – but those results were irrelevant in terms of the drivers' championship. Lewis had already done the business, and those three runner-up spots merely iced the cake for Mercedes as it also wrapped up their triumph in the constructors' championship, and left Nico feeling not as despondent as he had in Austin.

'I feel amazing,' Lewis told Sir Elton John on the winners' podium as his personal American dream started to sink in. 'I can't find the right words, I love you all,' he then told his crew and his adoring fans as they saluted his triumph. 'I'm just overwhelmed.'

He had matched his hero, Ayrton Senna, with those three titles, but his final thoughts in his moment of greatness were, appropriately, to recall just where he had come from, how he had achieved his dream from humble beginnings and how his family, and his dad in particular, had played a massive part in it all. Lewis said: 'It's just crazy to think that I'm now a three-time champion. I owe it all to my dad and family who sacrificed it all to see me here.'

CHAPTER 24

THE DUEL WITH VETTEL

No sooner had Lewis won his third world title, than he began plotting how he could make it four – an achievement that would propel him beyond Jackie Stewart as the most successful British F1 driver ever. This was no driver who was prepared to sit on his laurels and simply take the money until his deal with Mercedes ran out. No, he was a man who always needed to be doing something, to have a goal in mind, something to aim for. He wasn't somebody who could sit on a beach all day, lapping up the sun and counting his (now formidable) fortune. Lewis Hamilton had always been motivated by being the best – and that now meant plotting a path to that fourth title and overtaking the brilliant Stewart. In the event, he would secure that place in the history books, that was so important to him, with two races to spare, and the fourth world title would have another benefit: it would draw him equal with his arch- rival Sebastian Vettel, who had achieved the feat of four crowns during his mighty days in the Red Bull team.

Earlier in Lewis's career, almost a decade earlier, his main rival had been the Spanish ace and double world champion Fernando Alonso and the pair had duelled just as Lewis was starting out as the novice at McLaren. Given a seat in the team by Ron Dennis, Lewis had soon shown his fiery nature and commitment to being No. 1 by refusing to accept he was in the team as a back-up to Alonso. He had raced him and refused to back down on the track on one occasion, until Dennis had personally intervened on the radio. Eventually, it had become clear that Lewis was not only Alonso's equal, but his superior, and that had led to the breakdown of the Spaniard's relationship with McLaren and his exit. That, in itself, was a remarkable turn of events. How the junior had taken on his senior and usurped him. But now, in the racing season of 2017, Alonso was very much yesterday's man and Lewis Hamilton was battling Vettel every race as both men pushed themselves to the limit to prove they were THE king of the modern era. It rankled with Lewis that Vettel had eased ahead in the titles stakes during his spell with Red Bull, when he had the vastly superior car. But now they were duelling on a much more even surface with Lewis in the Mercedes and Vettel in the Ferrari.

To emerge triumphant meant a great deal to Lewis. His

plan now, as he prepared for 2017's opening race in Melbourne, was to equal Vettel's four titles this season and then to surpass him the following campaign. It was an ambitious project – it would mean outpacing and outmanoeuvring the German over two seasons when Vettel's car was becoming quicker thanks to the tech kings at the Ferrari HQ in Italy. Luckily, so was Lewis's: the Mercedes boys were well aware that Ferrari had quietly been upping their game during the winter break and they too worked night and day to perfect the cars that Lewis and Valtteri Bottas would be driving in 2017.

Lewis was convinced that with a fairly equal playing field, he could beat Vettel and prove that he was the better, faster driver. It was game on as far as Lewis was concerned as he lined up at Melbourne for the Australian GP in March – but it would be the German who would draw first blood. Hamilton was runner-up, with Bottas third. It wasn't the statement of intent Lewis had wanted in the opener and it showed him just how fine a job the Ferrari mechanics had done on their cars and how increased a threat they would be. Lewis has fond memories of Melbourne and it is a circuit he enjoys. He had high hopes of winning after beating Vettel to pole but the German's car was just too fast. The final ignominy of the weekend came when Mercedes turned down Lewis's engine when it became clear he had no chance of catching Vettel, who took the first 25 points of the campaign, with Lewis notching up 18 and Bottas 15. Vettel was quick to pay tribute to his team after the race, telling reporters, 'The whole team has been working really, really hard. The guys didn't get much sleep here and back in the factory. The car is really behaving well, incredible to drive, a beautiful day. Thank you.' It was Vettel's forty-third GP win of his career but his first since Singapore in September 2015. It just showed how improved his car was – finally, he was back on the podium as race winner after what had been a challenging period for both him and his Ferrari paymasters.

For his part, Lewis was magnanimous in defeat, at the same time admitting things hadn't been quite right. He said, 'We had a really good start, which is fantastic. After that, I was struggling with the grip. Sebastian was able to always answer in terms of lap time and the majority of the time do faster lap times and then towards the end I got a bit in traffic and the car started to overheat the tyres and I was struggling with grip and it was to the point [where] that I needed to come in. Plus, the gap was closing up and I was sliding around. So it was my call because otherwise he probably would have come by anyway. After I came in I then got stuck in traffic, which is a little bit unfortunate but that's motor racing. But big congratulations to Sebastian and Ferrari. I know it's been a long time coming for them to get a result like this. It shows we are going to have a race on our hands, which we are very happy to have, and which is great for the fans. Unfortunately it's harder than ever to get close to cars, which is a shame. We can't even have a close battle.'

Mercedes had a problem with the new, improved Ferrari, but they were determined to get Lewis back on the podium as a winner and worked hard in the garage to soup up the car for the next race, scheduled for China a fortnight later.

That hard work clearly paid off. Hamilton took his sixth consecutive pole and went on to win the race, leading from start to finish and posting the fastest lap into the bargain. Vettel was second and they were now level on points, with forty-three apiece. The contest we had anticipated pre-Melbourne was now becoming a reality as the duo embarked upon a battle for supremacy that would long continue. It was just what the sport needed after Nico Rosberg's shock retirement in December 2016: he and Lewis had conducted their own personal contest to keep the fans on the edge of their seats, now a new, top-notch duo's rivalry was brewing nicely.

It had been a race that tested the teams and the drivers, both in terms of speed and reaction. The track had started off wet and then dried bit by bit as the race progressed, meaning decisions on tyres and tactics were as key as the men in the cockpits being absolutely spot on the mark. Lewis accepted as much afterwards, telling the press, 'I am very grateful for all the efforts that the team have put in to enable us to be where we are and where I am today. It's overwhelming when you have a weekend like this, because I'm just a link in the chain and, when you really think about it, there's thousands of people involved, hundreds and hundreds of people involved in me being up here and us being where we are. So, congratulations to all of them. I hope they're all celebrating back home. I hope they're feeling the spirit, I hope they're feeling the fight because it's on. Qualifying was great, to be able to pull that good lap out, it put me in a great position.

'The start of the race was fantastic, too. And then in the

race, it really was just a case of keeping my composure. Some really tricky conditions out there, particularly on the intermediate tyres. Then, after that, once we'd done the pit stop with the safety car, the speed was very low and the tyres were so cold. So it was very easy to make mistakes and I'm just grateful I didn't. The last twenty-odd laps me and Sebastian were just pounding around as fast as we could, exchanging lap times and I think that's what racing is all about.'

Lewis clearly enjoyed racing in China; this was his fifth victory there, having also triumphed in 2008, 2011, 2014 and 2015. It was his 106th podium finish, putting him on a par with Alain Prost. The win also meant Mercedes overtook Ferrari in the Constructors' Championship, so it was trebles all round as the team celebrated in the pits.

Hamilton and Vettel continued their topsy-turvy battle for top spot in Bahrain a week later. This time Vettel came out on top, with Lewis second and Bottas, who had started on pole, finishing in his now traditional third. Ferrari leapfrogged back over Mercedes in the Constructors' title. Lewis made it difficult for himself by driving slowly into the pits to delay Daniel Riccardio. That apparently deliberate act earned him a five-second penalty and meant he was unable to catch Vettel. There was also a problem within the team when the bosses ordered Bottas to let Hamilton pass to chase the German. Bottas was clearly unhappy with the decision, which rained on his parade after he had earned that maiden pole.

'It has been a challenging weekend,' Lewis said afterwards. 'The start was OK but Sebastian was in my blind spot so I didn't know whereabouts he was. I didn't know where anyone was behind me. Valtteri got a good start and it was really just about covering him. I obviously lost position to Sebastian there. I had very good pace and believed I would be able to catch Sebastian but the five-second penalty made it twice as hard as it was already going to be. As I said, apologies to the team but I tried the best I could to recover it and we still got good points for the team today with a second and third.'

The F1 teams packed their bags and headed to Europe for the next stage of races in the season. Lewis was confident he would overtake Vettel in the upcoming races and the mechanics were confident they had ironed out earlier problems with the car. He was second in the title race but it was looking good: he was well on track to that fourth title if he could maintain his calm and composure and race at the top of his game. It had been noticeable during the early races that Lewis did appear much more at ease with himself and the sport. He had been gracious to Vettel when he had been beaten, and to his own team when the car had perhaps not been at full throttle. He was not blaming anyone as he trailed Vettel by seven points. His confidence was such that he knew he could and would prove to be the better driver as the season wore on. This was a more mature Lewis Hamilton; a man who knew he was at the very peak of his powers and who had lost the insecurities that had seemed to affect him after the split with his father all those years ago.

Yet it would be a difficult first weekend in Europe in

2017, as Lewis came home fourth in Russia, with Bottas first, Vettel second and the German's team-mate Kimi Raikkonen third. This was Bottas's maiden F1 win and, you could argue, karmic retribution after he had been ordered to pull over and let Lewis through in Bahrain. Valtteri's joy was clear to see afterwards. He said, 'It took quite a while, more than eighty races for me, but definitely worth the wait, worth the learning curve. The opportunity to join this team came in winter and they made it possible today, so I really want to thank the team. Without them it wouldn't be possible, it feels amazing.'

The pressure was now on Lewis as the show moved from Russia to Spain, and Barcelona. He was thirteen points adrift of Sebastian but remained calm and sure of himself, certain that he would overwhelm his rival. He was convinced that he could handle the pressure better than Vettel – and so it would prove, as he raced home to win in Barcelona. Lewis showed his intent by claiming pole. The lead went from one driver to another but Lewis stormed past Vettel on lap forty-four, the faster tyres proving key, and there was no catching him then. The win reduced Sebastian's lead in the title race to just six points. The rivalry between the two giants of motor racing was hotting up – and the difference in class between them and the rest of the field could be seen in the points total in the championship. Vettel was on 104, Lewis 98 while Bottas, in third place, trailed Lewis by 35 points with his total of 63.

Lewis had lost out to Sebastian at the start of the race, but that was the only negative he took from his second win at

Barcelona. He complimented his team on the continuing improvements in the Mercedes and admitted he loved the 'raw' battles he and Vettel were having. Lewis told reporters: 'Thanks to everyone back at the factory with the upgrades enabling us to be as close as we are to Ferrari. It has been a really good weekend, bouncing back from Russia is a great thing. But I obviously lost out on the start. I'm not quite sure exactly what it was. The initial phase was good, just got wheelspin later on and saw Sebastian fly by.

'Then he was so fast up ahead, it was such a push to try to keep close to him and not let him pull away. I think it was the rawest fight I can remember having for some real time, which I loved. This is what the sport needs to be every single race. This is why I race and this is what got me into racing in the beginning. To have that close battle with him, with a four-time champ, is awesome.'

And so on to Monaco, one of Lewis's favourite circuits and destinations. He was aiming to win on the Prinicipality's roads but, once again, it was Vettel's turn to cross the finishing line first. It wasn't a win without controversy; Ferrari called Kimi Raikkonen in for a pit stop early when Vettel was well behind him. The move enabled Sebastian to move ahead of the team's No.2 driver – and win the race. Raikkonen was unhappy about the move; he had led from pole and was hoping for another F1 victory in a colourful, successful career. The Finn finished second with Hamilton seventh (not bad considering he had started thirteenth on the grid and grabbed six points).

Vettel tried to play down the controversy over

Raikkonen. 'From the team point of view there was no plan of any team orders or anything,' he said. 'When Kimi stopped I was just going flat out as fast as I could. I was surprised when I came out ahead. It worked well for me to stay out longer. We're racing, we get on well but I can understand that Kimi's not entirely happy today. He drove well in the first stint and then got the message to go in. You do the pit stop and then you push. Obviously it's a bad surprise when somebody comes out ahead. I'll take it, there's no reason to lie or anything. I'm very happy about it today but I can understand he's upset.'

It was Ferrari's first win in Monaco for sixteen years and they were starting to believe that Vettel could indeed lift the drivers' trophy. In Lewis's opinion they were clearly favouring Vettel as their number-one driver to achieve that ambition. He said, 'It's clear to me that Ferrari have chosen their number-one driver. They are pushing everything to make sure Sebastian will maximise all his weekends. In strategy that just doesn't happen. For the leading car it's very hard for him to get jumped by the second car unless the team decide to favour the other car – so that is very clear.' As a sidenote, the race was tinged with a certain feeling of nostalgia and sadness as it was the final GP for Britain's former world champion, Jenson Button.

Of more concern to Mercedes, and to Hamilton, was that he now trailed Vettel by twenty-five points. He admitted the car wasn't as fast as Vettel's but remained adamant he could, and would, still be champion for a fourth time at the German's expense. Lewis added, 'Of course I can't afford another weekend like this. The Ferraris are quick and seem to work everywhere, so these next fourteen races are going to be very, very difficult. They have arguably the strongest car all year, like our car last year where it worked everywhere.'

Lewis wasn't moaning: he was simply being realistic. But, as we have often noted in this book, he works best when the heat is on. It showed in the results that would follow that disappointing weekend in Monaco. Of the next eleven races, he would win seven, a run that included Vettel winning just one. And in the twelfth race he would finish a lowly ninth – yet still lift the title that weekend in Mexico, courtesy of his incredible run of victories. That run would begin the race following Monaco, at another of his favourite circuits, Canada. Lewis was dominant throughout the weekend, taking pole, setting the fastest lap and emerging with the full points for his win – while Vettel could only finish fourth. Vettel still led the championship but his lead had been cut to twelve points. The Brit was coming after him – and fast.

Lewis secured yet another pole when the championship moved on to Azerbaijan. Daniel Ricciardo would win the race, Vettel was fourth and Lewis fifth. Both had been handed penalties, which allowed Ricciardo in for the victory. After Vettel steered into the back of Lewis's Mercedes under the safety car, Lewis was fuming mad and even seemed to challenge Sebastian to a duel. He said, 'Deliberately driving into another driver and getting away pretty much scot-free as he still came fourth, I think that's a disgrace. I think he disgraced himself today. Imagine all the young kids that are watching Formula One today and see that kind of behaviour from a four-time world champion. I think that says it all. If he wants to prove that he's a man, I think we should do it out of the car face-to-face.'

The duel between the pair was reaching boiling point, but Vettel would be the ultimate loser as it seemed to motivate Lewis for the remainder of the season. It would be Vettel who suffered more rushes of blood to the head over that season, and the one that followed, mistakes that would cost him the chance of two titles, which Lewis gladly snatched for himself. Vettel finished ahead of him in Austria, with Bottas clinching his second win. Lewis was third but knew the wins would come if he kept up his momentum; the fact he had once again set a fastest lap showed him that. He just needed the back-up team to give the car that extra edge over the Ferraris.

Sure enough, the turning point came in the very next race – and how sweet it was for Hamilton as he roared to victory on home territory, the British GP at Silverstone. And what a fabulous day it was for the British hero. He won in real style, achieving his fifth grand slam in the process. He started from pole, set the fastest lap, led on every lap and triumphed with a fourteen-second lead over his team-mate Valtteri Bottas. It was his fifth British GP victory, which equalled the feats of Alain Prost and Jim Clark. To top it all, Vettel could only finish in seventh after suffering a puncture with two laps remaining. The weekend's outcome meant his lead over Lewis in the title race was now cut to a single point and

Mercedes increased their lead to fifty-five points over Ferrari in the Constructors' Championship.

Lewis's perfect race was his fourth consecutive win at Silverstone and he paid tribute to the fans who had cheered him on, saying they 'make me go faster'. He joined the adoring crowds in the paddock, shaking hands and thanking them personally. Lewis told them, 'The support has been incredible this weekend. I am so proud I could do this for you all. Now the plan is to win the championship.' At the post-race press conference he explained how the race had gone so well: 'The team did an exceptional job this weekend. The car felt great and really was generally faultless. So proud of everyone at the factory. Perfect weekend for us as a team. I was up front, got a very good start and after that I was really able to manage the gap between myself and Kimi and just bit by bit, extend.

'We were planning on stopping on lap nineteen so I was able to extend it by quite a bit and then at the end, I had a decent gap to Kimi. I also heard that there were some tyre blow-outs and I had some graining and vibration on mine, so the last couple of laps I took it easy. I think we really had the legs this weekend. You just saw the crowd. I'm sweating, not necessarily because of the race but because I was just running outside and got to crowd-surf with everyone. The support has been immense this weekend.'

He was asked if he might retire if he won the title – little chance of that, of course! He said, 'At the moment I'm loving driving. I feel like I'm at my prime. I feel like I'm driving better than ever and I'm loving driving with the team. So there's no reason to stop. I'm still enjoying it and I still have a contract with the team for at least a year so I plan to see that out.'

Two weeks later Vettel would win in Hungary but it would be his last victory before Lewis wrapped up the title in Mexico. The Mercedes ace won the next three GPs – in Belgium, Italy and Singapore. The victory at Monza was particularly galling for Vettel as, of course, Ferrari see that race as their own, with it being the pride of Italian motor sport. Lewis led from pole and dominated the race, finishing 4.4 seconds ahead of team-mate Bottas, with Vettel a massive 36.3 seconds behind Hamilton in third. It was a key victory on the way to that fourth title as it meant Lewis had taken the lead outright in the drivers' championship for the first time in the 2017 season. His sixth victory of the campaign put him three points ahead of Vettel, which left him, understandably, on a real high, although he could still manage a subtle dig at Vettel for being off the pace. He said, 'We've gone from strength from strength and the way we have come together in this second half of the season is exceptional. I'm not really sure why the pace of the Ferraris was not as close as it usually is, particularly as it was in practice, but today the car felt fantastic, particularly in that first stint.

'I guess because we had a bit of breathing space behind us initially it was easier to extend the life of the tyre. I suppose if we had a Ferrari behind we would have been pushed more to the limit. And Valtteri did a fantastic job just to get through and get a one-two here.

'I know it's not easy for the Italian fans to accept but ultimately we did the better job this weekend, collectively, as a team. But it's still close and there's still a long, long way to go. The Ferrari should be quite quick at the next track [Singapore] with the extra downforce they generally are able to add on, so the fight will continue. But it is amazing to come and have the back-to-back wins. It's been a long, long time that Sebastian has been leading the championship, so with all the ups and down to now be just slightly ahead is a great feeling.'

Lewis's aim for a fourth consecutive GP win in the season was dashed in Malaysia at the start of October, with Max Verstappen taking first place. But victories in Japan and the United States put Hamilton on the very brink of that fourth drivers' crown. He travelled to Mexico at the end of the same month ready to claim the title and finally end up on equal terms with Vettel, who had achieved that same magnificent feat in his glittering time at Red Bull. Hamilton came into the race with a sixty-six-point lead over Vettel and needing a fifth place finish to claim that fourth title (assuming Vettel won). It meant the pressure was off – although Lewis being Lewis, he had arrived in Mexico City determined to win the race. In the event, it was something of an anti-climax. Vettel finished fourth so Lewis's ninth place finish was enough to have him crowned champion. The race had started controversially for the pair, when Vettel hit his rear right wheel. Both drivers pitted but it was Vettel who ultimately stayed ahead, albeit being unable to grab the second place finish that would have delayed

Lewis's coronation until the next race. Red Bull's Verstappen won the race but all eyes were on Lewis, now a four-time champion.

He told reporters of his joy and pride at the achievement, saying, 'I did everything I could. I had a good start and I don't really know what happened at turn three with Sebastian but I gave him plenty of room, but I tried my hardest to come back. A big thank you to my family and my team. Mercedes have been incredible over the last five years and I am so proud to be a part of it. I never gave up. Obviously it wasn't the finish I wanted, being forty seconds or behind or something. I kept going right to the end. I just want to lift it up to my family, and God and my team.'

He'd done it: Lewis had matched Vettel with the fourth title and was now behind only Michael Schumacher, the all-time record holder on seven, and Argentine Juan Manuel Fangio on five. He'd also done it with two races to go; he wouldn't win in Brazil or Abu Dhabi but it didn't matter, for Lewis was now planning how to lift a fifth crown the following season. That would be enough to equal Fangio and leave him just two short of Schuey. But it wouldn't be easy – the feud with Vettel had been hotting up throughout the 2017 season and Sebastian had his own dreams and ambitions. He also wanted that fifth title so fireworks were guaranteed for the 2018 season as the duo would do battle once again. And only one could emerge victorious.

CHAPTER 25

GIMME FIVE

Every Formula One season had been important and informative for Lewis, both in terms of personal and career development, since that opening campaign back in 2007. As success followed success, so he matured as a driver and a person – although he still loved to live life in the fast lane away from the circuit. He dated one pop singer, Nicole Scherzinger, long-term, and was linked with others including Rihanna, Nicki Minaj and Rita Ora, By 2018 he was living in Monaco, owned luxury cars, had the use of a private jet and spent a lot of his time away from the races carrying out fashion commitments, holidaying and escorting beautiful women.

His lifestyle prompted critics to question his commitment to Mercedes and Formula One. The easy answer to that was, of course, to cast an eye over the results he racked up in races and the title he was still winning. However, in September of that year, it all came to a head when some pundits criticised him before the Singapore GP. He had returned to Monaco and then flown to China for the unveiling of his Hilfiger collection in Shanghai. He then returned to for a wedding in Italy, before heading to another event in New York from where he finally travelled to Singapore.

The critics argued it would affect his performance in the race but he proved them wrong in style by claiming pole and winning the race. That led his boss at Mercedes, Toto Wolff, to speak out on his behalf, aiming a broadside at those critics. Toto said, 'For six years I have heard, "How can you allow Lewis to get off and fly around the world?" You know what? He did it to his most extreme in the last 10 days, he loved it, he was in Shanghai on the catwalk, he was in New York a couple of days later. He came here, rock and roll, and blew everybody away.

'Let's just be non-judgemental and allow everybody to judge how they perform best. He knows best what's good for him.'

Lewis also hit back at the critics, telling reporters his work always came first, however busy he may seem away from the track. He said, 'I definitely feel my approach and the balance that I have in my life in general is really good. I know some of you asked questions at the beginning of the weekend. And you actually asked quite nicely rather than aggressively which you could have done, but I am glad you have seen this performance. I said to Toto, "Just don't for a second ever believe or let it creep into your mind that I don't want to win this championship more than anything." So that is my priority. You can see that from my drive. That won't change.'

And even his team-mate Bottas felt it necessary to speak out, saying, of Lewis, 'He works hard. Many people might look sometimes from the outside and think he just goes and does whatever. But I know how many factory days we each have and the Skype meetings and so on, so it's not like he's not working between races. But of course he's very talented.'

Lewis's career highlights in F1, as he headed towards that legendary fifth title, only served to highlight his development and how strong his commitment was, and remained, to being the best in the world. In 2008, he became the youngest ever world champion, then there were the challenging years up to 2013 when he could have been forgiven for wondering if he would ever win the crown again, as Sebastian Vettel ruled supreme. At the end of 2012 he would leave McLaren to join Mercedes – and even then he would need a season to bed in before he could confidently challenge for the title again. His season finishes from 2007 to 2014 read like this: 2nd in 2007, 1st in 2008, 5th in 2009, 4th in 2010, 5th in 2011, 4th in 2012 and 4th in 2013. After that initial burst of glory at the start of his F1 career, he had finished no higher than fourth during the five years that followed his 2008 triumph. It was a time of reflection and hard work, mixed with hope and determination that his luck would change. In footballing terms, he was Arsenal, finishing fourth regularly, rather than Manchester City, who are now expected to win the league every year.

But in 2014, having settled at Mercedes and started to believe in the car and his backroom team, he was back in business. It had taken six years but he now, finally, added to that first title success. The second followed the year after, the third in 2015 and the fourth in 2017. Four of the six 'wilderness' years had happened as Vettel secured his four titles, but Lewis had then reversed the process – confining Sebastian to a relative wilderness as he joined him on four. The 2017 campaign had been demanding and seen the duo feud for supremacy – as Vettel tried for a fifth title and Lewis a (successful) fourth – and the 2018 season would be no different. Only now, there was added spice, and an added incentive for the conqueror: for he would collect that fifth title crown at the expense of the other. And that would make their rivalry all the more intense, and compulsive viewing for F1 fans around the globe. For some, it was Britain v Germany, for others it was Mercedes v Ferrari, but for both combatants it was a chance to prove who WAS top dog, given both cars were similar in speed and reliability. It was also the first time in F1 history that two drivers would be going head to head for a fifth title.

So, much was at stake as the duo headed to Melbourne for the season opener in March 2018. Lewis gained the upper hand initially, winning pole at the circuit for a record-breaking seventh time. But Sebastian would have the last laugh, winning the race for the second successive year with

Lewis runner-up and Raikkonen third. Lewis had looked in command but Sebastian took advantage of a virtual safety car period to register a victory that had looked unlikely. Lewis said later, 'I was keen to recover from whether it was a mistake or not and I was risking it all but eventually I had to make the sensible choice there is a long way in the championship and it is not all won in one race.' While a much happier Vettel added, 'Obviously we got a bit lucky with the safety car but I really enjoyed it.'

And Lewis was under no illusions that Vettel would be any less of a threat in the next race, in Bahrain. He said, 'There will be ups and downs. Ferrari are really quick on the straight. They will be rapid in the next race. I can tell you it is going to be close.' As well as a brilliant driver, Hamilton remained a top-class tactician: he understood racing cars better than any driver in the pitlane. And so it was no real surprise when his words proved prophetic about Bahrain, as Vettel stormed home in the desert, making it two wins from the first two GPs of the new season. Lewis came in third behind team-mate Bottas, meaning Vettel extended his early lead over the Brit in the drivers' championship to seventeen points. Ferrari also now held a ten-point lead over Mercedes in the Constructors' Championship. But it could have been a lot worse for Lewis. He had started ninth on the grid and afterwards admitted he was happy to have made it on to the podium – that had been his aim. He also said he had a few radio link problems which had made the task still harder: 'I started ninth, so third is not bad at all. It's damage limitation. I think there were some frustrating points during the race where they couldn't hear me, so I had to choose particular points during which I could speak to them. So communication was really difficult. When you're trying to catch Sebastian, who was 25 seconds ahead, to know exactly what you need to do in order to not kill your tyres but make it so that you can catch him at the end, it's difficult. And if you're not getting that feedback, it makes it kind of frustrating.'

Lewis had one other talking point from the race; Verstappen had touched his car trying to get past Lewis on lap four. Lewis survived the scare, but the Dutchman was forced out. Lewis told reporters of his displeasure with the youngster: 'Ultimately, I had a coming together with Max and it was an unnecessary collision. There needs to be a certain respect between drivers. Maybe I need to go and watch the manoeuvre again, but it didn't feel like a respectful manoeuvre. Ultimately, it was a silly manoeuvre for himself, because he didn't finish the race. And obviously he's tending to make quite a few mistakes recently, so it was just unnecessary for him to do that.'

China was next up and Lewis needed to start clawing points back from Vettel. It was still early days, but a win, or at least beating the German, would surely be of major psychological benefit. Yet Lewis did not get off to a good start as the weekend got underway. He was only fourth on the grid behind the two Ferraris and his team-mate Bottas and he finished in the same place. There was a consolation: Vettel did even worse, finishing eighth after a run-in with

Verstappen. That came on lap forty-three, with the Dutchman shunting Vettel off the track. Both drivers suffered, Vettel falling to eighth as he had to drive with a damaged floor. And although Max escaped the crash scot-free he was hit with a ten-point penalty for causing the crash, which meant him losing fourth place to Lewis. The race was won by Ricciardo with Bottas second and Raikkonen third. And Vettel's pain was Lewis's gain, as he now moved within nine points of him in the title race.

A fortnight later that pain was compounded for Sebastian as Lewis won in Azerbaijan and he finished fourth. It meant Hamilton leapfrogged him at the top of the leaderboard for the first time that season. And Vettel's downfall was of his own making after he tried to overtake Bottas in a restart after the safety car had appeared. He locked his left front tyre and ran wide. Vettel told reporters, 'S*** happens. Without a safety car it would have been a different race. I saw the gap on the side and unfortunately it did not work out for me. But that is easy to say now. I went over a bump and had front locking but I'm not blaming that – I am captain of my own ship.' Lewis had more luck when Bottas suffered a puncture as he looked set to win. It was his first win since the US GP the previous October and put him four points ahead of Vettel. Afterwards, a relieved Lewis admitted that fortune had certainly favoured him in Baku: 'I struggled throughout the weekend and I'm definitely struggling to extract the car's potential, but also my potential. It's been a little difficult, particularly the last two races but also with the tyres in Bahrain.

'But I have to be happy with today. I have to be thankful and grateful because it is such a tricky race and you don't know what's going to happen. Safety Car comes out and you can lose out but what's important is just to keep your head down and keep going and live to fight another day. I came out in the lead and honestly I couldn't believe that I was where I was. I was just praying that I could keep it together, stay focused and bring it home. We've definitely got a lot of work still to do; we still are behind [the Ferraris]. Kimi was nearly on pole yesterday, two-tenths ahead of Sebastian – their pure pace is a lot ahead of ours at the moment.'

That may have been the case, but it didn't account for the fact that he was an incomparable talent: Lewis now proved just how good he was by winning in Barcelona a fortnight later against the faster Ferraris. He took pole and led from start to finish in a masterful driving show. His joy was doubled when Bottas followed him home in second place – the first Mercedes 1–2 of the season and a win that increased his championship lead over Vettel, who could only finish fourth, to seventeen points. Later, Lewis said he felt a little easier about the car now he had won two races in succession, even though the threat from Ferrari would remain a major one on faster circuits. He said, 'I'd like to hope that this could be part of a turning point. Race by race we're understanding the tyres more. But we could just as easily go to the next race and struggle getting our tyres working and be nowhere. We do, after the five races so far, now have a much, much better understanding of the car, of what we need to do to get it working – but we still have learning to do, improvements to be made. We still need to add performance to the car throughout the year, so that's what we're going to continue to be working on.'

Lewis had broken Michael Schumacher's record with this win; it was his forty-first win from pole. He admitted he was proud to be mentioned in the same breath as the man who remains the greatest ever F1 driver with those remarkable seven title wins. Lewis added: 'Well, I didn't know about it. It's surreal. It just doesn't register because I remember like it was yesterday, sitting at home, playing a computer game as Michael! There was this game that you could do the whole Thursday, Friday practice and then Saturday qualifying – and I used to do the whole process through the weekend on a computer. I didn't have a steering wheel, I did it on two keys and I remember playing as Michael. It's surreal that every now and then I keep coming up against Michael in terms of records and it just reminds me of just what a great he was. It's taken a long time to be where I am today and he has some serious records. It's hard to beat a lot of the records he had. It's always an honour when his name and mine are brought up at the same time.'

There you had it: the respect Lewis has for Schuey, but also the determination to try to match him. To try to keep up with a legend by making inroads into the history books. For Lewis, the money was no longer the key motivation: he was a millionaire many times over and was set up for life even if he packed it in there and then. No, this was a man who lived for motor sport, whose life from an early age had been built around it and who now wanted to leave a legacy that would be remembered forever. As the greatest racer of all time. There was still a way to go if he were to achieve that, but that in itself was a motivation to continue. To try to match Schuey's seven titles. It would be tough but he was up for the fight, beginning with the current one, his attempt to keep Vettel at bay and lift that fifth title.

The pendulum now swung back Sebastian's way. He finished runner-up to Ricciardo in the next race, in Monaco, a place ahead of Lewis, and then won the following one in Canada. That put Sebastian a point ahead of Lewis, but it then swung back the Brit's way when he triumphed in France, with Vettel coming home in fifth. The to-ing and fro-ing between the duo was making for one of the most exciting F1 seasons since, well, the last one when they had also battled blow by blow to beat each other. The duo's rivalry, now season after season for supremacy, was bringing to mind the great rivalries of yesteryear – such as Ayrton Senna and Alain Prost and Niki Lauda and James Hunt.

At the start of July 2018, Sebastian had once again retained the lead in the championship but Lewis was revved up and more determined than any time in the season to win it back, and put Vettel in his place. The reason for his raised blood pressure? It was time for the British GP at Silverstone, his home race and the race he believed he owned and the one where he could pay tribute to the fans who backed him throughout the year: his own people. Inevitably, it was Lewis who took pole but he got off to a slow start in the race and had his work cut out to finish on the podium. A collision on the first lap with Vettel's team-mate Kimi Raikkonen left him at the back of the pack. It showed his extraordinary skill and ability that, at the end of the race, he had finished second. He had weaved in and out and overtaken superbly. Of course, it was a blow that it was Vettel who stood next to him on the podium as the race winner but Lewis had worked miracles to achieve runner-up. It was a bitter pill to swallow, losing to Vettel at his home and it didn't help that it was the other Ferrari that had cost him probable victory by crashing into the back of his car and sending him to the back of the race.

Raikkonen's guilt, and Lewis's innocence, was confirmed when Kimi received a ten-second penalty for his misdemeanour. Lewis was unhappy afterwards and hinted at a conspiracy to stop him by Ferrari, saying 'interesting tactics', although video footage and mechanical data confirmed Kimi had simply made a mistake. Raikkonen was honest enough to admit, 'I ended up hitting Lewis in the first corner. It was my mistake. I deserve it, and I took the 10 seconds and kept fighting.'

Lewis continued his conspiracy theory at the post-race press conference, saying, 'All I'd say is that it's now two races that the Ferraris have taken out one of the Mercedes, and a five-second penalty and a ten-second penalty. It's a lot of points that ultimately Valtteri and I have lost in those two scenarios. I couldn't see behind me but we've just got to try to position ourselves better so that we are not exposed to the red cars – because who knows when that's going to happen again. We've got to make sure that we work hard together as a team to try to lock-out the front row and make sure that we're fully ahead of these guys.'

Despite his anger, Lewis had still made sure he went to his adoring fans after the race, shaking hands and chatting to the crowds in the paddock. He paid tribute to them: 'The fans have been incredible this weekend. This is the greatest race of the year and this is the greatest crowd and I'm sorry I wasn't able to bring it home for you today, but thank you for your support. It's you guys that helped me get through today. We'll take it on the chin and keep pushing hard, because believe me I will not give up. I will not give up.'

He was true to his word, delivering morale-boosting wins in Germany and Hungary on the back of the British GP. The victory in Germany was particularly enjoyable for Lewis as he had got one over on Sebastian by winning in HIS home GP. It helped to take ease the wounded pride after Vettel had pinched his limelight by winning at Silverstone. It took Hamilton into the summer break on 213 points in the championship, 24 ahead of Vettel, which meant he had the luxury of an engine failure gap between them. If he failed to finish in a future GP and Vettel won, he would be just a point behind the German. Plus, Mercedes were ten points clear of Ferrari in the Constructors' Championship.

Vettel drew first blood after the summer break, winning in Belgium, but Lewis hit back with a knockout punch by sealing victory in Italy, Vettel's 'second home' as he worked for Ferrari. The rivalry between the pair remained intense and the race at Monza was hit by controversy after they collided as Vettel panicked when Lewis had an opportunity to pass him. Vettel claimed Lewis had blocked him from getting around a corner but replays clearly showed it was the German who had miscalculated and was at fault. Lewis said, 'I was a bit surprised Seb chose the inside and not the outside of Kimi. That was my opportunity. I stuck it down the outside and made sure I was far enough alongside. I had the experience a few years ago of being on the inside and it didn't come off too well.' Meanwhile Sebastian countered: 'Lewis didn't leave me any space and I had no choice but to run into him and make contact. I tried to get out from there but I couldn't. Unfortunately, I was the ___ around, which is ironic.'

At times they DID sound like two squabbling schoolboys, but you have to understand the pressure to win was intense. Not just from the team's bosses, but from the stress they heaped on themselves, each determined to prove they were No. 1 by lifting the drivers' title for a fifth time. It was an ambition that spurred them on and, inevitably, led to incidents like this. It is worth pointing out, though, that it was Sebastian who would lose most over the season through miscalculations on the track. It was his hot-headedness that would cost him dearly. He seemed often bedevilled by an 'all or nothing' mindset while Lewis realised that it wasn't the end of the world to sometimes go steadier and finishing second – rather than colliding with another car and finishing further down the field. Points did, indeed, make prizes.

Sebastian would later sum up the white-hot rivalry with Lewis in this way: 'The heat is there, the intensity is there. It's unavoidable for everyone, for me and him. It's very difficult for people watching who are not naturally in it to feel what we feel – the pressure is at its highest that I can ever remember. That's the pressure you put on yourself because you want to succeed, it's the pressure of all your desires and your fears and also of all the people that are depending on you.'

At Monza, Sebastian could only finish fourth – not the best of weekends in front of the fanatical Italian crowd. And Singapore now turned the screw even tighter by winning in surrounded Russia and Japan. The win in Sochi was controversy when Mercedes told Valtteri Bottas to let Lewis through when the Finn was in command. And that it was Lewis who prompted the controversy by saying he was unhappy with the decision says something about his character: that he wants to win fair and square, and does not condone 'below the belt' moves, as he told reporters afterwards: "It is definitely a win on my list of wins that I am least proud of. The strangest day I can remember in my career. I want to win the right way. As racing drivers we exist to win; if you tell us we can't, it is like you are taking our life away. I would never wish it on someone else and I would never ask for it ever. I made sure in a meeting that they knew this is not how I want to win.'

Vettel finished third, so the win gave Lewis a ten-point gain, as opposed to the three points more than Sebastian he would have gained by being runner-up. It also increased his championship lead to fifty points – he had a two-race comfort zone on his biggest rival, with only a handful remaining.

Lewis was clearly in command of the title: it was now his to lose and that was always unlikely given his nature.

By the time of the US GP towards the end of October 2018, he was in the enviable position of being able to lift the title if everything went his way. He held a sixty-seven-point lead over Vettel, an advantage he would need to extend by eight points at Austin to win the crown. If he won, Vettel would need to finish second to delay the inevitable. As it transpired, Lewis finished third and Sebastian was fourth, with Raikkonen winning.

The coronation was completed just seven days later in Mexico, which was where Lewis had won his fourth crown a year earlier. This time, he finished fourth, with Vettel second. It was enough to end any mathematical chance the German had of still lifting the title. He had amassed 358 points to Vettel's 294, with two races to spare. Lewis was world champion for a fifth time and the celebrations could begin. Lewis told the press, 'It is a very strange feeling right now. This was won through a lot of hard work through a lot of races. I am so grateful for all the hard work, for everyone who has been a part of it. To complete this, when Fangio has done it with Mercedes, it is an incredible moment. It was a horrible race. I got a great start and was working my way up and I really don't know what happened after that. I was just trying to hold on and bring the car home.'

Vanquished Vettel showed his sportsmanship by embracing his bitter rival and paying tribute, saying, 'Well deserved. Congratulations to him and his team. They did a superb job all year – we need to stand there and accept that. We would have loved to hang in there a bit longer but that wasn't the case.'

But he pledged he would be back the following year – and would be pushing Lewis even harder. The boy from Stevenage had written his name in the record books yet again with his fifth world title. But he knew right then that hitting Schumacher's seven would be a real test with Vettel in his slipstream. Yet who would back against him achieving just that – and even going one better? His remarkable story wasn't finished just yet...